THE
EMPERORS
OF ROME

THE EMPERORS OF ROME

THE STORY OF IMPERIAL ROME FROM JULIUS CAESAR TO THE LAST EMPEROR

DAVID POTTER

METRO BOOKS
NEW YORK

Contents

*Republican denarius (reverse) of Lucius
Antestius Gragulus, c.136 BC*

Marcus Aurelius (AD 121–180)

Trajan (AD 53–117)

*Denarius of Antoninus
Pius (r. AD 138–61)*

Being Caesar

One murdered his mother. Another fought as a gladiator. Two were philosophers, while yet another is revered as a saint in the Eastern Orthodox Church. What all these diverse personalities had in common was that they were emperors of Rome. Given the extreme behaviour exhibited by many of the holders of this office, it is little wonder that much of the political comment that has come down to us from Ancient Rome focuses on individual personalities. In polemical tones all too familiar to modern ears, Romans lambasted their leaders as lunatics, murderers or imbeciles or lionized them as heroes or geniuses.

An equestrian statue of Marcus Aurelius, in Rome's Capitoline Museum. Marcus was one of the chief exponents of collegial government. Rather than living as semi-divine creatures whose ethereal affairs were beyond the ken of ordinary mortals, Roman emperors were 'leading men' (principes) who were expected to deal reasonably with their colleagues.

Roman political discourse also resembled that of the present day in judging leaders and their achievements by an ideal standard. In the light of this, it is worth considering for a moment what a job description for a prospective emperor might look like.

Following the approved practice of human resources managers, in drafting this description we need to consult the best available literature, and keep in mind both the experience of previous holders and the needs of the organization. Aided by ancient works of political theory on kingship, and taking the average age of the incumbents as our yardstick of the level of experience required, we might well arrive at the following profile:

Wanted:
Dynamic and ambitious self-starter in his late thirties.
Skills required:
Good people skills; sharp legal mind; ability to handle an enormous volume of communication, make clear policy decisions, and deal ruthlessly with foreign peoples.
Experience:
Sufficient military background to act as commander-in-chief of world's most powerful army and preserve civilization as we know it.
Responsibilities:
Ruling the known world.
Job title:
EMPEROR OF ROME

Diverting though this exercise is, two basic problems bedevil any attempt to quantify the role of Roman emperor. First, the job as outlined above is fundamentally impossible, and second the material that we used to construct our job description is misleading. In writing about the 'perfect' emperor, the topic ancient commentators were actually addressing was the purpose of government. Emperors were representatives of the government as a whole, and the individual job description for each one might vary enormously from our norm. Even the notion of an ideal age for a new emperor is specious – in practice they fell into roughly three age brackets: one starting at around the age of 60, one around 40, and one in the early teens. These were largely conditioned by the needs of the age. There were periods when Romans did not need their emperor to do very much at all, and yet other times when his services were in great demand.

Communal power

It was quite remarkable that Romans should opt to be governed by emperors at all. Their state had done very well without a sole ruler and they were generally hostile to anything that smacked of kingship, for historical reasons that will presently become apparent. Moreover, temperamentally they were inclined to individualism, a trait which, when it has manifested itself in other societies, has sat uneasily with autocracy. Yet after hundreds of years of democracy, Romans found that their government could no longer keep pace with the speed of change and the special demands that came with being a superpower.

Foremost among these demands was that government should remain responsive to the needs of the majority of the people and not be hijacked by special-interest groups. The government of the Roman Republic failed to do this, and fell victim to men who took advantage of its weaknesses to further their own ambitions. That said, the men who usurped power in this way still found it impossible to do away entirely with the traditions of collective government that had existed for centuries under the Republic. The result was that Roman emperors always remained part of a governing group. What is even more extraordinary, however, and distinguishes the Roman empire from many more modern such polities, was that the post of emperor was not

A bust of the emperor Constantine. This early fourth-century ruler, the first Christian emperor of Rome, was one of the more long-serving and stable of the empire's many leaders. Roman emperors controlled an enormous state that stretched from the Atlantic to the borders of Iraq, and from the Rhine and Danube rivers to the Saharan and Arabian deserts. Their long period of rule over this vast domain, from the first century BC to the fifth century AD, witnessed momentous changes in society and culture.

reserved for people of Roman ancestry. Over time, it was filled by men from many different parts of the empire. Some only spoke Latin as a second language, while one was even the son of a freed slave.

At the root of these apparent idiosyncrasies of Rome's imperial system lie certain ingrained Roman attitudes. Notable among these was the great emphasis that Romans placed on an individual's relations with the community at large, plus their tendency to gauge personal happiness in terms of how other members of society saw them. These factors had a crucial bearing on Romans' perception of what it meant to be emperor.

The Roman fixation on communal participation is even enshrined in the official designation of the state – the *res publica populi Romani*, or 'public possession of the Roman people'. To be one of the people – a citizen – was therefore to be co-owner of an extraordinary entity. That said, not all the state's joint owners were created equal; every person's standing was reflected in the level of service that they devoted to the state. Being a wealthy Roman entailed taking an active role in government, holding public office and serving in positions of command in the army alongside one's peers. Middle-class Romans also undertook military service, while their appointed political role was to sanction the position of their social betters by voting them into office and affirming the proposals they put forward to the state's legislative bodies. The concept of serving the state even extended to the poor, who were expected to raise children and affirm the status quo by participating in the rituals of the state. To the Roman mind, there was nothing more abhorrent than the man who tried to shirk the duties that attended his station in life.

A key part of every prominent Roman's home, or domus, was his staff of slaves. When slaves became freedmen or freedwomen, it was accepted practice for them to publicly honour the master who freed them by taking his name and having his image incorporated on their tombs alongside their own. This funerary relief frieze from c. 30 BC shows the freedwoman Gessia Fausta (left) and the freedman Gessius Primus (right) flanking their former master, Publius Gessius.

Virtus and domus

An essential quality required by a Roman citizen was that of *virtus*. Its English derivative 'virtue', defined as 'the quality or practice of moral excellence or righteousness', does not successfully convey the meaning of the Latin concept. To the Romans, the word *virtus*, which was cognate with the Latin term for man (*vir*), denoted specifically male qualities of service to the state. So prevalent was the notion that *virtus* was essential to the community as a whole that women were also expected to demonstrate their own particular form of *virtus* by playing a supporting role to their menfolk. This role required them to maintain a stable environment within the man's home, or *domus*. The *domus* housed the family, who lived under the control and protection of a *paterfamilias*. His role was to represent the group in public and make sure that its members comported themselves in a fitting manner. To this end the *paterfamilias* was granted *patria potestas* – the power of life and death over every member of his family. Being invested with this draconian power meant that the Roman male was not truly a private person even within the bosom of his family. Rather, he was a representative of the community, supervising the actions of women, children and slaves to ensure that their behaviour conformed to the norms of Roman society. The fact that the *domus* was filled with sundry individuals who were subordinate to, and excluded from, the male world of public life, meant that it was also a potential threat to the order of society. In Roman thought the back rooms of the *domus* were places where un-Roman activities could occur. The antithesis of open public life was conspiracy, and conspiracies tended to be hatched by slaves and women in places that were out of sight of the community.

This exquisite fresco painting of a man and his wife was uncovered during the excavation of a house and attached bakery in the devastated city of Pompeii. The husband is wearing a toga, the traditional sign of Roman citizenship.

It was within the *domus* that a man might give vent to unacceptable passions, where he might be dominated by women or slaves, indulge excessively in sex with his subordinates, eat to excess, or waste the resources that should be at the disposal of the state in times of need. To the poor Roman who could not afford a *domus*, living in one room with a spouse and children in a rickety tenement, or in a hut in the country, the real test of the worth of a prominent citizen was how he behaved within his domestic setting. Did he live up to his public image or disgrace himself when he thought no one was looking? Be nice to your slaves if you are thinking of running for office, one politician advised another – they're the ones the people who hang around the forum will be talking to. It was in reaction to crimes committed within the *domus* that the Romans believed that their *res publica* was shaped.

From monarchy to republic

By the time the Romans started writing their own history in the third century BC, it was generally believed that kings had ruled them between the foundation of the city and the end of the sixth century. According to legend, in 509 BC the son of an odious king by the name of Tarquin the Proud (Tarquinius Superbus, reigned 535–510 BC) raped a woman called Lucretia. Lucretia revealed the crime to her brother Brutus before committing suicide. This outrage sparked a popular uprising; Brutus summoned the Roman people to the forum and called on them to depose the royal family, declaring the king and all members of his *domus* outlaws. In their place, he instituted a government based on annually elected colleges of magistrates. The working principle of this system was the devolution of *imperium*, the power to rule that the people had once conferred upon the king. The new government, where *imperium* was not only shared but also subject to checks and balances through legislation passed by the people, was seen as the polar opposite of one-man rule and autocracy, which came to be known simply as *regnum*, or 'royal power'.

The government of the Roman Republic proved astonishingly successful. During the fourth century BC the Romans conquered almost all of Italy south of the Po river. Rome then humbled Carthage, the North African city-state that had long controlled the sea-lanes of the western Mediterranean. The victory over Carthage and its great general Hannibal, which only came after decades of fierce fighting and terrible defeats, was the defining struggle in Roman history. It transformed Rome from a regional into a Mediterranean power and precipitated the rapid defeat of the Greek kingdoms that had dominated the eastern rim of the Mediterranean since the death of

THE KINGS OF ROME

Roman tradition held that the city had been ruled by seven kings:

ROMULUS
NUMA
TULLUS HOSTILIUS
ANCUS MARTIUS
TARQUIN
SERVIUS TULLUS
TARQUINIUS SUPERBUS

Mythology and history are inextricably intertwined in this list, but there is some evidence to suggest that Servius Tullus and Tarquin the Proud were historical figures.

ROMAN MAGISTRATES

Elected offices of the Roman state (magistracies) were:
  CENSORS (two, elected every five years for an
    eighteen-month term)
  CONSULS (two)
  PRAETORS
  AEDILES
  QUAESTORS
  TRIBUNES OF THE PLEBS

Advancement through the hierarchy of the offices (a career path called the *cursus honorum*) proceeded as follows: quaestorship, praetorship, and consulship. Several years had to elapse before the end of one tenure of office and the beginning of the next. Being aedile, a public-works office equivalent in rank to quaestor, was not a legal part of the cursus, but could be used as a stepping-stone to the praetorship.

The censors, consuls, praetors, aediles and quaestors all held *imperium*. The office of the tribune of the plebs was created as a check on the *imperium* of other magistrates, with tribunes having the power to veto any action by any other magistrate (including another tribune). All men who had been elected to the tribunate of the plebs or the quaestorship were eligible for membership in the senate, which approved measures to be voted on by the people.

The censors drew up the list of Roman citizens, reviewed the qualifications of sitting members of the senate, and issued contracts to corporations of equestrians for public services.

Consuls depicted on the Arch of Trajan, Benevento. Consuls were the two senior Roman magistrates, who were endowed with equal authority for the period of office.

Alexander the Great in 323 BC. By 146 BC, Rome had become the greatest power in the region's history. So why, given the signal success of their republican form of government and their hatred of autocracy, did the Romans even entertain the possibility of imperial rule? This was a question that even the Romans had difficulty answering.

Who was the first Caesar?

The most significant difference between Romans who wrote about the empire and modern authors who make the Caesars their subject matter is that latter-day commentators tend to assert as incontestable fact that the first emperor was Augustus (r. 31 BC–AD 14). Yet the only ancient Roman historian we know of who explicitly dated the start of the

'Tarquinius Superbus Founds the Temple of Jove on the Capitol' by the Italian Renaissance artist Perino del Vaga (c.1525). Tarquin the Proud's despotic reign was the catalyst for Romans to dispense with monarchy and institute a republican system of government. Even under imperial rule, the notion of kingship, and the absolutism it implied, remained anathema to Romans.

imperial system at 31 BC was Cassius Dio (c. AD 155–229), who was writing almost 300 years after the event. Among the many precursors and contemporaries who disagreed with Cassius was the biographer Marius Maximus, who was also active in the early third century. Maximus' book on the 'next' 12 Caesars (from Nerva to Elagabalus) implicitly takes its point of departure from the famous *Lives of the Twelve Caesars* by Suetonius (*c.* AD 69–130), which ended with the death of Domitian. Suetonius' first Caesar was Julius Caesar.

In turn, Suetonius' account of the Caesars also excited opposition from his contemporaries, such as the Greek biographer Plutarch. Plutarch included Julius Caesar in his work on prominent Greeks and Romans who lived before the advent of the empire. Another first-century historian, Cornelius Tacitus (*c.* AD 56–117), chose to begin his account of the development of the imperial system with the death of Augustus.

The lack of unanimity among these historians is mirrored in texts connected with the emperors themselves. A portion of a law conferring supreme power on Vespasian in AD 70 backdated his accession to his rebellion against the reigning emperor in AD 69, and listed only three previous emperors as having had powers comparable to those conferred on him. These were Augustus, Tiberius (AD 14–37), and Claudius, the grand nephew of Augustus (AD 41–54). The state's official record thus effectively airbrushed from history five men who had previously occupied the same post as that now held by Vespasian – and had been listed as such by Suetonius – while Julius Caesar wasn't even deemed part of the group.

A fundamental tension

What, then, became of these five missing leaders? The answer lies in Roman attitudes to power and the appropriate behaviour of an individual. The Roman ruling classes were supposed to set positive examples for their fellow citizens through their exercise of *virtus*. If they succumbed to the unbridled passions of the *domus*, they were not fit exemplars for others, and could therefore be struck off the list of 'approved' emperors. The emperor did not rule through divine right, but by virtue of a legal process that entitled him to wield power over other members of the governing class. For all his imperial pomp, he still remained a representative of that class – a first among equals, so to speak. This fact is echoed in his title of *princeps*, or 'leading man'.

'All power passed from the people and senate to Augustus, and from this time on there was, strictly speaking, a monarchy.'

CASSIUS DIO (ROMAN HISTORY, 53.17.1)

Tacitus expressed this point lucidly when comparing the task of the historian in republican Rome to his role in the imperial age. Whereas historians were formerly required to be well versed in all the diverse aspects of public life, 'now, with public affairs transformed so that there is no salvation for the state unless one man rules', their sole subject of study was this sole ruler and his dealings with those around him. This sea-change in the mode of governance came about as a result of the political crises that shook the Roman state to its very core in the century before Augustus. The advent of one-person rule must be seen in the context of a wider process of change affecting the nature of government in the Roman world.

The fundamental tension between the individual ruler and the system that Tacitus drew attention to would remain central to the history of Rome from the first century BC to the point at which the system failed to provide for the needs of society at the end of the fifth century AD. In the light of this, the conventional view of the Caesars as a succession of more or less colourful autocrats needs to be revised. First and foremost, they were representatives of the changing needs of the Roman people.

GREAT CAESAR'S GHOST

The Forum was the hub of commercial, judicial and political life in ancient Rome. Over time, many emperors embellished this space with new temples, triumphal arches and basilicas.

A Succession of Strongmen: Rome from Gaius Marius to Caesar (107–44 BC)

Rome's transition from a republic into an empire took place in the period of social turmoil that followed the infamous assassination of Julius Caesar by his former political confederates. Yet while all ancient historians see Caesar as a pivotal figure in this transformation, they disagree over his precise historical position. While some regard him as the last of the triumvirate of strongmen who dominated the political landscape of the Roman Republic in the first half of the first century BC, others prefer to see him as the progenitor of a dynasty of emperors that endured until AD 68 and included some of the most illustrious and notorious holders of the office.

A bust of Julius Caesar. The outstanding military commander of his age, Caesar rose to political prominence by portraying himself as virtuous and incorruptible. However, his increasingly autocratic control made him enemies among the Roman ruling classes, who conspired to be rid of him. He was assassinated on the fateful Ides of March in 44 BC.

Ancient writers' views of Caesar's assassination depend very much upon their attitude to the imperial system. Suetonius (AD 69–140), who hoped that his accounts of the lives of the emperors would provide examples for future rulers , was in no doubt that it was fully justified: Caesar, he claimed, had abrogated his leadership responsibilities by failing to pay due respect either to fellow members of Rome's élite or to the institutions of the Republic. By contrast, the Greek biographer Plutarch (*c.* AD 46–120, in his *Parallel Lives*) described Julius Caesar's death as a catastrophe that upset the natural order of the world. As for Caesar himself, he is reported to have said, with characteristic acuity and foresight, that if he were assassinated the result would be chaos. But what were Caesar's origins and how had both his own life and that of Rome in general proceeded up to his untimely death in 44 BC?

The Julii Caesares

Gaius Julius Caesar was born into the patrician class – the hereditary aristocratic ruling élite of Rome – in 100 BC. His family claimed descent from extraordinarily exalted ancestors, in the shape of both of

This 16th-century painting, by Giuseppe Cesari, shows the mythical founders of Rome – Romulus and Remus – being suckled by a she-wolf. After the shepherd Faustulus and his wife Acca Laurentia (centre) found the boys, they raised them to manhood. Romans were extremely proud of their city's origins, and it was a badge of honour to be able to claim ancestry from these legendary twins.

TIMELINE

107 BC Marius elected consul for the first time

104 Marius institutes army reforms

91 Questions of land reform and Roman citizenship spark the Social War (to 88)

89 King Mithridates of Pontus attacks Roman territory; First Mithridatic War (to 85)

82 Sulla installs himself as dictator of Rome

73 Outbreak of the slave revolt in Italy under Spartacus

67 Pompey is tasked with ridding the Mediterranean of pirates

66 Pompey granted extensive command against Mithridates

60 Caesar elected consul; creates informal alliance with Pompey and Crassus (First Triumvirate)

58 Caesar fights the Gallic Wars (to 51)

53 Crassus is killed fighting the Parthians at the Battle of Carrhae

49 Caesar crosses the Rubicon and invades Italy

44 Murder of Caesar on the Ides of March

the legendary founders of Rome – Aeneas and Romulus. Furthermore, through these mortal forebears they were also connected to two deities: Aeneas was thought to have been born to the goddess Venus and a man named Anchises, while Romulus was the offspring of a woman of noble background, Rhea Silvia, who gave birth to him and his twin brother Remus after being raped by the god Mars. The legend goes on to relate how the twins were set adrift on the River Tiber but were saved by divine intervention and went on to found the city of Rome.

With two gods in the family tree, most of the early Julii Caesares lacked any real incentive to enhance the earthly status of their family. For most of their history they pursued a languid aristocratic lifestyle that left almost no mark on the annals of Rome. It was only with the election of Julius Caesar's uncle as a consul and the later accession of his father to the office of praetor that the family attained any kind of prominence. However, the most significant of all Caesar's immediate forebears was not a male relative at all but rather his aunt Julia (*c*.130–69 BC), who in *c*.110 BC raised the profile of her family at a stroke through her marriage to Gaius Marius, the most renowned Roman of the age.

The career of Gaius Marius (157–86 BC) was as glorious as it was unexpected. He was not born a patrician and so could not call upon a long lineage of illustrious ancestors to advance his political career.

Plutarch tells a story that, when Gaius Marius fled to North Africa in 88 BC, he sent a messenger to the Roman governor to report that he had 'seen Gaius Marius sitting in exile among the ruins of Carthage', so linking his own fate to that of the destroyed city. This wistful, romantic image became a favourite subject of later painters, as in this fanciful 19th-century print.

A further handicap was that he came not from Rome but from the town of Arpinum, some 60 miles (100 kilometres) distant. Rather, Marius' rise to power was based on sheer personal ability combined with a talent for ruthlessly eliminating anyone who stood in his path. In the 20 years before Caesar's birth, Marius carved out a niche for himself as an expert on military affairs, at a time when the governing élite was experiencing a dearth of talented military tacticians and commanders from among its own ranks. Exploiting the political scandals sparked by a series of military fiascos, including a disastrous war in North Africa and several badly botched campaigns in southern France, Marius succeeded in getting himself elected consul in the face of determined opposition from the patrician establishment. In his new role, he swiftly brought the war in Africa to a successful conclusion. As if to underline Marius' skill and his opponents' ineptitude, just as he was ending his campaign, two Roman generals in southern France saw their armies wiped out by invading German tribesmen on the same day; this disaster arose from their pigheaded refusal to cooperate with each other.

Marius was elected consul for a second time in 105 BC (and would be re-elected every year thereafter until 100 BC – his final tally of seven consulships was unparalleled in Roman history). That same year, he took command of the demoralized armies in southern France and northern Italy. In developing his career through his military prowess, Marius moulded himself into the first *princeps*, a military strong man who used his army power base to exert political control. Marius' example would prove a potent model for his as yet unborn nephew.

PATRICIANS AND PLEBEIANS

In the earliest period of Roman history the Roman people were divided between an ancient hereditary nobility – called the patricians – and the broad mass of the common people, who were known as the plebeians (or plebs, for short). The distinction between these classes was one of blood rather than wealth. In the early years of the Republic only patricians were entitled to hold public office. However, in 368–367 BC the constitution was amended to allow plebeians to be elected as well. Any plebeian who was elected consul was automatically raised to the nobility, and was known as a 'new man' (*novus homo*).

By 100, Marius had defeated the German invaders and shortly thereafter retired from public life, since he was by then in his sixties. Yet the situation in Rome continued to worsen, for which Marius himself may have been partly to blame. The major reforms he instituted in the Roman army had forged a strong bond between himself and his men that far outstripped the loyalty they felt towards the government of the Republic (a term originating from the Latin *res publica*, literally meaning 'public thing'). The principal reason for their disaffection had to do with money. The average period of service for a Roman soldier had grown considerably over time; moreover, many men spent much of their tour of duty in provincial garrisons and no coherent plan existed for their retirement. Whether soldiers ultimately received any recompense for their years of service depended entirely upon how well connected their commanding officers were in political circles. A general with influence would secure special terms – usually land grants – for his men when they retired from the army. Marius had been one such commander, and his generosity had even extended to granting non-Romans citizenship in recognition of their loyal service.

Land and citizenship

The issue of who was entitled to be a Roman citizen was fast becoming the burning question of the day. In 100 BC, most inhabitants of Italy were not actually citizens of Rome. The towns where they lived were nominally allied to the Roman state through treaties imposed on them during Rome's victorious wars of expansion in the fourth and third centuries BC. Since then, they had reluctantly taken the role of Roman vassal states. But in 133 BC this uneasy peace had been shattered by the agitation of a plebeian tribune named Tiberius Gracchus (163–133 BC).

Concerned at the decline he perceived in Roman *virtus* (the quality of manly courage and steadfastness), Gracchus concluded that this was the upshot of many Romans abandoning traditional life on the family farm. His suggested remedy was a law redistributing land that Rome had originally seized from the cities of Italy, but which had since been left largely under their control. Gracchus' legislation infuriated not only the inhabitants of the vassal cities but also many Roman senators, who disapproved of what they regarded as his wilful disruption of the status quo. Although the divisive law was passed, its chief architect promptly paid with his life, murdered by political enemies.

Ten years later, Gracchus' younger brother Gaius (154–121 BC) introduced a series of laws designed to further reorganize the state. One of his proposed reforms was that all Italians should be made

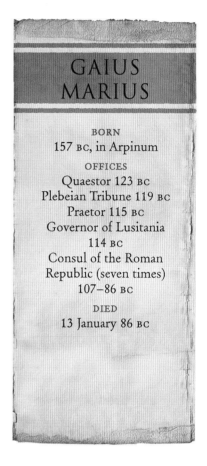

GAIUS MARIUS

BORN
157 BC, in Arpinum

OFFICES
Quaestor 123 BC
Plebeian Tribune 119 BC
Praetor 115 BC
Governor of Lusitania
114 BC
Consul of the Roman
Republic (seven times)
107–86 BC

DIED
13 January 86 BC

A floor mosaic from a Roman villa, showing a pastoral scene of agricultural workers threshing by driving horses and cattle over a pile of wheat. The second and first centuries BC witnessed bitter disputes over who had the right to settle and work the land in Italy.

citizens of Rome. Conservative senators (*optimates*) who had opposed Tiberius were just as outraged by Gaius' proposals, and, when he failed to win re-election for a third term, they summoned troops into Rome to massacre him and his supporters.

Over the next two decades, the related issues of land distribution and Roman citizenship arose time and again, but were never resolved. The basic problem was that, while many poor Romans were attracted by the prospect of receiving free land from the state, they were not prepared in return to share the advantages of Roman citizenship with other cities of Italy. Conversely, the Italians would not stand for massive land redistribution unless they were given a stake in governing the country. Marius was thrown headlong into this long-running controversy in

100 BC, when he deployed his troops to crush the supporters of yet another tribune who was agitating in favour of radical agrarian reforms.

The rise of Sulla

The spectre of land distribution and citizenship reared its head once more in 91 BC. When the tribune who was sponsoring the new reform bill suddenly turned up dead, the Italians, incensed by years of foot-dragging and abortive attempts at legislation, rose in revolt. Gaius Marius came out of retirement to command one of the armies that Rome put into the field to face them. At the head of another army was Lucius Cornelius Sulla (c.138–78 BC), formerly a lieutenant of Marius, but now opposed to his former commander. In the course of this so-called Social War – named for the *Socii*, the Latin term for Rome's erstwhile Italian allies – Sulla soon proved to be an outstanding general in his own right.

Two momentous events marked the year of 89 BC. First, the Roman state split the Italian resistance by passing a bill offering citizenship to the inhabitants of any city that lay down its arms. Many accepted the offer, and the war turned decisively against those who chose to fight on. At the same time, King Mithridates VI (132–63 BC) of Pontus (a state on the Black Sea coast of modern Turkey) launched an attack on Roman lands in the eastern Mediterranean. The senate voted that command in this war, which promised to be a far more profitable and glorious venture than the ongoing mopping-up operations in Italy should go to one of the consuls for the following year. Sulla was duly elected and put in charge of the campaign against Mithridates.

Sulla did not hold on to his prize for long. A tribune introduced a group of bills which, in addition to offering Roman citizenship to the Italians on far more favourable terms than before, also transferred command of the Mithridatic War to Marius. Sulla, outraged at what he regarded as an illegal act by the tribune, turned to his army for support. He was easily able to exploit the troops' anger at being deprived of a chance to share in the spoils that would flow from reconquering the eastern provinces. And so Sulla and his legions marched on Rome to force the senate to rescind its decision. Encountering only minimal resistance, he occupied the city and sentenced his political opponents to death before marching east once more. Meanwhile Marius, who barely escaped with his life, fled to North Africa.

> ### DICTATORS
>
> The constitution of the Roman Republic contained a special provision for the appointment of an individual to deal with specific crises facing the state; this position was known as the dictatorship. Elected by the consul, the dictator had the authority to overrule all other magistrates for a period of six months during times of emergency. Sulla was the first dictator whose term of office was unlimited. Later, Caesar also consolidated his power by assuming the dictatorship in perpetuity.

Mithridates VI of Pontus, portrayed on a contemporary coin. After overrunning western Anatolia (Turkey) in 88 BC, Mithridates is reputed to have ordered the death of all Roman settlers there, an atrocity that cost 80,000 people their lives. Rome finally defeated him in 65 BC.

SULLA

BORN
138 BC, in Rome

MARRIED
(1) Cornelia Sulla, born
c. 109 BC
(2) Aelia
(3) Caecilia Metella
Dalmatica, died c. 80 BC
(4) Valeria Messala

CHILDREN
(by 1) Faustus (I) Cornelius
Sulla
(78–47 BC)
(by 4) Postima Cornelia Sulla

OFFICES
Quaestor 107 BC
Praetor 94 BC
Governor of Cilicia 93 BC
Consul of the Roman
Republic 88 BC, 80 BC
Dictator of the Roman
Republic 82–79 BC

DIED
78 BC, Puteoli, near Naples,
southern Italy

Before resuming command of the Mithridatic War, Sulla had tried to secure his position in Rome by getting his supporters elected to the two consulships for 87 BC. Yet he failed in this and was forced to witness the election of his sworn enemy Lucius Cornelius Cinna (d. 84 BC) to one of the posts. Sulla had the military might to remove Cinna, but instead let him remain in office provided he swore to uphold the legislation that Sulla had introduced. Cinna lied; shortly after the start of his consulship, he broke his oath and led his own army against Rome. Marius returned from North Africa to join the armies that were now fighting their way into the city, massacring all of Sulla's supporters who did not flee or go into hiding. At the end of the year, Marius was elected consul for the seventh time, but died soon after taking office.

Over the following years Sulla succeeded in defeating Mithridates. The spoils of victory were great; not only did he loot vast treasures from the eastern provinces, but his coffers were also swelled by money from Mithridates, whom he had permitted to remain as king of Pontus in return for huge reparations payments. These finances enabled Sulla to reinvade Italy. By the end of 82 BC he had defeated his main enemies and had himself installed as dictator for as long as he wished. Sulla's dictatorial rule provided an object lesson for later rulers of Rome.

The bloody regime of Sulla

Sulla immediately embarked on a reign of terror. During his advance on Rome, he had committed a string of atrocities, including massacring prisoners, executing opposing generals and destroying districts that held out against him. Once installed in the city, Sulla posted lists of men who were 'proscribed,' namely condemned to death. Although the first targets of Sulla's proscriptions were his political opponents, soon anyone with property or wealth began to be included. Sulla personally presided over this bloodbath, encouraging bounty hunters to bring him the severed heads of proscribed men in return for a reward. The estates of the victims were confiscated by the state, and for the most part were sold off at knockdown prices to Sulla's supporters. Those districts of Italy that had supported Sulla's enemies were subject to massive confiscations of land, which were then divided up into sizeable farms for Sulla's retired veterans. In the dictator's savage reckoning, since he could never hope to reconcile his enemies to his newly purified Roman state, the only logical course of action was to kill them and eradicate their former power bases. Yet perversely the sheer brutality of Sulla's campaign actually succeeded in hardening opposition against him. And so, even though the civil war ended on the main Italian front in 81 BC, desperate men fought on for nearly a decade in more remote Roman outposts such as North Africa, southern France and especially Spain. Further sporadic revolts even occurred in Italy itself. The last and most famous of these was the great rural uprising led by the gladiator Spartacus (c.100–70 BC); while many of the rebels who took part in it were slaves, it was notable that Spartacus also managed to attract many dispossessed former soldiers to his ranks.

Sulla lived until 78 BC, resigning his dictatorship a few months before his death, which was probably hastened by his excessive fondness for drink. In a cynical comment on absolute power, Julius Caesar later claimed that Sulla's decision to retire simply proved that he didn't know what he was doing. In fact, Caesar was extremely fortunate to have survived Sulla's reign of terror. According to a story that Caesar himself later put about, he had been on the list of people that Sulla wanted killed. He was only saved by the intervention of friends and the Vestal Virgins. In pardoning him, Sulla is alleged to have remarked that there were 'many Mariuses' in the young man. What is beyond dispute is that Caesar found it prudent to complete his higher education in Greece until the situation in Rome calmed down.

The irresistible rise of Caesar

Caesar's defining character trait was his great ambition. He won renown as a junior officer in the eastern Mediterranean – Mithridates never gave up his desire to conquer Rome's eastern holdings, and launched another attack there in 76 BC. Having proved his *virtus* in war, Caesar returned to Rome and began to rally support among opponents of the political establishment by cultivating a personal style that marked him as a radical. He wore clothes that were generally regarded as too modish and became known as something of a ladies' man. He also ran up huge debts, and was forced to borrow heavily from

On entering service, Vestal Virgins spent ten years as students, ten as keepers of the sacred fire and ten as teachers. This ancient statue of a Vestal Virgin, which stands in the Roman Forum, shows the ceremonial robes worn by office holders – a simple shroud, the palla, and the long headdress known as the infula.

THE VESTAL VIRGINS

Vesta was the patron goddess of the hearth, the centre of the Roman home, and was universally worshipped by Roman citizens at shrines in their own houses. In addition, in the Roman forum an eternal flame was kept alight at the Temple of Vesta (the ruins of which can still be seen). The fire was tended by six Vestal Virgins, who were chosen from noble families at the age of seven and served the goddess for 30 years. It was a great honour to be made a Vestal Virgin, and any transgressions were severely punished. For example, if a Vestal Virgin allowed the flame to go out – an event that the superstitious Romans thought foretold disaster for the city – she was whipped. Worse still, if she lost her virginity, she would be buried alive.

POMPEY

BORN
29 September, 106 BC, in
Rome

FATHER
Gnaeus Pompeius Strabo

MARRIED
(1) Antistia
(2) Aemilia Scaura
100–82 BC
(3) Mucia Tertia
(4) Julia Caesaris 82–54 BC
(5) Cornelia Metella

CHILDREN
(by 3) Gnaeus Pompeius
(75–45 BC) Pompeia, Sextus
Pompeius (died 35 BC)

OFFICES
Consul of the Roman
Republic 70 BC, 55 BC, 52 BC

DIED
29 September, 48 BC, in
Egypt (murdered by envoys
of Ptolemy XIII)

one of Sulla's former generals, Marcus Licinius Crassus (*c.*115–53 BC), who had been responsible for suppressing Spartacus' revolt. Crassus had amassed a vast personal fortune through trading in slaves, mining interests and property speculation. Yet he was an intemperate personality who made many enemies, even falling out with his former ally Sulla. In particular, Crassus was almost pathologically jealous of Gnaeus Pompeius Magnus, better known as Pompey (106–48 BC). Though still only in his twenties, Pompey had displayed great military skill in Sulla's service – earning himself the nickname *adulescentulus carnifex* ('the teenage butcher') – and carved out a reputation as Rome's coming man, despite never having held political office.

Unfazed by the envy of Crassus, with whom he shared the consulship in 70 BC Pompey spent most of the 60s commanding Roman armies abroad. When pirates raided the coast of Italy and kidnapped two Roman magistrates, Pompey was charged with the task of sweeping them from the Mediterranean. Within a year, he was claiming outright victory and had engineered his own appointment as commander-in-chief of the Mithridatic War. Pompey brought this conflict to a successful end three years later.

Caesar, meanwhile, continued to groom his political career. Elected aedile in 65 BC, he restored the trophies of Marius' victories against the Germans – destroyed by Sulla – to their former place of honour. In the same year he held a lavish public funeral for his aunt, Marius' widow, and laid claim to the political mantle of Marius himself. During his lifetime, Marius had been anything but a radical, but he now became a rallying point for enemies of the post-Sullan regime. Caesar made sure that he was identified closely with the myth he spun around his uncle. In 63 he was elected as praetor, setting up a run for the consulship three years later (the interval between the two offices had become statutory for everyone except Pompey, who had never held any office other than consul), and as *pontifex maximus*, the high priest of Rome.

> 'Soon Gaius Marius, from the lowest class, and Lucius Sulla, the most savage of the nobles, turned free government, conquered by arms, into tyranny. Gnaeus Pompey came next, less obvious but no better, and now nothing was sought except domination of the state.'
>
> TACITUS (HISTORIES 3.38)

This latter office was more political than religious. The Roman state religion was overseen by several collective priesthoods, of which the most influential were the pontiffs, whose leader Caesar now became. Their main function was to oversee other groups of priests. The office of *pontifex maximus* also brought with it several perks, chief among which was occupancy of the Regia in the heart of the Roman Forum. Residing here put Caesar quite literally in the centre of the city's political life. Yet the two election campaigns also left him deep in debt.

Manoeuvring for power

By the end of 62 BC Caesar's financial problems were so serious that Suetonius recounts that he was obliged to slip out of town in the dead of night to avoid being seized by his creditors. Like many Romans of his day, Caesar saw the opportunity to govern a province – a privilege accorded to praetors either during or after their year in office – as a chance to recoup the enormous sums he had spent while running for office. Political campaigns, then as now, were extremely expensive undertakings, and Caesar had earned a reputation for extravagant spending. In 65 he had purchased so many gladiators for the shows which his post of aedile obliged him to stage that his enemies in the senate passed a law restricting the number of performers any one person could engage. Caesar's successful contest of the two elections in 63 would have entailed even more lavish outlay. According to Roman law, a man standing for election was permitted to offer a cash gift to every member of his tribe. In Roman eyes, this did not constitute a bribe. Rather, it was regarded simply as 'munificence', and displays of such generosity guaranteed a person popular acclaim in Rome. By contrast, what Romans found truly distasteful was excessive private luxury, and so Caesar was careful to make it clear that the vast sums of money he borrowed were for the benefit of the Roman people rather than his own pleasure.

Aside from Caesar's fondness for fancy clothes and his vanity (by this stage he was trying to conceal his incipient baldness with a combed-over hairstyle) he was notably abstemious in his private life. One enemy even remarked that he was the only sober man who ever tried to ruin the Republic.

Pompey experienced a meteoric rise to fame as a brilliant general. Over time, however, his achievements were overshadowed by those of Caesar and conflict between the two became inevitable. In the civil war of 49–48 BC, Caesar contemptuously dismissed his adversary's skill: 'The enemy would have won if they had had a commander who was a winner.'

ROMAN NAMES

Roman names were an outward sign of the bearer's biological and legal relationships. Each person's name had three parts: a *praenomen* or first name, a *nomen* or family name and a filiation, which indicated both the individual's relationship to the authoritarian head of the family, the *paterfamilias*, and the 'tribe' to which he or she belonged. All Roman citizens were members of one of 35 tribes. Freed slaves took their *praenomen* and *nomen* from their master, but, in place of filiation, the third part of their names simply indicated that they had been freed. The names of wealthy Romans customarily included a fourth element, or *cognomen*. For example, Gaius Julius, son of Gaius, Caesar of the Polline tribe is a typical four-part aristocratic name.

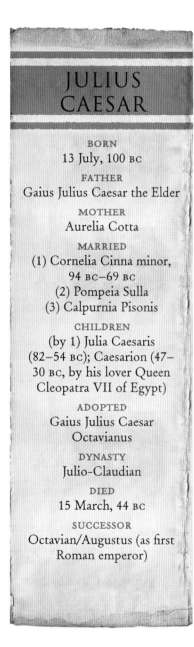

JULIUS CAESAR

BORN
13 July, 100 BC

FATHER
Gaius Julius Caesar the Elder

MOTHER
Aurelia Cotta

MARRIED
(1) Cornelia Cinna minor,
94 BC–69 BC
(2) Pompeia Sulla
(3) Calpurnia Pisonis

CHILDREN
(by 1) Julia Caesaris
(82–54 BC); Caesarion (47–
30 BC, by his lover Queen
Cleopatra VII of Egypt)

ADOPTED
Gaius Julius Caesar
Octavianus

DYNASTY
Julio-Claudian

DIED
15 March, 44 BC

SUCCESSOR
Octavian/Augustus (as first
Roman emperor)

Caesar's studied frugality stood in marked contrast to the profligacy of the old regime. Many of Sulla's friends had become as self-indulgent as their former general, erecting enormous villas and throwing extravagant private banquets. Caesar also appears to have treated his slaves humanely and was popular with his gladiators, perhaps owing to his unwillingness to expose them to fights to the death. Where his personal life was open to criticism was in the bedroom, and it was this Achilles' heel that his enemies targeted. They declared his public displays of *virtus* through generosity a sham, pointing instead to his immodest conduct in the very heart of the *domus*.

Personal indiscretions

On one occasion Caesar even arranged for a love letter from the sister of one of his fiercest political opponents, Marcus Portius Cato the Younger (95–46 BC), to be ostentatiously delivered to him while the senate was in session. Thinking that Caesar had just received a secret message that would implicate him in a conspiracy against the state, Cato demanded that he read it aloud, only to be humiliated by the public airing of its contents.

Caesar's enemies claimed to have proof that, while serving as an ambassador at the court of Nicomedes IV of Bithynia in 80 BC (a kingdom bordering the former lands of Mithridates in northern Turkey), he had allowed himself to be sodomized by the king. Their objection was not so much that Caesar had had sex with another man, but that he had taken the passive role. He was not, therefore, a 'real man,' but a *cinadeus* – a man who played the 'female part' during lovemaking. One enemy even quipped that he was 'every woman's husband and every man's wife'. Caesar was furious, and remained intensely defensive on the subject for the rest of his life. Yet he failed to prevent the rumour from spreading, and even his soldiers, who seem genuinely to have admired him, later sang lewd ballads about Caesar as the 'Queen of Bithynia'. This scurrilous story was all the more hilarious to Caesar's contemporaries since it was totally at odds with his carefully groomed public persona of the virtuous, clean-living man.

Caesar managed to weather both his financial problems and the slanders of his opponents. His one-year term as governor of Spain netted him enough money to enable him to discharge his debts and stand for the consulship of 59 BC. He easily won the election and began to consolidate his position. In this he was aided by the ineptitude of his enemies, who had managed simultaneously to alienate both Crassus and Pompey. Crassus had tried to establish a power base in Rome by representing the interests of the equestrian corporations. However, these bodies were soon embroiled in a financial scandal concerning taxation in the province of Asia (western Turkey). The senate refused to remit the money they owed the state, threatening them with bankruptcy. For his part, Pompey found himself at loggerheads with the senate when it refused to authorize retirement payments to his soldiers and blocked his administrative reforms in the eastern provinces. Spotting an opportunity for an advantageous alliance, Caesar first arranged for his only child, Julia, to marry Pompey, and then made political overtures to both Pompey and Crassus. Exploiting his position as consul (in which capacity he was allowed to put bills before the people without prior approval from the senate), he promised to introduce legislation to help the two men overcome their present difficulties if they, in return, would give their backing to a bill granting Caesar a five-year command in the province of his choice.

This naked political skulduggery provoked scenes of uproar in the senate, during which Caesar's consular colleague and leader of the faction opposing his legislative programme was doused with the contents of a chamber pot. It seems likely that Caesar himself

Guests at a Roman banquet. From late Republican times, as the prosperity of the upper classes grew, such gatherings became a byword for gluttonous excess. An account of one especially lavish meal describes: 'A hare decked out with wings to look like Pegasus, a wild sow with its belly full of live thrushes, quinces stuck with thorns to look like sea-urchins, and roast pork carved into models of fish, song birds and a goose'. However, Caesar recognized early on that anyone who ran for public office in Rome did well to profess a frugal lifestyle.

engineered this furore as a diversionary tactic, testifying to the fact that he was already well versed in the black arts of politics. In any event, the manoeuvre achieved its aim, with Pompey and Crassus getting what they wanted and Caesar securing not one but three provinces. At the start of 58 BC he left Rome to govern the provinces of Transalpine Gaul (southern France), Cisalpine Gaul (northern Italy, also known as Gallia Togata, or 'Toga-wearing Gaul') and Illyricum (present-day Croatia).

Caesar the general

This period – from 58 to 50 BC – laid the foundation of Caesar's reputation as the greatest general in Roman history. His enemies hoped that his lack of experience as a military commander would prove his undoing and that he would fall victim to one of the many fierce tribes in the badlands beyond Rome's borders. Yet Caesar soon confounded them, showing himself adept at transferring to the battlefield the skills that had brought him political success. Behind the often deceptively simple accounts that he wrote of his campaigns – ultimately collected together in his work *The Gallic Wars* (*De Bello Gallico*) – lay a boundless capacity for forward planning, a keen understanding of the psychology of his opponents, an impressive flexibility when confronted with new problems and a profound confidence in his own ability.

Time and again in Caesar's narrative, an apparently throwaway remark reveals that supplies were being prudently laid up in advance, detailed intelligence gathered and strategic plans altered to exploit changing circumstances or to respond to unforeseen challenges. Above all, Caesar knew that absolutely no faith should be placed in intelligence offered by people who stood to gain from supplying information, that wars are won not on the battlefield so much as at the conference table and that the enemy was watching and reacting to his every move.

THE EQUESTRIAN CLASS

The term 'equestrian' was originally applied to wealthy members of Roman society who could afford to serve as cavalrymen. This group steadily gained in influence as their economic power increased. Equestrians who chose not to hold public office were permitted to form corporations to provide services for the Roman state. They tendered for work by estimating the cost of providing this service and offering this sum to the censors. If the revenue they amassed during their employment exceeded the estimate, they were entitled to keep the profit. But if they estimated too low, they were personally liable for making up any shortfall to the state.

Roman territory, *c.* 201 BC

gains by 100 BC

gains by 44 BC

gains by AD 14

gains by AD 117

temporary gain, with dates held

kingdom of Pontus under
Mithridates VI, 112–63 BC

● Roman provincial capital

*The growth of Rome from the late
Republic to the end of Hadrian's reign in
AD 117, showing most of the provinces of
the expanding state. Rome discovered to its
cost that interventions in areas completely
unsuited to assimilating Roman institutions
were costly failures, and Hadrian was
content to consolidate existing boundaries.*

GERMANIA
12 BC–AD 9

Rhine

Elbe

Oder

● Colonia Agrippinensis

MANIA
ERIOR

LGICA

rocortorum

● Moguntiacum

Danube

● Augusta
Vindelicum

● Carnuntum

GERMANIA
SUPERIOR

RAETIA NORICUM

● Aquincum

● Virunum

unum

● Axima

Po

● Segusio

LIA

BONENSIS

● Cemenelum

ssilia

PANNONIA

Sava

DACIA

● Sarmizegethusa

Black Sea

DALMATIA

● Viminacium

Danube

Tiber

CORSICA

● Aleria

● Rome

ITALIA

SARDINIA

● Carales

MOESIA
SUPERIOR

MOESIA
INFERIOR

THRACIA

Perinthus
●

BITHYNIA
AND PONTUS

● Nicomedia

● Thessalonica

MACEDONIA

ASIA

● Ancyra

● Caesarea

CAPPADOCIA

GALATIA

● Tarsus

CILICIA

● Antioch

ARMENIA
AD 115–117

SICILIA

● Syracuse

● Corinth

● Ephesus

● Myra

CYPRUS

SYRIA

● Carthage

CRETE

● Gortyn

● Paphos

Mediterranean Sea

JUDEA ● Bostra

● Caesarea

● Cyrene

● Alexandria

ARABIA

FRICA

CYRENAICA

AEGYPTUS

Nile

'It is often the case that, motivated by rumours, the Gauls make decisions about the most important matters, which they often change their minds about very quickly, since they are slaves to rumour and many people make things up to tell them what they want to hear.'

CAESAR (THE CONQUEST OF GAUL, 4.5)

For this reason, he never employed the same tactics twice in battle. He also spent a great deal of time before and after the campaigning season winning hearts and minds among those Gauls who saw that their own interests were best served by supporting him.

Yet despite his overall record of success, there were also setbacks, which proved that even Caesar had human failings. For example, he was sometimes too quick to assume that his solutions were acceptable to everyone. In the winter of 54–53 BC he divided his legions into several camps to avoid any single Gaulish tribe having to shoulder the burden of tens of thousands of Roman legionaries billeted on its territory and exhausting its food and fodder supplies after the bad harvest that year. He may well have thought that this concession went far enough, since no tribe would surely be foolish enough to stage a revolt on its own. This was a fatal miscalculation: a force of up to 8000 men was wiped out when their commander was tricked into abandoning his camp. Caesar had plainly not devised any contingency plan for his officers to follow in case of trouble. Similarly, he is quick to blame a Roman defeat during the siege of a Gallic city in 52 BC on his men panicking. But an aside by Caesar on this incident paints a different picture; he concedes that the terrain made it hard for commanders to adapt his orders to events as they unfolded on the ground. Caesar spent a great deal of time trying to communicate his strategic and tactical vision to his subordinates, but seems to have felt, at times, that people ought to read his mind. In the long run, this style of leadership would prove fatal to Caesar when he applied it to the running of the Roman state.

This coin, with suitably martial symbols of a warrior with a shield and a hatchet, was minted in c.48–44 BC in commemoration of Julius Caesar's military conquests. During this period, the senate showered Caesar with many honours, including naming the month of his birth after him.

While Caesar was away campaigning in Gaul, several events had conspired to change the political landscape in Rome dramatically. For a start, one of Rome's triumvirate of strong men was dead, killed ignominiously in battle in a far-off land. Jealous of both Caesar and Pompey, Crassus had embarked on a military adventure of his own by launching an illegal invasion of the Parthian Empire. This realm, which included modern Iraq and Iran, was the only remaining major power on Rome's borders. Crassus was dismissive of enemies whom Rome had never fought and made no effort to grasp their strategy or tactics. Predictably, his ill-advised campaign ended in a crushing defeat, as his large army was routed outside the city of

Carrhae, the present-day city of Harran in Turkey, in 53 BC. Crassus himself was cut down in this bloody fiasco. The only consolation for Rome was that the Parthians, excellent though they were in holding their own ground, as yet lacked the organization to pose any real threat to its eastern provinces.

While Crassus' death removed a major rival to the ambitions of Caesar and Pompey, it crucially also meant that there was now no longer any figure of comparable stature who could act as a mediator between them. In any event, even before Crassus' demise, the bond between Caesar and Pompey had already been dealt a fatal blow by the death of Julia, Caesar's daughter and Pompey's wife, in 55 BC. Increasingly alarmed at Caesar's inexorable rise, Pompey formally severed all links with him in 52 BC and began to prepare for the possibility of war.

Crossing the Rubicon

By the summer of 50 BC Caesar had united all of what is now modern France, along with parts of Germany and Belgium, under his rule. Proud of his achievements, the illustrious general felt that he was entitled to dictate the terms on which he would return to the Roman political arena. In particular, Caesar's demand that he be allowed to stand for the consulship while remaining in Gaul put him on a direct collision course with the senate. This was a crucial sticking point; to prevent any recurrence of the kind of dictatorship imposed by Sulla, Roman law had long since required army commanders to relinquish control of their legions before entering the city – a prerequisite to running for political office there. But if Caesar obeyed, so divesting himself of his military muscle, he knew that his enemies would waste no time in arraigning him on charges of abuse of power during his first consulship. Although, as the returning hero, he was fully confident of winning an election, a trial would instantly annul his candidacy.

Caesar's fiercest adversary in his conquest of Gaul was Vercingetorix, chief of the Averni tribe. He won a notable victory against the Romans at the siege of Gergovia, but was defeated at the Battle of Alesia in 52 BC and executed.

Caesar resolved this dilemma by confronting his enemies in Rome head-on with an invasion of Italy. On 11 January, 49 BC he crossed the Rubicon River, which marked the southern boundary between his province of Cisalpine Gaul and Rome's Italian provinces. His famous reported comment on his action was 'The die is cast' (*Iacta alea est*). As Caesar advanced, Pompey staged a tactical withdrawal to the port of Brundisium (modern Brindisi, on the 'heel' of Italy). From there, he planned to embark the force of more than 20,000 men that he had mustered to Greece to join other armies he was assembling in the eastern provinces. However, Pompey's authority was beginning to crumble by this stage. One of his subordinates ignored several urgent messages from his commander and was cut off and forced to surrender 10,000 men at Corfinium in central Italy.

This proved to be the defining moment of the war. When the garrison at Corfinium – which included many leaders of the political opposition – surrendered, Caesar took the soldiers into his service and released the rest. This act of clemency, unheard of in previous civil wars, was a propaganda coup that rallied many people to Caesar's cause. The war lasted until August 48 BC, when Pompey's army was routed at the Battle of Pharsalus in northern Greece. During 49–48 BC, Caesar consolidated his political position, being briefly made dictator in late 49 BC (when he also secured the consulship for a second time) and again, for a longer spell, after Pharsalus.

'Caesar was stabbed with twenty-three dagger thrusts and uttered not a word, but only a groan at the first stroke, though some have related that when Marcus Brutus rushed at him, he said in Greek, "You, too, child?"'

SUETONIUS (LIFE OF CAESAR, 82)

Caesar had always displayed a weakness for alluring women, and Cleopatra VII of Egypt proved more seductive than most. Legend has it that she presented herself to him rolled in a rug. In 47 BC she bore him a son – Caesarion – but Caesar, ever mindful of public opinion in Rome, refused to recognize paternity of the boy.

The deaths of Pompey and Caesar

Meanwhile, Pompey fled to Egypt, where agents of King Ptolemy XIII, knowing that Caesar was already on his way there, assassinated him. Arriving in Egypt, Caesar soon became embroiled in a dynastic power struggle between Ptolemy XIII and his sister, Cleopatra. Siding with Cleopatra (whom he lost no time in making his mistress), he quickly defeated Ptole my and installed his lover and her brother on the throne. This affair scandalized Rome, since it suggested Caesar had an unhealthy interest in royal power. However, by May of 47 BC, he was on the move once more, this time to Asia Minor to quell a revolt in Pontus led by Pharnaces, a son of Mithridates (the occasion of Caesar's famous boast *veni, vidi, vici*: 'I came, I saw, I conquered').

The civil war dragged on after Pompey's death; his supporters raised an army in North Africa, which was only defeated in 46 BC. That same year saw further outbreaks of trouble, as Pompey's sole surviving son Sextus rallied support in Spain. Yet while Caesar's military skills showed little sign of waning, his political acumen now began to desert him. During a brief stay in Rome in 46 BC, he had accepted the dictatorship for ten years and was granted the office in perpetuity two years later. He was also made consul continuously from 46 BC. All the while, his autocratic attitude to power was alienating fellow members of the ruling class.

Having put down all the major insurrections, Caesar finally returned to Rome in August 45 BC. The senate voted him divine honours and the month of his birth was renamed July. He pointedly refused the title of *rex* ('king') but ruled henceforth as the king of Rome in all but name.

Caesar planned to leave Rome again on 18 March, 44 BC to campaign against the Parthians. Just prior to his departure came the Ides of March, the 15th day of the month, which a soothsayer had warned him to beware of. Spurning her advice, he attended a meeting of the senate, where he was approached by a group of men apparently presenting a petition. As they surrounded him, they drew their daggers and stabbed him to death. More than 60 senators were involved in the conspiracy against Caesar – including men he had spared and some of his own officers. Like Suetonius after them, these men were adamant that Caesar had effectively signed his own death warrant by riding roughshod over the cherished traditions of the state. It now remained to be seen how many in the Roman world shared their view.

THE BATTLE OF PHARSALUS

This decisive showdown between Julius Caesar and Pompey in the summer of 48 BC had a swift and brutal outcome. Both commanders were in no doubt that Caesar's veteran infantry, although outnumbered, would have little trouble in overcoming Pompey's inexperienced foot soldiers. However, Pompey gambled that he could win the battle by deploying his more numerous cavalry on his left flank. His plan was to use them to swiftly neutralize Caesar's cavalry before attacking the rest of his army from the rear. But Caesar second-guessed his adversary's game plan, forgoing the customary three-line formation of his infantry in favour of a fourth line, which he used to attack Pompey's cavalry head-on as soon as it had, as expected, overrun his own cavalry. When Pompey saw his cavalry decimated, he realized that defeat was inevitable and fled the battlefield. Meanwhile Caesar's troops completed their rout of his forces. Behind him, Pompey left 6000 of his men dead, while a further 24,000 were taken prisoner.

A coin showing a Parthian ruler of the first century AD. Following Crassus' disastrous campaign in 53 BC, the Parthians remained a thorn in the side of Rome until Trajan and Septimius Severus crushed them in the second century AD.

A Time of Turmoil: Octavian and Antony (44–30 BC)

Thirteen years separate Caesar's murder from the Battle of Actium, the naval engagement off the coast of Greece that ushered in the final demise of the Republic and the accession of Rome's first emperor. Many later Roman writers recognized the key significance of this battle; for example, the historian Cassius Dio (c. AD 155–after 229) asserted that it marked the point when the Roman monarchy began.

The tale of these intervening years is dominated by two men whose fortunes changed radically as a result of the events of 15 March, 44 BC. The first was Mark Antony (Marcus Antonius; c. 83–30 BC), the scion of a distinguished family, many of whose members had entered public life. For instance, Mark Antony's father had held the post of consul 19 years before the death of Caesar. The second was born Gaius Octavius (63 BC–AD 14). His father, an equestrian, was the first member of the family to become a senator. But far more significantly, his mother was a niece of Julius Caesar.

In the power vacuum left in Rome after the assassination of Julius Caesar, one of the key players to come to the fore was Mark Antony. His alliance with Octavian (and Lepidus) in the Second Triumvirate was always an uneasy affair, and the rift between the two men became permanent when Antony abandoned Octavian's sister Octavia for Cleopatra.

Contenders for power

Antony had long been a protégé of Caesar and in 44 BC followed in his own father's footsteps by being chosen as Caesar's partner for his fifth consulship. That same year, the 19-year-old Octavius was awaiting his great-uncle's arrival in Greece to join him on his Parthian campaign. When Caesar was assassinated, Antony automatically became the head of the Roman state for the duration of the year he was consul, while Octavius was made Caesar's son and heir through an adoption noted in the dictator's will. He duly assumed the name Gaius Julius Caesar. Roman tradition suggests that he might also have had the *cognomen* Octavian to indicate his biological family. Political enemies continued to refer to him by this name throughout his life, by way of emphasizing his humble beginnings, while he refused absolutely to use it.

In this print, Mark Antony is shown eulogizing Julius Caesar at the dictator's funeral in 44 BC. Snatching the toga from Caesar's corpse, he showed the crowd the stab marks in the garment to back up his accusation of murder.

The evolving relationship between Antony and the Octavian splits roughly into three phases. The first, in which Antony was the dominant partner, spans the period from the assassination to around 37 BC. In the second phase, lasting for the next three years, the two men held equal power, while in the years immediately leading up to Actium – the final phase – Octavian's star was in the ascendant. In many ways, the men were polar opposites, and their diametrically opposed characters played a major role in determining their career trajectories. So, while Antony was capable of displaying great *virtus* on the battlefield, his reputation was undermined by scandalous conduct in his private life. Octavian, by contrast, was pusillanimous in battle (tending to fall violently ill whenever danger threatened) but proved himself extremely adept in the political arena, especially in cultivating a popular public persona. The one trait that the two did share was utter ruthlessness.

The seven years that followed the assassination of Julius Caesar saw a continuation of the internecine strife that Caesar had sparked with his civil war against Pompey. What was at stake was not a restoration of the Republic – even Caesar's assassins, who may well have taken their drastic action with this aim in mind, seem rapidly to have realized that it was an impossible dream – but rather which faction should succeed Caesar, and what precise form this succession should take. Both sides soon abandoned the notion of one-man rule in favour of a limited collective style of leadership that was less offensive to Roman tradition.

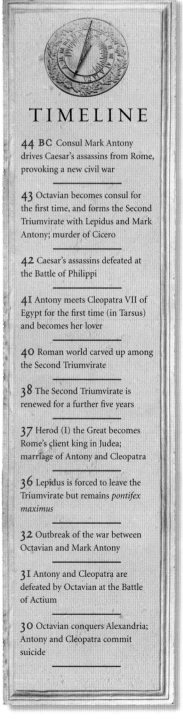

TIMELINE

44 BC Consul Mark Antony drives Caesar's assassins from Rome, provoking a new civil war

43 Octavian becomes consul for the first time, and forms the Second Triumvirate with Lepidus and Mark Antony; murder of Cicero

42 Caesar's assassins defeated at the Battle of Philippi

41 Antony meets Cleopatra VII of Egypt for the first time (in Tarsus) and becomes her lover

40 Roman world carved up among the Second Triumvirate

38 The Second Triumvirate is renewed for a further five years

37 Herod (I) the Great becomes Rome's client king in Judea; marriage of Antony and Cleopatra

36 Lepidus is forced to leave the Triumvirate but remains *pontifex maximus*

32 Outbreak of the war between Octavian and Mark Antony

31 Antony and Cleopatra are defeated by Octavian at the Battle of Actium

30 Octavian conquers Alexandria; Antony and Cleopatra commit suicide

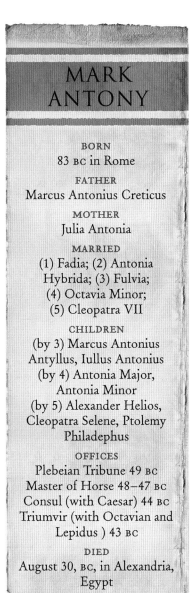

MARK ANTONY

BORN
83 BC in Rome

FATHER
Marcus Antonius Creticus

MOTHER
Julia Antonia

MARRIED
(1) Fadia; (2) Antonia
Hybrida; (3) Fulvia;
(4) Octavia Minor;
(5) Cleopatra VII

CHILDREN
(by 3) Marcus Antonius
Antyllus, Iullus Antonius
(by 4) Antonia Major,
Antonia Minor
(by 5) Alexander Helios,
Cleopatra Selene, Ptolemy
Philadephus

OFFICES
Plebeian Tribune 49 BC
Master of Horse 48–47 BC
Consul (with Caesar) 44 BC
Triumvir (with Octavian and
Lepidus) 43 BC

DIED
August 30, BC, in Alexandria,
Egypt

When, during his funeral oration for Caesar, Mark Antony openly condemned Caesar's death as murder by conspiracy, public opinion turned against the party of the assassins, and its leading members Brutus and Cassius were driven into exile. After initial power struggles among the leading members of the Caesarian faction, they settled their differences and promptly assumed control of the state through a triumvirate (often called the Second Triumvirate to distinguish it from that of Caesar, Pompey and Crassus).

The leaders of this triumvirate were Octavian, Antony and Marcus Aemilius Lepidus (d. 13 BC), the former deputy of Julius Caesar in the dictatorship of 44 BC. Like Crassus before him, Lepidus seems to have acted as a counterbalance to the competing ambitions of his colleagues. At the end of 43 BC they made their position legally unassailable by passing a law proclaiming them *triumviri rei publicae constituendae*, or 'board of three for putting the Republic back in order' – a piece of political 'spin' of breathtaking temerity in any age. While claiming to be acting in the best interests of the Republic, they were in fact writing its obituary. Through this legislation the three men had, in effect, appointed themselves dictators.

The triumvirate tightens its grip

It was not long before the triumvirate faced its first crisis. Each man commanded his own army, making a total of some 100,000 men under arms. This was almost half as large a force as that later deployed by Rome's first emperor to control his entire empire, and there was simply not enough money to pay the troops. The solution of the triumviri was, in the manner of Sulla, to spread a climate of fear by reinstating the dreaded proscriptions. History, subsequently manipulated by the victorious Octavian, apportions blame for this new spasm of bloodshed to Antony. Even so, the accusation may well be grounded in fact. Not only was Antony the senior partner in the triumvirate at this stage, but his immoral private life was also closely modelled on that of Sulla. Like him, Antony drank to excess and enjoyed the company of dissolute actors. He also followed his dictator predecessor in regarding the eastern part of the Roman world as his natural power base.

The Second Triumvirate's proscriptions were responsible for one of the most brutal periods in the entire history of Rome. More than 3000 members of the upper classes were summarily executed, including one of the most notable Romans of all time, Marcus Tullius Cicero (106–43 BC). Cicero was the greatest orator of his age, a relatively principled and conservative politician and the most vociferous opponent of

THE LIFE AND DEATH OF CICERO

Marcus Tullius Cicero was born into the equestrian class in the provincial town of Arpinum in 106 BC. He first came to prominence in around 80–70 BC as a lawyer, acting as both prosecutor and defender in a number of high-profile cases. Elected consul, in 63 BC he was responsible for suppressing the conspiracy of Catiline, who had plotted to overthrow the Republic. Yet the fact that Cicero had Catiline and his co-defendants executed without trial would later bring about his exile from Rome. On his return in 57 BC, he re-entered public life. As the rift between Caesar and Pompey grew wider, Cicero favoured Pompey but at the same time avoided alienating Caesar.

Following Caesar's murder, Cicero became a popular figure for his attacks on corruption and lawlessness. His scathing criticism earned him the enmity of Mark Antony, and when the Second Triumvirate began its reign of terror, Cicero found himself on the proscription list. He was tracked down by bounty hunters, who seized and decapitated him on 7 December, 43 BC. His body was then mutilated and used for the ghoulish amusement of Mark Antony and his politically ambitious third wife Fulvia; she is said to have stuck needles in the dead orator's tongue to punish it for having 'slandered' her husband.

The second-century AD historian Appian was unsparing in his account of Cicero's grisly end:

Cicero was the most renowned orator of his age, and his name has since become closely associated with eloquent legal advocacy.

'Cicero was proscribed along with his son, his brother, his brother's son and all his household and friends ... The centurion drew his head out of the litter and cut it off; he also struck off the hand with which Cicero had written the speeches against Antony as tyrant ... Antony was delighted beyond measure ... the head and hand of Cicero were suspended from the rostra in the forum where he had formerly made his public speeches. It is said that even at his meals, Antony would place Cicero's head before his table, until he became satiated with the horrible sight'.

Antony in the confused months after Caesar's death. His violent death and its gruesome sequel testified to the savagery that was meted out daily during this new reign of terror.

Meanwhile, Brutus and Cassius were rallying support in the east – sometimes using violent coercion – to mount a challenge to the rule of the triumvirate. The core of the army they assembled comprised legions that Pompey had once raised for the war with Caesar, and that Caesar had left in the east, hoping to win their loyalty in his forthcoming Parthian campaign. But the memory of Pompey had remained strong among these troops, making them willing recruits to the assassins' cause.

In the late summer of 42 BC, Octavian and Antony defeated the party of the assassins in two battles near Philippi in northern Greece. During these engagements, Antony covered himself in glory, while Octavian disgraced himself by taking to his tent with an 'illness' shortly after the first action commenced, and only just making good his escape when Brutus' soldiers overran the camp. Following his victory, Antony absorbed the army of the assassins into his forces and set about founding an Antonian empire in the east. Meanwhile, other Pompeians now emerged in the west. Pompey's only surviving son, Sextus, joined together various fleets that had been assembled over time to fight the Caesarians and began a war off the coast of Italy that would last until the summer of 36 BC.

Key events in the period 42–36 BC included a civil war in Italy; two meetings of the triumviri in 40 and 37 BC to reconfirm their authority; and an ongoing see-saw struggle with Sextus Pompey. For Octavian, the greatest of these challenges was the civil war of 41 BC, which erupted when he tried to settle veterans from the Philippi campaign on land that had been confiscated from Italian towns. The rebellion was fomented and led by Antony's younger brother Lucius, who was consul for that year, and Antony's wife Fulvia. Victory for Octavian was only assured when armies led by allies of the elder Antony failed to pledge their support to his brother. The conflict ended with a siege of the city of Perusia (modern Perugia), which was eventually starved into submission. Lucius was exiled to Spain, and Fulvia to Greece, where she died.

'The triumvirs joined in making a list of those who were to be put to death – those whom they suspected because of their power, their own personal enemies, and they exchanged their own relatives and friends with each other for death.'

APPIAN (C. AD 95–C.165; ROMAN HISTORY, BOOK 4.2)

An uneasy peace

When Antony returned in September 40 BC the two men patched up their differences. Antony sealed the reconciliation with Octavian by marrying his sister, Octavia, before returning east. In 37 BC, following military setbacks for both Octavian (fighting Sextus Pompey) and Antony (against the Parthians) they renewed the triumvirate once more. When Octavian finally managed to defeat Sextus the following year, he summarily stripped the vacillating Lepidus of his authority as a triumvir without consulting Antony. Lepidus was banished to an undistinguished retirement within Italy.

Now the power struggle was free to develop unimpeded between the two main players. Antony's problems continued to grow after 36 BC. Although he and Octavia had two daughters, their relationship was strained. Even before he married Octavia, Antony had become besotted with Queen Cleopatra of Egypt. Cleopatra encouraged this infatuation, and in the years that followed Antony's passion for her, and for life in her capital of Alexandria, became a scandal, just as it had once been for Julius Caesar. Antony dressed and partied as a Greek, and martial, virile Rome had always regarded Greece as the home of lewdness and effeminacy. Not even the most lurid propaganda that Octavian spread about Antony's conduct came close to conveying the real state of affairs. A contemporary dedication to 'Antony the Great' from a local drinking club that archaeologists found carved on a stone at Alexandria provides eloquent proof of his debauchery. Antony's overindulgence had long been infamous; one of Cicero's most memorable attacks on his character includes a description of the hung-over Antony vomiting while attempting to attend to public business in the Forum.

The luxurious lifestyle of Antony and Cleopatra, as imagined by the 19th-century Belgian artist Alexis van Hamme. In the power struggle with Octavian, Mark Antony's self-indulgent posturing as an Eastern potentate lost him much support in the Roman world.

Even more damagingly, Antony's opponents now began to accuse him of infecting other Romans with his vices. Stories spread of wild parties, including one at which a senior officer stripped naked, painted himself blue, and flopped around on the floor wearing a fish tail in imitation of a sea god. Antony even tried to respond in a self-justifying essay, *On his Own Drunkenness*, sadly now lost. But Antony's conduct only fuelled Roman distrust of the licentious East and gave credence to Octavian's image of him as a wilful despot who would, given the chance, rule Rome like a foreign potentate.

Octavian, in the meantime, managed to bring a semblance of order to the government of Italy. He stopped settling veterans on confiscated land and made sure that the people had enough to eat. In one

THE CLOACA MAXIMA

One of the earliest known examples of a sewerage system, the Cloaca Maxima (literally 'Greatest Drain') is thought to have first been constructed in around 600 BC to drain the marshlands around the Tiber and discharge waste from the growing city of Rome through an outfall into the River Tiber. Pipes from bath houses, public toilets and other official buildings connected to the sewer; most private houses, except those of the very rich, were not linked to the Cloaca, but instead used cess-pits to dispose of their waste. In 33 BC, the Cloaca Maxima was given a major overhaul by Marcus Agrippa, whose public works programme also included building aqueducts to supply fresh water to the city and laying out public baths and gardens. The Romans endowed all places with their special protector-deities, and the Cloaca Maxima was no exception; Cloacina, goddess of the sewer, presided over the continued efficient functioning of this important utility.

particularly striking display of public service, Marcus Agrippa (*c.* 64–12 BC), Octavian's chief lieutenant and the architect of the victory over Sextus, accepted a reduction in rank – having already been consul – to serve as an aedile. During his term of office, Agrippa made great improvements to the city's water and sewerage systems, including rebuilding the main drain, the Cloaca Maxima. Octavian now tried to project an image of himself that was in accord with the traditional Roman ideals of frugality and self-reliance. Although it is hard to imagine that anyone seriously believed his claim to have given up sex in his late teens for the good of his health, or his contradictory claim that he had only indulged in adulterous relationships with the wives of his enemies to learn their secrets, he had settled into a stable marriage with a woman of impeccable aristocratic heritage named Livia. They had become a model couple, and Romans favourably compared their life of uncomplicated domesticity to the licentious behaviour of Antony and Cleopatra.

Octavian makes his move

The legal authority of the triumviri was due to expire on 31 December, 33 BC. When several Italian towns pledged their allegiance to him in 32 BC and urgently petitioned him to lead a campaign against Antony and Cleopatra, Octavian made a decisive move to seize power. In February of 32 BC, after one of the consuls attempted to read a letter from Antony to the senate, he entered Rome at the head of an armed guard, marched into the senate house, seated himself between the consuls and proclaimed his continuing authority as head of state. Shortly thereafter he produced what he claimed to be a copy of Antony's will, in which Antony made clear his intention to move the capital to Alexandria. The consuls fled to Egypt, and Octavian took advantage of the crisis that he had engineered to obtain a further grant of supreme authority in the war that he now declared against Antony.

Antony anticipated Octavian's actions and, in the late summer of 31 BC assembled a huge force with the intention of invading Italy. Cleopatra joined him on this campaign. Octavian now showed

'The whole of Italy, unprompted, swore to obey my commands, and asked me to be their leader in the war that I won at Actium.'

OCTAVIAN/AUGUSTUS (DEEDS OF THE DIVINE AUGUSTUS, 25)

ACTIUM – THE ARCHAEOLOGICAL EVIDENCE

Historical accounts of Actium are sketchy and confused, with some hinting that the outcome was something of a foregone conclusion, while others speak of a fierce fight. Yet there exists one compelling piece of evidence suggesting that a full-scale naval engagement did indeed take place. Shortly after his triumph, Octavian founded the settlement of Nicopolis (literally 'Victory City') on a peninsula jutting into the Ionian Sea (in what is now Greece). Here, a monument commemorating the victory was discovered by archaeologists. It was decorated with the prows of ships taken in the battle, indicating that Antony's losses were heavy. It appears that Antony tried to break through the centre of his opponents, and that, as he did so, Cleopatra's squadron hoisted its sails and fled. Antony first followed in his own massive flagship, which he later abandoned for a faster vessel. The remainder of his fleet that survived the battle retreated into the bay, where it later surrendered.

An artist's impression of the Battle of Actium, showing Cleopatra's ships (background) fleeing the fight.

consummate skill in directing his commanders' response. They cut Antony's supply lines and blockaded his force in the Bay of Actium on the east coast of Greece. Octavian's army, led by Statilius Taurus, won an initial skirmish, while his fleet, under Marcus Agrippa, dominated the sea-lanes. As food ran out and disease became rife, on 2 September, 31 BC Antony made a desperate bid to break out. His and Cleopatra's squadrons soon gave up the unequal fight and fled. Octavian was now the undisputed master of the Roman world. His victory was sealed a year later when his armies entered Alexandria as Antony committed suicide in Cleopatra's arms. The queen also later took her own life by clutching a venomous snake to her breast.

Foundations of the Empire: The House of Augustus (29 BC–AD 14)

Octavian came back to Rome in 28 BC; many in the city feared that his return would herald a consolidation of his position as dictator, backed as he was by a huge army. However, on the Ides of January, 27 BC, he convened a meeting of the senate at which he renounced the extraordinary dictatorial powers granted him to command the armies of Rome in the war against Antony. But at this same session, the senate, alarmed that he was about to relinquish his wise guardianship of the state, urged him to carry on as consul. As an additional honour for his service to Rome, the grateful senators bestowed on him the name Augustus, or 'revered personage'.

Augustus was a shrewd ruler who carefully balanced personal myth-building with pragmatic measures. Among the many titles bestowed on him, he particularly valued the office of proconsul, as it suggested his power derived from the will of the people. The title Augustus remained the designation of the rulers of the Roman and Byzantine empires for 14 centuries.

In naming him Augustus, the senate completed a process of transformation in Octavian that had begun several years before; in 42 BC, when Julius Caesar had been declared a god, his adopted son Octavian had taken the names 'Gaius Julius, son of the divinity Caesar'. Six years later he had changed his first name, or *praenomen*, from Gaius to *imperator*, or 'victorious general', in celebration of his victory over Sextus Pompey. Now his new name, Caesar Augustus, while acknowledging a debt to the older Caesar, also proclaimed to the entire world that Octavian was a new man whose *virtus* outstripped that of any other mortal. Unlike his adoptive father, however, he was not divine. He kept his feet very firmly planted in the world of mortals, despite the fact that people throughout the Roman world now offered sacrifices to him in gratitude for his defeat of Mark Antony. He attended dinner parties with his friends, was scrupulous in consulting the senate and was generally accessible to the average Roman. His unofficial title of *princeps* ('first citizen') had been bestowed on

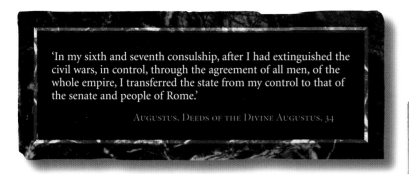

'In my sixth and seventh consulship, after I had extinguished the civil wars, in control, through the agreement of all men, of the whole empire, I transferred the state from my control to that of the senate and people of Rome.'

AUGUSTUS, DEEDS OF THE DIVINE AUGUSTUS, 34

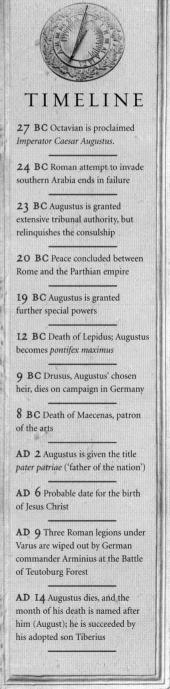

TIMELINE

27 BC Octavian is proclaimed *Imperator Caesar Augustus*.

24 BC Roman attempt to invade southern Arabia ends in failure

23 BC Augustus is granted extensive tribunal authority, but relinquishes the consulship

20 BC Peace concluded between Rome and the Parthian empire

19 BC Augustus is granted further special powers

12 BC Death of Lepidus; Augustus becomes *pontifex maximus*

9 BC Drusus, Augustus' chosen heir, dies on campaign in Germany

8 BC Death of Maecenas, patron of the arts

AD 2 Augustus is given the title *pater patriae* ('father of the nation')

AD 6 Probable date for the birth of Jesus Christ

AD 9 Three Roman legions under Varus are wiped out by German commander Arminius at the Battle of Teutoburg Forest

AD 14 Augustus dies, and the month of his death is named after him (August); he is succeeded by his adopted son Tiberius

prominent citizens before him (such as Pompey), and he made it clear that he could wish for no higher accolade. In accordance with this, he also modestly referred to the various duties that the senate delegated to him, and the people confirmed, as his *statio*, or allotted station in life.

The making of Augustus

Yet, by any measure, Augustus' accomplishments in the years after Actium had been truly impressive. Not the least of these was to bring the long period of civil war to a definitive close. This was a signal success, and may have stemmed from the fact that Augustus had not followed the pattern of Sulla and Caesar. They had imposed their authority on Rome only after first having established their power base in the provinces, and in so doing had never really been able to impose their will throughout the empire. Augustus, on the other hand, had made Rome his constituency from the outset. The fact that he defeated Antony as the legitimate head of a functioning government enabled him to integrate the former supporters of his rival into the state.

At the same time, his difficult early years had taught him a valuable lesson about the thorny problem of disbanding and resettling a large force of armed men. First, he was careful to ensure that those demobilized soldiers who still retained connections to the Italian homeland were resettled at his own expense, and not by confiscating land from Italian towns. In addition, since many of the soldiers, especially those who had served under Antony, had no real roots in Italy any more, Augustus met little resistance in resettling them in far-flung military colonies abroad. In this way, hundreds of thousands of men were successfully discharged, thereby reducing the army by more than half its strength to a permanent force of 28 legions – roughly 150,000 men. The remainder of Rome's armed forces were made up of supporting 'auxiliary' units recruited from the provinces, whose numbers were roughly equal to the legionary force.

When the senate conferred his new station on Augustus, they also endowed him with a variety of different powers. The two most important of these were *imperium maius*, the power to intervene over the heads of all other provincial governors, and *tribunicia potestas*, the powers of a tribune of the plebs. These latter powers included the right

This statue of Augustus, found at his villa at Prima Porta in Rome, presents an idealized image of the emperor. It shows him in military garb; on his breastplate are scenes showing the return of the standards Crassus lost at Carrhae. There are also hints at the divine nature of Augustus, such as the small Cupid at his feet, an allusion to the Julian family's claim to be descended from Venus.

to summon assemblies of the people to vote on laws, the right of intercession and the right to veto any action taken by another magistrate. They also rendered him sacrosanct, so that anyone who dared to raise a hand against him would be committing a crime against the gods (though, given that more than a few tribunes from Tiberius Gracchus onwards had been murdered, the protection this offered was more symbolic than real). Finally, the senate made him titular governor of several provinces, including Spain, Gaul, Syria and Egypt. Since these provinces were also the ones that had garrisons, the upshot was that Augustus now commanded 26 legions, the vast bulk of the Roman army.

Augustus consolidates his rule

The legal powers vested in him in 27 BC effectively made Augustus the head of state, but he did not dare govern the empire on his own. In the course of the civil wars he had come to depend heavily upon two close friends, Agrippa and Maecenas (70–8 BC), to help him. These two men were a study in opposites. Maecenas, who never held public office, was a wealthy patron of the arts and something of a party animal. Agrippa, a masterful soldier, had been consul in 37 BC and shared the consulship with Augustus when the structure of government was reformed in 28 and 27 BC. It was common knowledge that Agrippa and Maecenas disliked each other, but the very fact that the emergent Augustan regime could accommodate two such contrasting figures attested to its collective nature, further dispelling fears that Augustus was imposing monarchical rule.

In addition to Maecenas and Agrippa, there were a number of other men who retained very powerful positions within the senate. These included Asinius Pollio (76 BC–AD 5), who had secured Augustus' friendship by refusing to support the younger Antony in 41; Messalla Corvinus (64 BC–AD 8), who had served both Cassius and Antony before declaring his undying support for Augustus in the early 30s; Statilius Taurus (c. 60 BC–c. AD 10) who had commanded the land army in the Battle of Actium; and Munatius Plancus (87 BC–AD 15), the man who had once humiliated himself by performing the drunken fish dance for Antony but had judiciously switched sides just before Actium. Augustus' pardoning of men such as Munatius Plancus was reminiscent of Caesar's clemency, but unlike Caesar, he ensured that those he spared would stay loyal by giving them prestigious and useful roles within Roman society.

THE ROMAN ARMY AND ITS TACTICS

A key distinction in the Roman army was between the professionally trained heavy infantry, known as legionaries, and the support forces, or auxiliaries.

A detail from Trajan's Column in Rome showing Roman auxiliary archers clad in leather jerkins and conical helmets. A wide variety of specialist soldiers were recruited from different parts of the empire, with most archers coming from Asia Minor and Syria.

The standard strength of a Roman legion was around 5500 men in the early days of the empire, but became far smaller (c. 1000–2000) over time. Legions were recruited solely from among the ranks of Roman citizens. They consisted of heavily armed infantrymen whose primary tactical purpose was to lure the main battle line of an enemy into hand-to-hand combat and destroy them. One of their most famous tactics was the *testudo* or 'tortoise' formation. This involved the legionaries closing ranks and grasping their shields at the sides to form a protective shell all around the body of soldiers, including over their heads to make them invulnerable to arrow or javelin attack from above. However, this formation severely limited their manoeuvrability in close-quarters combat, and so was used primarily as a siege tactic. When an army was in trouble, the formation that it tended to adopt was a square.

Auxiliaries were drawn from the various provinces of the empire or even from client kingdoms. Often, these regions contributed forces that specialized in particular fighting techniques. The Gauls of France and the Batavians (a Germanic tribe from the modern Netherlands), for example, provided cavalrymen, while the kingdoms of Syria and Scythia (the Black Sea region) supplied men who were skilled at archery and the Balearic Islands contributed excellent marksmen with the slingshot. Initially, auxiliaries had their own leaders and equipment, though later they became more integrated into the Roman army.

Auxiliaries also included more lightly armed infantrymen than the legionaries. In battle, the auxiliaries' task was to pin down an enemy force so that the legions could then crush them. This style of fighting, which evolved in the course of the second century BC and was refined by Pompey and Caesar, would remain the basis of Roman tactical doctrine for two more centuries, until Rome's enemies finally devised ways of defeating it.

Augustus was also keen to avoid Caesar's mistake of micro-managing and antagonizing his trusted lieutenants in Rome, and so decided to absent himself from Rome for a while on campaign. Ever prudent, he wanted to avoid taking on a truly dangerous enemy (which for the present ruled out Rome's nemesis, the dreaded Parthians) but nevertheless wanted to find a suitably worthy opponent to justify the major logistics of raising and moving an army. And so he fixed his gaze on Spain. Spain had been the springboard from which Hannibal had launched his invasion of Italy at the end of the third century BC. After finally ousting their Carthaginian foe, the Romans established two provinces in the country, but had continued to meet significant resistance from the Spaniards. In particular, ever since Pompey had campaigned there in the 70s BC, it had become a hotbed of Pompeian sympathies. With their long history of turbulence and disloyalty to the Caesarian cause, the independent tribes of Spain therefore provided Augustus with a tempting target. With much public fanfare, he duly declared war on them in 27 BC; they proved a tougher nut to crack than he had anticipated, but his generals gained enough ground by 25 BC for Augustus to claim that he had solved a problem that was more than a century and a half old. Even so, it took a further 15 years, and the intervention of such high-profile generals as Agrippa, to bring Spain firmly to heel and integrate it fully within the provincial system.

Essential reforms

By 23 BC, it was becoming clear to Augustus that he needed to effect changes in his mode of governance. Some voices of discontent began to be raised about his tenure of the consulship for every year since 31 BC. He had mooted the idea of replacement ('suffect') consuls stepping in during the course of the year, but this did not satisfy the ambitions of aristocrats who still yearned for consular office and the kudos it brought. Augustus' protracted occupancy of the consulship also placed a major question mark over his claim to have 'restored' Republican government in 28 BC.

Following a serious illness, therefore, Augustus surrendered the consulship halfway through the year. Yet this by no means signalled that he was relinquishing his hold on true power. The senate now voted him further honours, including a renewed grant of the *imperium maius* and confirmation of the *tribunicia potestas* for life. The subtle interplay between these two roles testifies to Augustus' political sleight of hand and his keen appreciation of the tenor of public opinion in Rome. While his proconsul's right of *imperium maius* handed him effective control over the provinces, the *tribunicia potestas* equipped him with all the legal authority he needed to administer Rome itself. Since Augustus could not, technically, invoke the *imperium maius* in Rome or Italy, the *tribunicia potestas* became the symbol of his civil authority. Indeed, Augustus' reign later came to be dated from when he was first granted this particular power. This underlines the extraordinary nature of the position that Augustus had fashioned for himself: an office originally created to protect the Roman people from the wilful acts of a magistrate had become the defining power of the emperor.

Moreover, in terms of public relations, the title *tribunicia potestas* was infinitely more palatable to Roman sensibilities than that of dictator, as Sulla and Caesar had styled themselves. As if to underscore this point, Augustus refused the dictatorship at the end of 23 BC when the senate offered it to him to help solve a threatened grain shortage. He was concerned to maintain the illusion that his authority was dependent on the will of the people. This may all have been political theatre, but it was an extremely convincing performance.

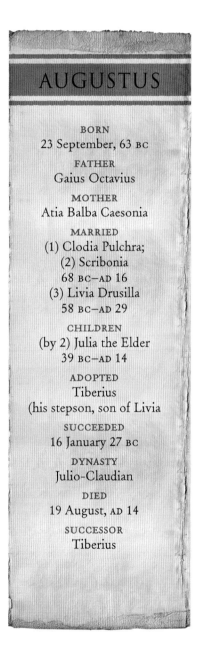

AUGUSTUS

BORN
23 September, 63 BC

FATHER
Gaius Octavius

MOTHER
Atia Balba Caesonia

MARRIED
(1) Clodia Pulchra;
(2) Scribonia
68 BC–AD 16
(3) Livia Drusilla
58 BC–AD 29

CHILDREN
(by 2) Julia the Elder
39 BC–AD 14

ADOPTED
Tiberius
(his stepson, son of Livia

SUCCEEDED
16 January 27 BC

DYNASTY
Julio-Claudian

DIED
19 August, AD 14

SUCCESSOR
Tiberius

'The masters of the Roman world surrounded their throne with darkness, concealed their irresistible strength, and humbly professed themselves the accountable ministers of the senate, whose supreme decrees they dictated and obeyed.'

EDWARD GIBBON, THE DECLINE AND FALL OF THE ROMAN EMPIRE, CHAPTER 3.

Securing the succession

Political theatre of another kind was played out the following year, when a group of senators plotted to kill Augustus. Several of the conspirators were extremely prominent citizens – one was even Maecenas' brother-in-law – a fact that sent shock waves through the establishment. By this stage, Augustus was 41. Agrippa was possibly a year older and the life expectancy of most Romans did not extend far beyond 50. As bungled as the conspiracy of 22 BC turned out to be, it was a timely reminder to Augustus that he had still not truly ensured the long-term security of his rule or made provisions for a successor. It was clear that he urgently needed to start looking for younger heirs to carry on his legacy.

The system of succession that took shape over the next few years was based on the familiar Roman principle of collegiality. Augustus' eldest nephew Marcellus (born 42 BC), recently married to his only daughter Julia, had died suddenly in 23 BC. During his own life-threatening illness that same year, Augustus had indicated that Agrippa should succeed him, and now arranged that he should marry Julia, while also promoting the careers of the two sons of Livia by her first marriage. Her elder son, Tiberius (42 BC–AD 37) was earmarked for prominent military responsibilities during the campaign that Augustus was planning to mount in the east.

A relief showing a legion presenting its standard, or aquila ('eagle,' from the silver or bronze bird on top of the ensign), to the emperor. The standard was a rallying point on the battlefield and to lose it to the enemy was a serious disgrace.

Rome's arch-enemy Parthia had recently been torn apart by a dynastic power struggle, and in the course of these upheavals the pretender to the throne had decamped to Roman territory with two sons of the ruling incumbent as hostages. This presented Rome with a golden opportunity to put pressure on Parthia. Augustus and Agrippa headed east, and, after tough diplomatic wrangling, the Parthian king made a number of important concessions in return for his sons' release. These included officially recognizing the River Euphrates (in present-day Syria and Iraq) as the border between the two empires, granting Rome the power to appoint the king of Armenia – whose realm occupied much of what is now eastern Turkey – and returning military standards captured from Crassus and Antony. The return of the legionary standards was an easy gesture for the Parthians to make, but was of huge symbolic significance to the Romans, who still regarded their loss by the previous generation as a source of profound national shame. Augustus proclaimed the peace that he concluded with Parthia as a great victory, and not without some justification, since it removed at a stroke any potential grounds for Rome having to wage war on its old enemy. No Roman army could possibly have occupied Iraq and Iran, or even a significant portion of that territory, without getting bogged down in endless warfare. There were simply not enough soldiers to control an area that was culturally and politically too complex for the Romans to manage.

Indeed, Augustus avoided imposing direct Roman administration upon many Semitic borderlands of the empire where traditions of Graeco-Roman government, based upon city-states, were wholly alien and liable to stir up local resistance. If Augustus felt that Palestine was better off with Rome's client king Herod (I) the Great (74–5 BC), then it was obvious that he would not even entertain the thought of sending Roman governors to Iraq.

Augustus' wife Livia Drusilla, the most powerful woman in the early empire, and her son, the future emperor Tiberius. Livia set the tone for the noble Roman matron, firmly controlling the royal household and cultivating an image of modesty and marital loyalty. Contemporary coins even portrayed her as the living embodiment of 'Pietas' – the goddess of duty to the state and the family.

VIRGIL AND HORACE

Among the writers of the Augustan Age whose careers were promoted by Octavian's wealthy advisor Maecenas were two of the greatest of all Roman poets – Virgil and Horace.

Virgil (Publius Vergilius Maro; 70–19 BC) was born into a noble farming family near Mantua. His first major work, the *Eclogues* (42–37 BC), consists of ten poems set in a mythical landscape of herdsmen. Though they were based on a well-known Greek poetic form, Virgil breathed new life into these poems by subtly contrasting the world portrayed with the sufferings of the present, and even dwelling on hopes for a better future. His second work, the *Georgics* (36–29 BC), was a hymn of praise to life in the countryside, implicitly comparing this mode of existence favourably to the corrupt urban society of Rome. Virgil's third and greatest poem was the *Aeneid*. Recognized immediately as a work of extraordinary genius, the 12 books of the *Aeneid* tell the story of the mythical foundation of Rome by the Trojan leader Aeneas. During his wanderings, the hero wages a long, hard struggle to find the right path to the future, wrestling with his conscience over whether to obey the dictates of his humanity or blindly pursue glory. Aeneas and the men who followed him from Troy when it was destroyed by the Greeks

On this third-century mosaic from North Africa, Virgil is seen composing his famous epic poem the Aeneid, which tells of the mythical founding of the city of Rome. He is flanked on the right by Melpomene, the muse of tragedy, and on the left by Clio, the muse of history.

are forced to fight a war against native peoples when they finally arrive in Italy. The epic poem ends with Aeneas' slaying of the leader of the Italians, and a brief vision of the unity of the two peoples. The *Aeneid* was an allegory of the painful, bloody path that Roman history had taken up to that point. Yet its vision of a brighter future was clearly meant to praise the greatness of Rome and extol the virtues of the Julian dynasty and in particular of Augustus, who through Julius Caesar claimed direct descent from Aeneas.

As the son of a freed slave, Horace (Quintus Horatius Flaccus; 65–8 BC) came from a much humbler background than Virgil. Horace backed the side of the assassins of Julius Caesar during the civil war, but was treated indulgently by Augustus. He repaid the favour by including flattering references to the emperor in his poems. Horace had been educated in Greece, and his works are finely crafted lyrical poems (odes) that express the joy of life and a great love of nature. In 17 BC, Horace was accorded a major public honour when Augustus asked him to compose a 'secular hymn' to commemorate the 800th anniversary of Rome's founding that year and to mark the dawning of a new age (*saeculum*).

Back to basics

Returning to Rome in 19 BC, Augustus embarked on a new phase of his reign. Even so, he would still spend most of the next decade away from the capital. Rather than pursue military glory for himself, he was now intent on focusing all his efforts on the moral regeneration of the Roman state by reviving the customs and traditions of the past. At the same time, he cemented his legacy by giving his stepsons free rein to display *virtus* in war, a vital quality if they were to be presented as worthy successors. Over the next decade, armies under the command of Tiberius and Drusus (38–9 BC), the younger of his stepsons, occupied Switzerland and southern Germany.

A Roman couple in bed, from a marble bas-relief panel. Augustus' concerted campaign to clamp down on sexual misconduct and punish adulterers was designed to promote the virtues of marriage and strengthen the moral fibre of the Roman state. Even so, the emperor's own conduct in this regard was not beyond reproach.

Meanwhile, in Rome, Augustus initiated his campaign to clean up both public and private life. In 19 and 18 BC respectively, he introduced legislation to expel 'unworthy' men from the senate and to regulate the marital and reproductive habits of the city's upper classes. New laws were introduced governing marriage, and draconian measures were brought in to curb sexual offences. One law was specifically geared towards encouraging the élite to produce more children; men whose wives bore three or more children were given preferment in public office. By contrast, those who refused to marry were penalized, including being cut off from their inheritance. Another piece of legislation made adultery a crime for both sexes. The penalties it imposed were harsh; any man who refused to divorce a wife who was having an affair could be charged as a pimp. Many Romans resented this intrusion of the state into the realm of the *domus*, but these measures were important symbols of an imperial commitment to a more orderly society, and thus helped consolidate the new regime.

Around the same time, in 17 BC, Rome celebrated the 800th anniversary of its founding. The lyric poet Horace – one of several writers who flourished in a period of extraordinary literary achievement, the Latin Golden Age, which began in the late Republic and ended with Augustus' death – wrote a poem marking the occasion. This festival was the culmination of many years of work restoring temples and other public buildings that had fallen into disrepair. The years of civil war were decried as a period in which immorality had been allowed to run rampant, the cults of the gods had been ignored and personal expenditure on private luxury had replaced the pursuit of the common good. Augustus also staged a number of extraordinary spectacles for the Roman people and funded extensive construction of new venues

One example of the architectural enrichment of Rome during the reign of Augustus was the magnificent Ara Pacis Augustae ('Altar of Augustan Peace'). Located on the Campus Martius, it was commissioned by the Senate to celebrate the 'Pax Romana' established by the emperor. The altar, which was decorated with scenes of traditional Roman piety, was dedicated in 13 BC.

for shows. For example, a huge new theatre was built and named for his deceased nephew Marcellus; the Circus Maximus, where the hugely popular chariot races were held, was improved and the first permanent amphitheatre for gladiatorial shows was constructed by Statilius Taurus. Taurus' magnanimity was part of a trend whereby prominent citizens commissioned lavish public works. This had begun in 39 BC, with Asinius Pollio's patronage of the first public library in Rome, while Agrippa later built a gleaming new portico in which he encouraged members of the Roman élite to display their art collections. Augustus pointedly refrained from having his own name associated with new buildings because he wanted to emphasize that this investment in the welfare of the Roman people was a communal enterprise. Likewise, in financing the restoration of temples he made sure that he did not efface the record of the original builders – further demonstration of his interest in and reverence for the Roman past.

In 12 BC, Augustus assumed the role of *pontifex maximus,* celebrating this new honour by erecting a massive new Altar of Peace by the banks of the Tiber, near to the spot where he had already built his own mausoleum. Rome was now a very different place, bearing out Augustus' proud boast that he had found a city of brick and transformed it into one of marble. The many new public buildings had transformed the cityscape, while Roman possessions overseas had been enlarged by conquests in the Alps and Germany. Yet this new civic and imperial pride came at a price; Augustus now presided over a state where nonconformity was viewed with increasing suspicion.

'You Roman, remember to rule, these are your arts, to impose the habit of peace, to spare the submissive and humble the proud.'

VIRGIL, AENEID 6, 851–53

The reluctant heir

As Rome changed, so too did the regime. Agrippa died in March 12 BC, leaving the new generation as heirs apparent. Agrippa's widow Julia was remarried to Tiberius, who was forced to divorce Agrippa's daughter, whom he seems genuinely to have loved. The new marriage was not a success; the grim Tiberius was ill-matched to a younger woman who was notorious for her sexual promiscuity. In 9 BC, Drusus died when he fell from his horse while on campaign, and Augustus began to invest his hopes for the succession in two of the sons (Gaius and Lucius) that Julia had borne during her marriage to Agrippa. Tiberius, to whom the burden of military command of new campaigns in the Balkans now fell, became increasingly restive. In 7 BC, thoroughly disaffected, he announced that he was withdrawing from public life and retiring to Rhodes. His departure marked the start of a difficult decade.

With advancing years, Augustus seems to have become very hard to live with. Even when he and his wife Livia were both present in Rome, he continued to communicate with her by letter. A man of ostentatiously simple tastes, he delighted in dice games that the serious and academically minded Tiberius scorned. He was also shameless in his favouritism, doting on his grandsons but spurning Drusus' son Claudius (10 BC–AD 54), who stammered and had a club foot and whom Augustus banned from showing his face in public. He was also adamant that a woman's place was at home behind the spinning wheel, and his attempts to impose his abstemious lifestyle on those around him led to a serious rift with his daughter Julia. In 2 BC, just after her sons had been dispatched on campaign, Julia was found to have engaged in dubious activities with several members of the aristocracy. One of her misdemeanours was an orgy in the Forum, while there was also some suspicion of her involvement in a nascent plot to kill her father. She was banished into exile on an island.

Further crises rocked the state with the sudden deaths on campaign of Julia's two sons, and Augustus' preferred heirs, in AD 2 and 4. The reluctant Tiberius was recalled to Rome and installed on the Palatine Hill. Two years later he re-emerged as the heir apparent, was shipped off to fight in Germany, and then to command a major military operation in the Balkans (Illyricum), where recently conquered tribes had risen in revolt. In AD 8 the palace was shaken by another conspiracy, this time involving the daughter of Julia and Agrippa, also named Julia, and her brother, known as Agrippa Postumus since he was born after his father's death. Agrippa Postumus had already been sent into internal exile for allegedly deranged behaviour (open criticism of his grandfather seems to have been part of it), and was now dispatched to an island. Julia was found to be pregnant by someone other than her husband. Augustus saw to it that the child was killed and that she was exiled.

At the same time, Augustus lashed out at Rome's most brilliant living poet, Ovid (Publius Ovidius Naso; 43 BC–AD 17), whose works included a poem on the art of love, which had been in circulation for some seven years but which Augustus now suddenly denounced as offensive. To be sure, Ovid's poem celebrated extramarital love and also contained some wonderfully witty send-ups of Augustan propaganda – suggesting, for example that imperial processions provided excellent opportunities to meet lovers. But that was not enough, in and of itself to cause the poet's downfall – he refers also to an error that angered the emperor. We don't know what that error was, but we do know the result: Ovid finished his life in Tomis, a city on the Black Sea coast of what is now Romania.

A military catastrophe

In AD 6, Augustus introduced his last, but arguably one of his most important, reforms when he set up a new treasury to guarantee retirement bonuses to soldiers who had completed 20 years of service. Funded initially by a large gift from Augustus' private fortune, and thereafter by taxation (including an inheritance tax that was deeply unpopular with senators), this measure was the final step in creating a professional career structure for private soldiers and ensuring the army's loyalty to the imperial house. In Tiberius, the army also now

MASSACRE IN THE TEUTOBURG FOREST

Long lost to history, the site of the battlefield where Varus' legions – the Seventeenth, Eighteenth, and Nineteenth – were slaughtered in AD 9 was found north of the German city of Osnabrück in the early 1990s. Its discovery has helped historians gain a more accurate impression of how the engagement unfolded and puts in context the various sketchy Roman accounts of the battle. Traces of German fieldworks have been identified on the Kalkriese, a hill bordering on the road that the Romans were taking south when they were ambushed. Arminius and his tribes launched repeated attacks on the Romans from this vantage point in the course of a three-day running battle. The Roman infantry was badly hampered by being forced to fight on swampy, heavily wooded terrain poorly suited to their tactics; the Romans' fighting units could not manoeuvre successfully, and were split up and picked off by the Germans.

had a skilled commander, supported by a cadre of competent senior officers who all owed their positions to the regime. However, this period is chiefly known for one of the most devastating defeats in Roman military history, a disaster attributed to the strategic incompetence and naivety of the commanding officer. In AD 7, Quinctilius Varus, who was related to Augustus by marriage, was sent to govern the province of Germania, a region between the Rhine and Elbe rivers that Drusus had recently fought hard to subdue. In AD 9 Varus was deceived into believing intelligence supplied by a supposedly loyal Germanic chieftain named Arminius, who commanded an auxiliary cavalry unit. Varus was lured into leaving his camp and withdrawing his three legions to the Rhine to avoid being cut off for the winter by a rebellion among the tribes. Arminius then sprang his trap, ambushing and destroying the entire Roman force in the Teutoburg Forest.

The disaster in Germany hit the regime hard. Augustus is reported to have wandered the palace banging his head against the walls and crying 'Quinctilius Varus, give me back my legions!' He seldom appeared in public after the disaster and his health was plainly beginning to fail. Tiberius recovered the situation to some extent, reinforcing the frontier on the Rhine before handing over command to his nephew Germanicus, who was tasked with retrieving the standards that had been lost with Varus. The three legions, however, were never replaced. Augustus and Tiberius seem to have agreed that the period of expansion was over and that the empire should remain within boundaries marked by the Rhine and Danube rivers in Europe, the Euphrates in the east, and the Sahara in North Africa.

Five years later, Augustus left Rome to travel to Naples. He fell desperately ill, and died on 19 August, AD 14. Tiberius, who the year before had been accorded equal authority to Augustus everywhere throughout the empire but Rome, now succeeded him.

A Germanic tribesman offering his surrender, from a coin minted during the reign of Augustus. Although Roman armies had enjoyed some success in trying to pacify such tribes, after the disaster of the Teutoburg Forest, expansion was halted and the empire fell back on its border along the River Rhine.

Eccentric Stability: Emperors from Tiberius to Nero
(AD 14–68)

Augustus put the imperial system on such a firm footing that even the dysfunctional behaviour of his four successors could not overturn his achievement. The pillars of the new regime were the army's loyalty to the *princeps*, concern for the welfare of the population of Rome and the emperor's patronage of loyal members of the ruling class. The overarching ideological principle that informed all the regime's policies was domestic propriety. Romans recalled that the years before Actium were haunted by violence and uncertainty, and the ideals of the Republic became inextricably linked with civil war.

A coin from the early years of Tiberius' reign, with the heads of the emperor and his nephew Germanicus emerging from cornucopiae. Tiberius grew increasingly jealous of the younger man's evident popularity with both the army and the citizens of Rome.

Augustus' very success in promoting his mode of governance as the only effective antidote to anarchy resulted in widespread fear that civil war would erupt as soon as he died. This fear was not even allayed by the fact that Tiberius already held a firm grip on power, and persistent rumours of impending turmoil continued to circulate. Some people wondered if Agrippa Postumus might break free from his island prison to challenge the new regime (the rumours were not even scotched when Postumus was executed by his guards, an act of gratuitous brutality for which Tiberius denied all responsibility). Others speculated whether Tiberius' popular nephew Germanicus (15 BC–AD 19), now commanding the powerful army on the Rhine, might choose not to bide his time and wait to succeed Tiberius but instead make an immediate bid for power.

Tiberius and Germanicus

In the event, matters came to a head when four Roman legions stationed on the Rhine and three on the Danube (the province of Pannonia) staged mutinies at the news of Augustus' death. The immediate catalyst of the mutinies was anger over harsh conditions of service; men were being forced to serve beyond their due retirement date, while also suffering brutality at the hands of their centurion officers and receiving derisory pay. Yet the underlying cause that made the troops' simmering grievances boil over into open insurrection was their uncertainty about the future. The Danubian mutiny was swiftly and decisively put down by Tiberius' son Drusus (13 BC–AD 23) and Aelius Sejanus (20 BC–AD 31), the newly promoted commander of the Praetorian Guard, who were dispatched to deal

'The first crime of the new regime was the murder of Agrippa Postumus, whom, ignorant of what was happening and unarmed, but firm of heart, a centurion slew with difficulty. Tiberius said nothing about the matter to the senate.'

TACITUS (ANNALS 1.6)

with the crisis in the Balkans, around the time of Augustus' funeral in September. However, the mutiny in Germany was a far more serious affair; Germanicus' men murdered several brutal centurions and there were mutterings in the ranks that he should seize the throne. Yet although Germanicus refused to accede to their demands, the histrionics he displayed in quelling the unrest in his ranks called his judgement and leadership into question. At one point, the general drew his sword and threatened to commit suicide unless the men returned to their proper loyalty; one soldier was so unimpressed by this display that he offered his own sword, saying that it was sharper. Eventually, through some persuasive last-ditch rhetoric, and concessions to the troops on pay and conditions, Germanicus calmed the situation.

Despite some shortcomings as a commander, Germanicus ultimately turned out to play a key role in the dynastic succession of the Julio-Claudian family. His wife, Julia Agrippina, was exceptionally fecund and gave birth to nine children, no fewer than six of whom survived infancy. These offspring of their union ensured the continuation of the imperial house – one as the emperor Caligula, the other as the mother of Nero. Germanicus himself disappeared from the historical stage in October, AD 19 when he suddenly fell ill and died in Antioch, Syria.

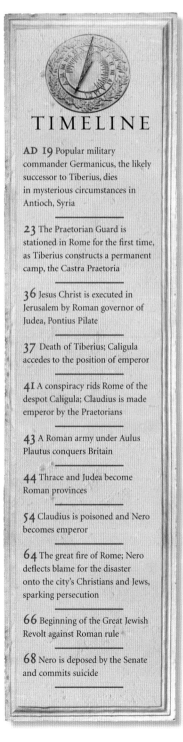

TIMELINE

AD 19 Popular military commander Germanicus, the likely successor to Tiberius, dies in mysterious circumstances in Antioch, Syria

23 The Praetorian Guard is stationed in Rome for the first time, as Tiberius constructs a permanent camp, the Castra Praetoria

36 Jesus Christ is executed in Jerusalem by Roman governor of Judea, Pontius Pilate

37 Death of Tiberius; Caligula accedes to the position of emperor

41 A conspiracy rids Rome of the despot Caligula; Claudius is made emperor by the Praetorians

43 A Roman army under Aulus Plautus conquers Britain

44 Thrace and Judea become Roman provinces

54 Claudius is poisoned and Nero becomes emperor

64 The great fire of Rome; Nero deflects blame for the disaster onto the city's Christians and Jews, sparking persecution

66 Beginning of the Great Jewish Revolt against Roman rule

68 Nero is deposed by the Senate and commits suicide

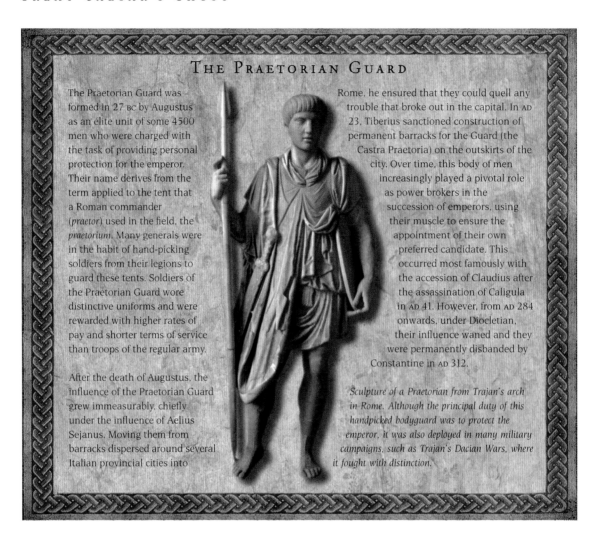

THE PRAETORIAN GUARD

The Praetorian Guard was formed in 27 BC by Augustus as an elite unit of some 4500 men who were charged with the task of providing personal protection for the emperor. Their name derives from the term applied to the tent that a Roman commander (*praetor*) used in the field, the *praetorium*. Many generals were in the habit of hand-picking soldiers from their legions to guard these tents. Soldiers of the Praetorian Guard wore distinctive uniforms and were rewarded with higher rates of pay and shorter terms of service than troops of the regular army.

After the death of Augustus, the influence of the Praetorian Guard grew immeasurably, chiefly under the influence of Aelius Sejanus. Moving them from barracks dispersed around several Italian provincial cities into Rome, he ensured that they could quell any trouble that broke out in the capital. In AD 23, Tiberius sanctioned construction of permanent barracks for the Guard (the Castra Praetoria) on the outskirts of the city. Over time, this body of men increasingly played a pivotal role as power brokers in the succession of emperors, using their muscle to ensure the appointment of their own preferred candidate. This occurred most famously with the accession of Claudius after the assassination of Caligula in AD 41. However, from AD 284 onwards, under Diocletian, their influence waned and they were permanently disbanded by Constantine in AD 312.

Sculpture of a Praetorian from Trajan's arch in Rome. Although the principal duty of this handpicked bodyguard was to protect the emperor, it was also deployed in many military campaigns, such as Trajan's Dacian Wars, where it fought with distinction.

Meanwhile, Romans were becoming ever more alarmed at the tyrannical turn Tiberius' rule was taking. In particular, he increasingly resorted to invoking the *lex maiestatis*, the law governing actions that might 'diminish the majesty of the Roman people' (that is, high treason) to silence his enemies, real or perceived. There was widespread abuse in the application of this capital offence, since anyone who accused a person subsequently found guilty stood to gain a share of the convicted man's estate. Tiberius' overuse of this extreme sanction was just another manifestation of his aloofness and disdain for the finer arts of political persuasion.

In public relations terms, Tiberius completely lacked his predecessor Augustus' personal touch in the exercise of authority and his flair for winning friends and influencing people. As a result, he maintained extremely poor relations with the Senate, whom, according to the testimony of the later Roman historian Tacitus, he derided as 'men fit to be slaves'.

The news that the people's champion and heir apparent was dead sent ripples of shock through the empire. Tiberius was reviled, and his likely successor Drusus was far less popular than Germanicus. The finger of suspicion for Germanicus' death pointed at the governor of Syria, Gnaeus Calpurnius Piso (*c.* 44 BC–AD 20). There was a long-running enmity between the two men, and just before the onset of Germanicus' fatal illness, he had forced Piso to resign his post. Worse still, there was some circumstantial evidence to suggest that Piso had poisoned his rival on the secret instruction of Tiberius. No one dared say this openly, but suspicions mounted when the former governor returned to Rome to defend himself on a charge of *maiestas* arising both from the assassination rumours and his subsequent efforts to retake the province from Germanicus' officers by force of arms. Piso's defence was that he was Tiberius' man on the spot and his fulsome protestations of unswerving loyalty may only have served to convince the emperor that his placeman was actually about to make incriminating revelations. Conveniently, following a visit by Sejanus, Piso was discovered to have committed 'suicide' by slitting his own throat.

Agrippina landing at the port of Brundisium (modern Brindisi) with the ashes of her husband Germanicus. Most Romans suspected Tiberius of being behind Germanicus' mysterious death in Antioch, but his alleged agent was murdered before he could expose the truth. This painting of the incident is by the American artist Benjamin West (1738–1820).

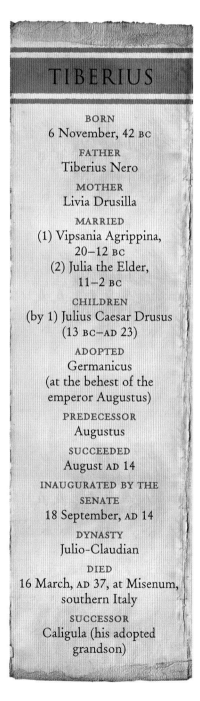

TIBERIUS

BORN
6 November, 42 BC

FATHER
Tiberius Nero

MOTHER
Livia Drusilla

MARRIED
(1) Vipsania Agrippina,
20–12 BC
(2) Julia the Elder,
11–2 BC

CHILDREN
(by 1) Julius Caesar Drusus
(13 BC–AD 23)

ADOPTED
Germanicus
(at the behest of the
emperor Augustus)

PREDECESSOR
Augustus

SUCCEEDED
August AD 14

INAUGURATED BY THE
SENATE
18 September, AD 14

DYNASTY
Julio-Claudian

DIED
16 March, AD 37, at Misenum,
southern Italy

SUCCESSOR
Caligula (his adopted
grandson)

The rise and fall of Sejanus

Drusus did not long survive Germanicus, dying in AD 23. A plot almost certainly lay behind his sudden demise, though unlike Germanicus' death, no rumours circulated at the time. However, after Sejanus fell from favour and was killed eight years later, clear evidence of a conspiracy emerged. From as early as AD 19, Sejanus had been conducting an affair with Drusus' wife Livilla. His political ambitions were also on the rise and he began to entertain hopes that, if he made himself indispensable to Tiberius, the emperor might begin to regard him in the same light as Augustus had viewed Agrippa and appoint him as his successor. Sejanus realized that it would immeasurably strengthen his hand if Drusus were to die and he marry his widow. Drusus duly fell victim to a mystery illness, but the second part of Sejanus' plan was thwarted when Tiberius refused him permission to marry Livilla. Even so, from this point Tiberius seems to have placed ever greater trust in the leadership powers of his lieutenant and had statues of Sejanus erected throughout Rome. At this stage, the only heirs to the throne were the two teenage sons of Germanicus, Nero and Drusus, but they and their mother Agrippina antagonized Tiberius by continuing to hold him responsible for Germanicus' death. Thoroughly sick of the business of governing, Tiberius retired to his villa on Capri in AD 28, leaving the day-to-day running of the state in Sejanus' hands. The following year, his patience with Agrippina and her sons finally ran out and he had all three banished to the same island where Augustus had once exiled his daughter Julia.

The succession now looked as if it must fall to Agrippina's third son, Gaius Caligula or the young son of Drusus, Tiberius Gemellus (AD 19–38) who were both favoured by Tiberius and who lived with him on Capri. Faced with these new obstacles, in AD 31 Sejanus appears to have decided to seize power for himself and hatched a plot to kill Tiberius and the surviving male members of the imperial house. The conspiracy was unmasked by Germanicus' mother, who sent a slave girl named Caenis to warn the emperor. Tiberius' response was swift and brutal; Sejanus was condemned by the Senate, strangled, and his body thrown to the Roman mob who had always hated and feared him in equal measure and who now delighted in tearing his corpse to pieces.

Tiberius spent the final years of his reign as an embittered recluse. His tendency to brooding introspection – a contemporary once characterized him as *tristissimus hominum* ('the gloomiest of men') – now assumed paranoid proportions. Members of the senate lived in fear they might be suddenly charged with treason, and some long-serving provincial governors lapsed into incompetence. One of these men was Pontius Pilate, the governor of Judaea, who was finally dismissed in AD 36, a few months after he had executed a teacher from Galilee at the behest of the religious authorities in Jerusalem. It was one of the few times that he seems to have been willing to go along with what they wanted, but Jesus of Nazareth was the sort of independent religious leader who had caused him trouble at various points during his years in office. His brutal response to the actions of another holy man in the course of the year would finally convince the governor of Syria that he had to go.

As for the emperor, surrounding himself on Capri with a coterie of academics and astrologers, he disengaged himself from all practical concerns, including the crucial question of his succession, as he began to have serious doubts about the fitness of his nephew Gaius Caligula to assume the mantle of emperor. These doubts gave way to study of the stars, which only confirmed his tendency towards helpless inertia, since it indicated to him that Caligula's accession was inevitable. In March of AD 37, aged 79, Tiberius fell ill and died of natural causes, though stories spread suggesting that he was actually smothered by Sejanus' successor as praetorian prefect, a man named Macro (21 BC–AD 38).

Four busts on a cameo from the first century AD portray the siblings Germanicus and Claudius together with their respective wives, Agrippina and Agrippina the Younger. Although Germanicus was groomed for leadership from an early age and seemed set to come to power, it was his ill-favoured elder brother Claudius who was fated to become emperor.

Caligula the monster

Tiberius' death provoked unbridled celebration among both the senate and the people of Rome. Yet the fact remained that when he came to power, he had been eminently well qualified to succeed Augustus; no-one had commanded more armies and provinces than Tiberius, nor been consul so many times. Moreover, despite his deep unpopularity, his reign had left the empire in a far stronger position. He had not embarked on damaging military adventures but had consolidated existing boundaries, and as a result the treasury was in a very healthy state on his death. He had therefore been, for all his growing eccentricity, a symbol of stability from the outset. The same could not be said for his successor. Caligula had held just one junior office, and had no official position when Tiberius died. So, whereas Tiberius had simply inherited the role of *princeps* from Augustus, to formalize this new accession the senate and people now took it upon themselves to define the legal position of the emperor by passing a bill to confer that position on Caligula. To those who did not know him, the young Caligula, the son of a popular father, seemed the perfect antidote to his great-uncle. Caligula instantly won great acclaim by abolishing treason trials.

After the dour reign of Tiberius, the new emperor Caligula seemed like a breath of fresh air. Crowds greeted his accession with wild enthusiasm, and he rewarded their adulation with chariot races, plays and gladiatorial displays. Yet it was not long before Romans came to realize that Caligula was a tyrant.

However, it soon became apparent that Rome's euphoric celebration of her new emperor was badly misplaced. Caligula had never had to demonstrate *virtus* in a collective environment. The formative period of his life had been spent at Tiberius' villa on Capri, and there his chief companions were the sons of eastern client-kings whose attitudes toward power were very different from those of the average Roman. Caligula had fully imbibed their imperious attitude. His closest friends were his sisters, and it was rumoured that he had incestuous relations with at least one of them, possibly all three. In response, Caligula's propagandists now sought to deflect public attention by disseminating lurid stories about how Tiberius had spent his waning years. He was alleged to have developed a taste for watching young people have sex; in the public mind, the image of the dour, academic ex-general was supplanted by that of the septuagenarian paedophile. This salacious smear campaign could not, however, mask the essential truth. The intelligence offered to Tiberius by his stargazing had been accurate; Caligula lacked experience of collective decision-making and was wholly unsuited to wielding absolute power.

Rome now witnessed a series of unsettling events. Macro was executed on a charge of treason within a year of Caligula taking power. Those who were tired of the overbearing influence of the Praetorian Guard's commander may have been glad to see him go, but there was now no voice to control the emperor. Caligula began to suggest that he was god, and began to indulge his whims (including sexual assaults upon female guests at his parties). It took less than a year before the first conspiracy against him came to light, and its aftermath revealed another unsavoury characteristic of the new ruler: he liked to watch people be tortured. Shortly thereafter, Caligula left Rome to campaign in the North. This escapade was meant to prove that the emperor really

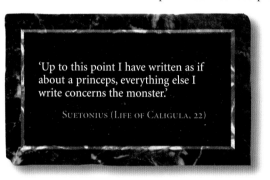

'Up to this point I have written as if about a princeps, everything else I write concerns the monster.'

SUETONIUS (LIFE OF CALIGULA, 22)

was a man of substance, but instead turned into a fiasco; a planned invasion of Britain was aborted and Caligula's troops were ordered to collect seashells to carry back to Rome as tokens of the emperor's glorious victory over the sea-god Neptune. Caligula announced his intention of making his favourite, pampered horse Incitatus a member of the senate. Anger mounted, and a number of senators and military men plotted to assassinate the emperor.

In January, AD 41, while Caligula was watching a gladiatorial show, a tribune of the imperial bodyguard stabbed him to death. Never before had this loyal body of men shown itself willing to betray the emperor, but Caligula had made the mistake of alienating them by surrounding himself with an exotic entourage of German troops. The plot against Caligula taught future conspirators an important lesson: first ensure the complicity of the Praetorian Guard.

An unlikely successor

Shortly after the assassination, the senate convened a meeting at which several of its members proposed a return to Republican government. This was clearly not going to be acceptable to the Praetorian Guard, who owed their privileges to the imperial system. Interestingly, despite the recent dashing of their hopes in Caligula and their long, painful experience of Tiberius' rule, the Roman people apparently had no wish to see the Republic restored either, assembling in the Forum and loudly proclaiming that they would not stand for a return to senatorial rule.

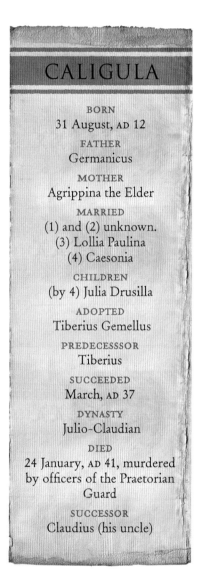

CALIGULA

BORN
31 August, AD 12

FATHER
Germanicus

MOTHER
Agrippina the Elder

MARRIED
(1) and (2) unknown.
(3) Lollia Paulina
(4) Caesonia

CHILDREN
(by 4) Julia Drusilla

ADOPTED
Tiberius Gemellus

PREDECESSSOR
Tiberius

SUCCEEDED
March, AD 37

DYNASTY
Julio-Claudian

DIED
24 January, AD 41, murdered by officers of the Praetorian Guard

SUCCESSOR
Claudius (his uncle)

CLAUDIUS

BORN
1 August, 10 BC

FATHER
Nero Claudius Drusus

MOTHER
Antonia Minor

MARRIED
(1) Plautia Urgulanilla
(divorced for adultery)
(2) Aelia Paetina (divorced)
(3) Valeria Messalina
(divorced and executed for
treason) (4) Agrippina the
Younger

CHILDREN
Claudius Drusus (died in
adolescence), Claudia,
Antonia, Octavia, Britannicus
(poisoned in adolescence)

ADOPTED
Nero (his stepson, son of
Agrippina the Younger)

PREDECESSSOR
Caligula

SUCCEEDED
24 January, AD 41

DYNASTY
Julio-Claudian

DIED
13 October, AD 54, murdered
by poisoned mushrooms
possibly administered by his
wife Agrippina

SUCCESSOR
Nero

Popular myth recounts that the Praetorian Guard discovered Caligula's uncle Claudius hiding behind a curtain and, on a whim, declared him the new emperor. The truth may be more prosaic; the officers of the guard knew that they were going to need an alternative to Caligula, and Claudius was the obvious choice was Caligula's uncle Claudius. In fact, he may well have willingly joined the praetorians in their camp as soon as he learned that Caligula was dead, suggesting that he had foreknowledge of the plot and colluded in his nephew's demise. After a day of intense negotiation between the various parties, the senate welcomed the appointment of new emperor.

Claudius is an intriguing figure. He is most familiar to contemporary readers through the historical novels *I Claudius* (1934) and *Claudius the God* (1935) by the British writer Robert Graves, which cover the reign of the first four emperors; drawing on Tacitus, Plutarch and Suetonius, Graves presents a man who learns to play up his disabilities, especially his supposed simple-mindedness, so as to avoid appearing a threat to his peers, and so survive. This portrait is probably well grounded in historical fact. Born with a club foot, and possibly also suffering from cerebral palsy, Claudius had been kept in the background throughout the reign of Tiberius. Caligula had deigned to share the consulship with him in AD 37, but thereafter had rarely missed an opportunity to humiliate him. The two men were fundamentally different characters. Claudius had spent his formative years in the palace reading widely, and writing. History was his particular love, and he seems to have developed a genuine affection for Roman antiquity. But, like Caligula, he had no real experience of political life, and reportedly found the company of senators difficult. Having no power base among the senatorial classes, he naturally turned for advice to the freed slaves who administered the increasingly complex affairs of the imperial household, which controlled vast territories throughout the empire. In modern terms, Claudius can be seen as a technocrat, valuing the company of other people who knew how to get things done. Conversely, his abiding weakness was his lack of political guile in not recognizing that many of those who served him did so not in order to further the public good but for their own ends.

Achievements and setbacks

Claudius was also keen to foster good relations with the Roman army. Two years after coming to power, he organized a highly efficient invasion of Britain, winning kudos for capturing a prize that had even eluded Julius Caesar. Although the military operation was subsequently hampered by the lack of an exit strategy (a problem that bedevils ill-considered invasions to this day) it did achieve its short-term political ends. Claudius hurried north to share in the glory of his forces as they completed their victory, and even gave his son the honorific Britannicus (offered to Claudius himself by the senate, but refused) in commemoration of the triumph. The highly competent freedmen he appointed as secretaries for state also ensured that the administration of Rome and her empire ran smoothly. One of his most impressive public works projects was the construction of the vital new commercial port of Portus north of Ostia at the mouth of the River Tiber. Linked by canal to the Tiber, Portus could handle year-round shipments of the grain needed to make bread, the staple of the Roman diet.

It was only in the later 40s that Claudius' turbulent private life began seriously to compromise the achievements of his administration. Claudius gradually became estranged from Messalina, his third wife, who was much younger than him. He took slave mistresses, and she in turn took lovers of her own. Messalina's licentious conduct began to scandalize Rome; there were rumours that she spent an evening in a brothel seeing if she could make love to more men than an experienced prostitute. In AD 48, while Claudius was out of town, she even went through a mock wedding ceremony with one of her partners, Gaius Silius. It is possible that the pair were plotting to usurp the emperor's power, or that they were simply set on defying the conventions of popular morality. In any event, the incident galvanized Claudius into drastic action, and Messalina was summarily executed along with several of her lovers.

After discovering that he had been cuckolded in the most outrageous manner, Claudius had his young third wife Valeria Messalina put to death in AD 48. This painting of 1875 – by the Austrian artist Hans Makart, depicting a well-known contemporary tragic actress in the role of Messalina – was clearly intended to convey the languid decadence for which Claudius' empress became notorious.

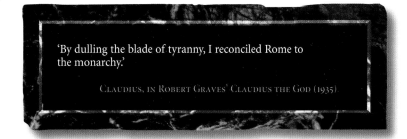

'By dulling the blade of tyranny, I reconciled Rome to the monarchy.'

CLAUDIUS, IN ROBERT GRAVES' CLAUDIUS THE GOD (1935)

Claudius' Invasion of Britain

Two years after coming to power, Claudius launched an invasion of Britain in AD 43. Several factors lay behind his decision to do so. First and foremost, Britain was by this stage a key trading partner with Rome, supplying the empire with valuable metals and ores, such as iron, silver, tin and galena (lead ore). There was also a political motive – the invasion would help demonstrate to a sceptical Roman senate and people that Claudius was a strong and decisive leader.

The operation was meticulously planned and executed. Four legions and several auxiliary units, including Batavian troops, took part. In all, the force comprised some 40,000 men. Their skilled commander, Aulus Plautius, quickly succeeded in establishing a bridgehead on the island. The decisive battle took place at the River Medway in southeast England, where the Batavians played outflanked the Britons under King Caractacus after fording the river in full battle gear. After two days, the Britons were defeated and the Romans gained a firm foothold from which they began the long process of pacifying the island.

Yet despite Claudius' success in achieving his initial objectives, the occupation – as always happens with military operations motivated by short-term political ambitions – turned out to be a costly and protracted affair with no thought-out endgame. Effective administration took nearly another 50 years to establish.

Heeding the advice of his freedmen, Claudius took a new bride straight away, and his choice fell on his niece Agrippina. The relationship was plainly incestuous, but Claudius had the law changed to accommodate his wishes. Agrippina moved into the palace with her son Nero (AD 37–68), who was three years older than Britannicus. A highly ambitious woman from impeccable stock (her grandfather by adoption was Augustus and her father Germanicus), Agrippina made sure that Nero was introduced to public life, and soon amassed enormous power for herself within Claudius' *domus*. She realized that Britannicus could not legally succeed Claudius until he had reached manhood at the age of 14 in February AD 55. In late AD 54 she arranged for Claudius to be fed poisonous mushrooms at a banquet. Nero was proclaimed emperor at the tender age of 16, and Britannicus was poisoned a few months later. The people and especially the senate, many of whose members had been unable to penetrate the charmed circle of freedmen who enjoyed Claudius' confidence, greeted the news of Nero's accession with delight.

The last of the Julio-Claudians

It took some time for it to emerge that Nero's appointment as emperor was a disaster. Initially, he had little interest in governing and left effective control of the state in the hands of competent people hand-picked for the task by his mother. This enabled him to devote himself to the pursuits he favoured – he fancied himself a poet and actor. The reins of power were held at this time by the famous Spanish-Roman philosopher and man of letters Seneca the Younger (4 BC–AD 65) who was Nero's former tutor, and the Praetorian prefect Sextus Afranius Burrus (d. AD 62). A clear measure of their practical competence was their appointment of a seasoned and gifted soldier, Domitius Corbulo

(AD 7–67), to take charge of a new conflict that had arisen with the Parthians over control of Armenia. Corbulo acquitted himself well in this role.

Nero fiercely resisted any attempts by others to regulate his private life. As part of his mother's succession project, he had been persuaded to marry Claudius' daughter Octavia, whom he found deeply uncongenial. As emperor he began to take concubines and play the field of senatorial women. Agrippina, who was well aware that such conduct had precipitated her brother Caligula's fall from grace with the Roman people, signalled her disapproval. Nero soon tired of his mother's interference, and communication between them broke down almost totally. It was at this point that Nero first met Poppaea Sabina, the daughter of one of Tiberius' generals, and a woman of powerful personality. He planned to divorce Octavia and make Poppaea his wife. Agrippina and the senior advisers counselled against this; Octavia was a valuable symbol of stability and continuity. Nero's response was to seek other counsel and hatch a plot to kill his mother.

> 'Even if [Nero] was not the instigator of the emperor's death, he was at least privy to it, as he openly admitted; for he used afterwards to laud mushrooms, the vehicle in which the poison was administered to Claudius, as "the food of the gods, as the Greek proverb has it."'
>
> SUETONIUS (LIFE OF NERO, 33)

In AD 59 Nero arranged for Agrippina to take a trip across the Bay of Naples on a boat that had been sabotaged so that its stern, where she would be seated, would break off during the voyage and sink. Yet Nero had failed to take into account that his mother was a strong swimmer. Having made it safely back to shore, the empress was an object of pity to the crowd that assembled as she dragged herself on to the beach. Her son showed no mercy. Learning of her escape, he planted a dagger on her freedman and, concocting a story that she had in fact planned to kill him, sent a detachment of guards to detain Agrippina and put her to death.

BOUDICCA'S REVOLT

Most of our knowledge about Boudicca's revolt against Roman rule in AD 60–61 comes from Tacitus, who blames the uprising on the arrogance and brutality of the province's bureaucracy.

When King Prasutagus of the Iceni in East Anglia died, a dispute arose over whether Rome was entitled to annex his kingdom, since the king had made his two daughters and the emperor Nero co-beneficiaries of his will. Roman law did not recognize female inheritance and the imperial procurator Catus Decianus intervened clumsily to enforce Rome's will. Prasutagus' widow Boudicca was beaten and her daughters raped. Meanwhile, the governor, Suetonius Paulinus, was directing military operations in Wales.

The treatment of Boudicca ignited the powder-keg of British resentment of the occupation. The founding of the settlement at Camulodunum (Colchester) incensed both the Trinovates, in whose territory the colony was forcibly implanted, and the Iceni, their neighbours to the north.

Inspired by Arminius, the hero of the Teutoburg Forest, Boudicca's forces attacked Camulodunum, Verulamium (St Albans) and Londonium (London). The scale of the destruction at these sites that has been unearthed by archaeologists testifies to the Britons' desire to wipe out all traces of Roman rule. Early in the revolt her forces also crushed a Roman force sent from Lincoln to relieve Colchester. She was less fortunate when she met Suetonius Paulinus' main force somewhere in the Midlands. Her army was destroyed, and Tacitus says that she committed suicide shortly thereafter.

NERO

BORN
15 December, AD 37

FATHER
Gnaeus Domitius
Ahenobarbus

MOTHER
Agrippina the
Younger

MARRIED
(1) Claudia Octavia
(divorced) (2) Poppaea
Sabina (killed by Nero in a
fit of rage)

CHILDREN
(by 2) Claudia, b. 63 AD

PREDECESSOR
Claudius

SUCCEEDED
13 October, AD 54

DYNASTY
Julio-Claudian

DIED
9 June, AD 68, committed
suicide after being deposed
by the senate

SUCCESSOR
Galba

According to Suetonius, the megalomaniac emperor Nero subjected his fellow Romans to interminable performances of song and recitation, which nobody was allowed to leave on pain of death.

The murder of Agrippina changed everything. Seneca's and Burrus' influence instantly began to wane, as Nero's megalomania took a firm hold. Seneca was fired in AD 60, while Burrus died a year later. Octavia was falsely accused of adultery, divorced and executed around the same time that Seneca was dismissed. Poppaea was installed as empress, and a man named Tigellinus (d. 69), previously a supplier of chariot horses for the circus, joined Nero's inner circle. Tigellinus would prove a loyal confederate in encouraging the worst of Nero's vices, and was rewarded in AD 62 by being made prefect of the Praetorian Guard.

Meanwhile, the foundations of the empire began to totter. In AD 60, a violent revolt broke out in Britain, led by Boudicca (d. AD 60/61), the queen of the Iceni tribe. Four years later disaster struck closer to home, when a fire destroyed most of Rome. The Roman version of disaster planning was sketchy, and relief efforts were not coordinated by Nero, who allegedly reacted very badly to news of the conflagration: it is said that he recited a poem on the fall of Troy even though his 'press office' claimed that he was instrumental in fighting the fire. Nero found a convenient scapegoat for the fire in the form of a minor religious sect – the Christians. Followers of this faith were subjected to hideous tortures for their alleged guilt, including being covered in animal skins and having dogs set upon them, crucifixion, and being burned alive.

Nero's regime lurched from crisis to crisis. A year after the fire, in a fit of rage, Nero kicked his wife Poppaea Sabina in the stomach while she was pregnant, causing her death. That same year, a conspiracy was uncovered among members of the senate and the guard to kill the emperor and install a new ruler. A round of executions followed, and Tigellinus and his confederates took advantage of the situation to settle old scores. Seneca was forced to commit suicide, and within the year other enemies were arraigned on trumped-up charges. In this orgy of bloodletting, Nero's advisers blundered by charging Corbulo, the all-conquering hero of the Parthian War, with treason and executing him. Yet Corbulo had many influential friends and admirers in Rome. In AD 67, when Nero left for Greece to demonstrate his skill as a charioteer in the Olympic Games (which were rescheduled to fit round his visit), a serious conspiracy arose among various generals and governors.

Nero's Greek trip was a great success, and he was crowned victor in all the events he entered. However, he was immmediately summoned back to Rome by a letter from his freedmen warning him of the conspiracy. Nero arrived too late to change the course of events. In March, AD 68, the governor of one of the Gallic provinces proclaimed his loyalty to the Roman government rather than to Nero; the governor of Judaea, who commanded a powerful army assembled to suppress the revolt that had broken out there in AD 66, suddenly suspended military operations, and Galba, the governor of a Spanish province, had himself proclaimed emperor. The commander of the major army in Germany switched sides to support Galba. Within Rome itself a fifth column was at work, which enjoyed the support of the Praetorian Guard. Its commanders may have grown weary of Nero and taken the pragmatic view that their troops were no match for a seasoned provincial army. On 9 June, AD 68, the guard declared for Galba and the senate deposed Nero, declaring him an enemy of the state. Nero fled the palace, making for the house of a freedman named Phaon, not knowing that Phaon had already betrayed him. As he heard his captors approach, Nero stabbed himself to death. Vain and deluded to the last, the emperor's reported last words were 'How great an artist dies with me!'

An 18th-century copy of one of the fresco paintings found at the ruins of the 'Golden House' hints at the opulent decor for the new imperial palace that Nero planned after the great fire of AD 64. Once built, this enormous edifice dominated the heart of Rome and must have created huge problems for people trying to get from one place to another.

CAESARS AND THEIR SUBJECTS

The Colosseum is the most famous symbol of ancient
Rome. Construction of this huge amphitheatre, which
could seat 45,000–55,000 spectators, was begun
by Vespasian and completed by his son Titus.

New Dynasties: From the Flavians to the Antonines (AD 68–180)

Between the deaths of Nero (AD 68) and Marcus Aurelius (AD 180), the century or so of stability that the Roman empire brought to regions under its control remains an astonishing achievement. While peace and prosperity were by no means universal, most crises were, by the standards of earlier and later eras, relatively short. One major exception to the general *pax Romana* was the province of Judea, covering the territory of the modern state of Israel, plus parts of Jordan and Syria. There, two major revolts, in AD 66–73 and AD 132–135, caused terrible destruction and loss of life.

Galba's accession as emperor brought to an end almost a century of imperial rule by the Julio-Claudian dynasty. Yet lack of political acumen, in particular his tendency to alienate potential allies, was to bring about Galba's downfall after barely three months in office.

Sixteen centuries later, at the start of his magisterial six-volume work *Decline and Fall of the Roman Empire* (1776–88), the English historian Edward Gibbon famously summarized this era in the following terms:

'If a man were called to fix the period in the history of the world, during which the condition of the human race was most happy and prosperous, he would, without hesitation, name that which elapsed from the death of Domitian to the accession of Commodus. The vast extent of the Roman Empire was governed by absolute power, under the guidance of virtue and wisdom. The armies were restrained by the firm but gentle hand of four successive emperors, whose characters and authority commanded involuntary respect. The forms of the civil administration were carefully preserved by Nerva, Trajan,

Hadrian and the Antonines, who delighted in the image of liberty, and were pleased with considering themselves as the accountable ministers of the laws. Such princes deserved the honour of restoring the republic had the Romans of their days been capable of enjoying a rational freedom.'

Context is everything. First, Gibbon was writing at a time when the burgeoning British empire was facing insurrection in its American colonies; the didactic thrust of his work was that governance must always proceed from civic virtue – a lesson that later rulers of the Roman empire forgot at their peril as, by implication, would the ministers of his own time. Second, the Enlightenment, with its stress on reason and order, which informed Gibbon's approach to his subject, followed on the heels of more than two centuries of turmoil in Europe marked by a succession of wars of religion and dynastic succession. Gibbon's glowing appraisal of this period of Roman history was tempered by his awareness that even the best of empires emerge from conflict and secure happiness for the many at the cost of the few. It is against this background that the accomplishment of the second century AD needs to be set.

Three brief reigns

It is unlikely that anyone in Rome in AD 68–69 would have predicted a century of stability. After Nero's suicide, a vacuum had opened up at the heart of the empire. It was filled by civil war – the first Rome had seen since the bloody struggle between Octavian and Mark Antony in 32–30 BC – and a succession of military pretenders, each of whose reigns lasted months rather than years. So ephemeral was their hold on power that AD 69 is remembered as the 'Year of the Four Emperors'.

Servius Sulpicius Galba (3 BC–AD 69), a former general and consul, was governor of the province of Hispania Tarraconensis in AD 68. His rise to power was not the result of a determined campaign, or indeed decisive action of any kind on his part. On the contrary, he vacillated when Julius Vindex, leader of the first major revolt against Nero in AD 68, announced that Galba was his chosen candidate to succeed Nero. It was only when he was certain that the praetorian prefect had declared in his favour that he marched to Rome. Galba had no outstanding leadership qualities or populist flair, and in his brief reign earned a reputation for being callous, mean and snobbish. One likely explanation for his succession was that ambitious men in the army and senate backed his appointment as a stop-gap measure, calculating that, aged 71 and with no children, he would be sure to die before long and

TIMELINE

AD 69 Vespasian made emperor

70 Vespasian's son Titus crushes the Great Jewish Revolt

74 Masada, stronghold of the Jewish Zealots, falls to the Romans

79 Eruption of Vesuvius

81 Domitian accedes to the throne

96 Assassination of Domitian; Nerva comes to power

106 Roman armies under Trajan complete conquest of Dacia

117 Death of Trajan and accession of Hadrian

122 Construction of Hadrian's Wall in northern Britain begins

132 Start of the Jewish Bar Kochba revolt against Roman rule

138 Hadrian dies and is succeeded by Antoninus Pius

161 Antoninus Pius succeeded by Marcus Aurelius and Lucius Verus

166 The Antonine Plague sweeps through the Roman empire

170 Marcus Aurelius' wars against the Danubian tribes (to 180)

180 Death of Marcus Aurelius; Commodus becomes sole ruler

*A Renaissance engraving of the emperor
Otho. Otho turned against his former ally
Galba and ousted him when he promoted
another man to be his chosen successor.
His turned out to be the briefest reign
in the period of bloodshed and turmoil
known as the 'Year of the Four Emperors'.*

leave the field open for more dynamic personalities.
As it turned out, his demise actually came far
sooner than anyone expected.

Galba was far along the path to self-destruction
even before he entered Rome in September AD 68.
Despite the fact that his position depended entirely
upon military backing, he set about alienating key
elements of the army. During Nero's vain attempt
to muster forces to crush the growing rebellion
against his rule, he had raised a legion from
marines serving in the fleet in the Bay of Naples,
promising these irregular troops equal pay to that
received by regular legionaries. Galba now refused
to honour this pledge and executed those who
protested. In his dogged concern to get state
finances back on an even keel at all costs, he even
countermanded loyalty payments due to the
praetorians who had ensured his rise to power. At the same time,
he lost the support of the army of southern Germany (Germania
Superior) by removing its popular commander, Verginius Rufus
(AD 14–97). Verginius had been responsible for putting down Vindex's
revolt against Nero, whereupon the army offered him the throne. He
refused and offered his services to Galba. Galba probably owed his life
to this decision, but was less than gracious. The soldiery regarded
the dismissal of Verginius and his replacement by a nonentity as a
calculated insult.

Trouble on the horizon

Meanwhile, changes were also afoot in the army stationed in Rome's
other German province (Germania Inferior). Unwisely, in late AD 68,
Galba appointed the ambitious Aulus Vitellius (AD 15–69), whose
father had been Claudius' closest associate, to reimpose discipline on
this force after their previous commander was murdered. Vitellius
immediately began to manoeuvre himself into a position to seize
power. Perceiving that Galba was weak, and that the army in Germany
had been insufficiently rewarded for its break with Nero, he ingratiated
himself with the general staff in Colonia Agrippina (Cologne).
Moreover, even before leaving Rome he had taken a sword that had
once belonged to Julius Caesar from the temple of the Divine Julius.
The fact that he was allowed to remove such a powerful symbolic
trophy was a sign that he had lost no time in organizing an efficient
fifth column in the capital. On 1 January, AD 69 matters came to a head

GALBA

BORN
24 December, 3 BC,
in Tarracina

FATHER
Servius Sulpicius Galba

MOTHER
Mummia Achaica

PREDECESSOR
Nero

OFFICIAL START OF REIGN
8 October, AD 68

DYNASTY
None

DIED:
15 January, AD 69

SUCCESSOR
Otho

when the legions at Mainz in Germania Superior refused to swear loyalty to Galba and smashed his statues. The next day the armies of both German provinces proclaimed Vitellius their new emperor.

Typically, Galba's response was to dither and, equally characteristically, to make an enemy of another erstwhile ally, Marcus Salvius Otho (AD 32–69). This Etruscan nobleman, prominent among the libertines who surrounded Nero, had once been involved in a wife-swapping arrangement with Nero – he had married Poppaea Sabina on the understanding that Nero would sleep with her until he could get rid of Octavia – and allegedly instructed Nero in the art of foot perfuming.

'He [Galba] seemed greater as a private citizen, when all would have agreed that he was capable of ruling, if only he hadn't done so.'

TACITUS HISTORIES 1.49

Then, it seems, Otho had fallen in love with Poppaea himself, with the result that Nero forced him to divorce her and sent him to govern Lusitania (modern Portugal). Accordingly, he had every reason to support Galba during the revolution, and joined him on his march to Rome. This loyalty, plus an astrological prediction that he would be the next emperor, encouraged him in the belief that Galba would name him his successor. However, his hopes were dashed when Galba adopted the young Lucius Calpurnius Piso (d. AD 69) as his heir on 10 January. Galba's decision was motivated by sheer snobbery; despite Otho's pedigree, Piso was the scion of an indisputably nobler house. The appointment galvanized Otho into high-speed plotting. On 15 January the Praetorian Guard and other troops stationed in Rome declared Otho emperor. Galba panicked and set off across the Forum to confront the rebels, but was instantly cut down by Otho's men. The unfortunate Piso was tracked to the temple of Vesta, where he had taken sanctuary, dragged out, and butchered.

While these dramatic events were unfolding, Vitellius' legions were on the march from Germany to Rome to install their man as emperor. While Vitellius' troops undoubtedly represented the cream of the Roman army, Otho still managed to muster a strong enough force from Nero's former troops, gladiators and the Praetorian Guard to mount a credible defence. His wider strategy was to hold Vitellius' advance units long enough to enable him to call up reinforcements from the province of Illyricum in the Balkans. The holding action

OTHO

BORN
25 April, AD 32, in
Ferentium (Etruria)

FATHER
Lucius Otho

MOTHER
Terentia Albia

MARRIED
Poppaea Sabina

PREDECESSOR
Galba

OFFICIAL START OF REIGN
8 October, AD 68

DYNASTY
None

DIED
16 April, AD 69

SUCCESSOR
Vitellius

The last of Nero's shortlived successors was Vitellius. His assassination in December AD 69 by troops loyal to Vespasian brought to an end more than a year of anarchy.

VITELLIUS

BORN
24 September, AD 15

FATHER
Lucius Vitellius

MOTHER
Sextilia

PREDECESSOR
Otho

BEGINNING OF REIGN
17 April, AD 69

DYNASTY
None

DIED
22 December, AD 69

SUCCESSOR
Vespasian

failed when Vitellius' army defeated Otho's men in a hard-fought engagement at the Battle of Bedriacum outside Cremona. When he learned of the defeat, Otho committed suicide on 16 April to spare Rome further mayhem. His reign had lasted barely three months.

Vitellius reached the capital at the start of June and began the process of establishing his own regime in the face of serious opposition. In particular, Vespasian (Titus Flavius Vespasianus; AD 9–79), a relatively low-born career soldier who had risen through the ranks to become commander of the force sent to pacify Judea during the Great Jewish Revolt, disputed Vitellius' appointment. He rapidly garnered support among the eastern garrisons. On 1 July, AD 69, Vespasian was proclaimed emperor by the Roman army occupying Egypt, and the armies in Judea and Syria swiftly followed suit. This was a powerful military coalition, and Vespasian's campaign soon gained momentum among other units closer to Rome. The Balkan legions in the provinces of Pannonia, Illyricum and Moesia, fearing retribution for their support of Otho, soon declared for Vespasian (moreover, in some cases, they were commanded by men with strong links to the eastern commanders, having served under Corbulo).

Faced with this growing rebellion, Vitellius tried to hedge his bets. He dispatched his main force to northern Italy to confront Vespasian, but at the same time kept potential sources of mediation in play by not arresting either Vespasian's brother Sabinus or his younger son, the future emperor Domitian. Even so, his position became increasingly untenable. Vespasian's army crushed his legions on almost exactly the same spot where Vitellius had earlier defeated the forces of Otho and then marched on Rome. During the fierce battle for the city, Domitian and Sabinus took refuge in the temple of Capitoline Jupiter, Rome's most sacred monument. Domitian managed to escape, but Sabinus was captured by Vitellius' troops and killed despite Vitellius' efforts to save his life. When Vespasian's men finally secured control of Rome, they were no more merciful, stabbing Vitellius to death and hurling his body into the Tiber. Vespasian was proclaimed emperor while he was still at Caesarea in Judea. It is a mark of how heavily Roman emperors had come to rely on the army as a power broker that Vespasian dated his rule not from when the Roman people voted to confirm his installation but from 1 July, AD 69, when his troops acclaimed him.

THE GREAT JEWISH REVOLT

The root cause of the Great Jewish Revolt was the long history of poor government by Roman procurators of Judea. One particularly bitter grievance was their failure to devolve any power to the province's Jewish élite. Instead of widening their local power base, the Romans preferred to control the region through client kings drawn exclusively from the Idumean family of Herod the Great.

The crisis began in May AD 66 when rioting broke out in the capital, Caesarea. Its immediate catalyst was the desecration of a synagogue by members of the Greek community there, but it was fuelled by pent-up rage at the brutal administration of Porcius Festus. The situation escalated when extremist opponents of Roman rule seized the fortress of Masada and the Jewish priesthood refused to continue offering sacrifices for Nero in the Temple. The initial response by Cestius Gallus, governor of Syria, was poorly organized and he was defeated at the Battle of Beth Horon outside Jerusalem: his legion even lost its standard during the retreat.

Vespasian was appointed to replace Gallus as military commander, and early in AD 67 arrived in Judea with three legions. Over the course of the next year, he crushed the insurrection in Galilee

Titus' troops stealing a menorah while desecrating the Second Temple of Jerusalem in AD 70. This relief forms part of a frieze on the Arch of Titus.

and isolated Jerusalem. The capture of the city was delayed for two years while Vespasian took part in the revolt against Nero and then wrested control of the empire from Vitellius. The honour of taking Jerusalem fell to Vespasian's son Titus, who captured the city after a long siege in AD 70 during which many of its inhabitants starved to death. Most of Jerusalem was ransacked and burned, including, most devastatingly for the Jewish people, the Second Temple. The day on which this desecration took place, 29 August – known as Tisha b'Av in the Jewish calendar – is often referred to as the 'saddest day in Jewish history.' The fall of Jerusalem marked the official end of the war, which was celebrated with a massive triumph at Rome in AD 71. Later, in AD 80, the emperor Domitian commemorated his deceased elder brother's sack of Jerusalem by erecting the Arch of Titus (the model for all subsequent such edifices, such as the Arc de Triomphe in Paris), which still stands on the Via Sacra south of the Forum in Rome.

The crushing of the revolt saw many Jews sold as slaves or transported as captives, while others escaped oppression by leaving Judea to join growing communities in the Jewish Diaspora.

The Flavian dynasty

On the face of it, the start of Vespasian's reign was highly inauspicious. He lacked a noble lineage; neither his former wife, the daughter of an obscure Roman equestrian, nor the freedwoman lover who replaced her were well connected. This freedwoman, Caenis, was the same person who in AD 31 had warned Tiberius of Sejanus' plot and who, according to rumour, had also shielded Vespasian from Nero's wrath on several occasions (for instance, when he dared to doze off during one of Nero's recitals). Yet Roman high society still looked down on her as a former slave. Compounding Vespasian's problems, the destruction

The triumph of Titus and Vespasian in AD 71, as depicted by the 16th-century Italian painter Giulio Romano. The lavish procession was held to mark the success of their suppression of the Jewish revolt. The Arch of Titus was later erected by the emperor Domitian as a permanent reminder of his deceased brother's greatest hour of military glory.

of the temple of Jupiter during the assault on Rome portended the ruination of the city in the eyes of its superstitious inhabitants.

Away from Rome, things also augured badly for Vespasian. Judea was still in flames, and a massive rebellion had broken out on the Rhine, as the Germanic auxiliaries turned on the legions that Vitellius had left behind. At the same time, the first of three fraudsters who tried to capitalize on whisperings that Nero was still alive appeared in the Aegean region, playing a lyre and claiming to be the emperor. Yet Vespasian was made of sterner stuff than Galba. Leaving his son Titus to deal with the revolt in Judea, he travelled from Judea to Rome to put things in order. He sent his nephew to suppress the revolt on the Rhine, which he accomplished successfully, and set about forging a genuinely warm relationship with the people of the capital.

A safe pair of hands

Vespasian had an unusual profile for a Roman emperor: he had two grown sons, worked hard at the job, and lived in a stable relationship with a woman he clearly loved. A first-rate soldier, his reputation for *virtus* had been earned on the battlefield as a legionary commander in Claudius' invasion of Britain in AD 43, and was confirmed by his sure handling of the hitherto chaotic Roman response to the Jewish revolt.

The new emperor's domestic lifestyle was austere by the standards of the Julio-Claudians after Augustus. Perhaps the most obvious sign of Vespasian's new approach was his decision to tear down the Golden

House of Nero and build a vast amphitheatre in place of an artificial lake that Nero had constructed within his palace. Although the official name of this new building was the Flavian Amphitheatre, it would become known to later generations as the Colosseum. It was conceived as a monument commemorating the suppression of the Jewish revolt, which finally came to an end when the governor of Judea, Flavius Silva, captured the last stronghold of the rebels at Masada in AD 74.

Vespasian consciously strove to present himself as a ruler in the tradition of Augustus. In particular, he eschewed government through a coterie of favourites among the palace staff, the style of rule that was favoured by his immediate predecessors in the post. Rather, in the manner of Augustus, his closest advisers were drawn from the senatorial and equestrian orders, and he was not afraid to promote people of genuine ability irrespective of their background. A good example of his egalitarian attitude was the promotion of Ulpius Traianus (c. AD 30–100) a Spaniard of Roman descent who had commanded a legion during the Jewish revolt, to supreme commander of the eastern provinces.

VESPASIAN

BORN
17 November, AD 9

FATHER
Titus Flavius Sabinus I

MOTHER
Vespasia Polla

MARRIED
(1) Flavia Domitilla; (2) Caenis (mistress and de facto wife)

CHILDREN
(by 1) Titus, Domitian, Domitilla

PREDECESSOR
Vitellius

BEGINNING OF REIGN
1 July, AD 69

DYNASTY
Flavian

DIED
June, AD 79

SUCCESSOR
Titus (eldest son)

MASADA

Between 37 and 31 BC, on a rocky plateau at the edge of the Judean Desert, Herod the Great erected a citadel known as Masada (a Romanized form of the Hebrew *metzuda* 'fortress') to serve both as a redoubt and as a pleasure palace. The site was well chosen as a defensive location, with precipitous 90-metre (300-ft) high cliffs plunging down to the shores of the Dead Sea. During the Great Jewish Revolt, in AD 65, Masada was seized by a group of Jewish rebels known as the Zealots. In AD 70, their numbers were swelled by sympathizers and their families, expelled from Jerusalem just before the razing of the city by Roman forces. The palace now became the last refuge for a band of 900 men, women and children. A Roman legion under the governor of Judea, Flavius Silva, laid siege to Masada in AD 73–74, building an enormous rampart with Jewish slave labour that enabled the attackers to position a siege tower against the walls. When the defensive walls were breached, the defenders of Masada committed mass suicide rather than fall into Roman hands. The siege rampart can still be seen at Masada, along with the outlines of Roman camps in the valley.

Since the founding of the modern state of Israel in 1948, the resilient defence of Masada has become a powerful symbol of national identity and absolute determination to resist invasion. Troops of the country's armed forces attend swearing-in ceremonies on the plateau, during which they take the vow that 'Masada Shall Never Fall Again'.

TITUS

BORN
30 December, AD 39

FATHER
Vespasian

MOTHER
Flavia Domitilla

MARRIED
(1) Arrecina Tertulla; (2)
Marcia Furnilla

CHILDREN
(by 2): Julia Flavia

PREDECESSOR
Vespasian

BEGINNING OF REIGN
24 June, AD 79

DYNASTY
Flavian

DIED
13 September, AD 81

SUCCESSOR
Domitian (younger brother)

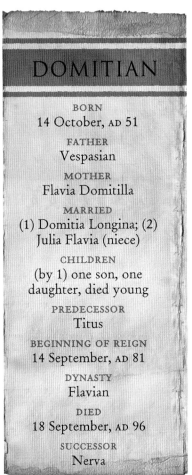

DOMITIAN

BORN
14 October, AD 51

FATHER
Vespasian

MOTHER
Flavia Domitilla

MARRIED
(1) Domitia Longina; (2)
Julia Flavia (niece)

CHILDREN
(by 1) one son, one
daughter, died young

PREDECESSOR
Titus

BEGINNING OF REIGN
14 September, AD 81

DYNASTY
Flavian

DIED
18 September, AD 96

SUCCESSOR
Nerva

In AD 79, after ten years of energetic and generally successful rule, Vespasian died, just before completion of the Colosseum. It was Titus (AD 39–81), his eldest son and successor, who inaugurated the new amphitheatre in AD 80 with one hundred days of spectacular games.

This is one of the defining moments of Titus' brief reign. The other took place on 24 August, AD 79, barely two months after his accession, when Mount Vesuvius on the Bay of Naples erupted violently, burying the city of Pompeii under tons of volcanic ash, while the settlement at Herculaneum was hit by a mudslide. Titus visited the scene of the disaster twice and reportedly spent large amounts of his personal wealth on relief for the victims. This and his similar efforts following a major fire in Rome the following year helped endear him to his subjects, who mourned his loss when he succumbed to a fever on 13 September, AD 81.

Domitian (AD 51–96) the younger brother of Titus, was a very different sort of person from his father and brother. Although he retained many of Vespasian's advisers, his relationship with the court and the senate was strained by his overweening sense of imperial grandeur mixed with an unappetizing tendency to prurient self-righteousness. The former trait was manifest in his insistence on being addressed as 'master and god,' an extreme variation of the polite Roman form of address *dominus* ('master', or simply 'sir'). The latter came to the fore when he assumed the title of censor for life in AD 84 and used this position to conduct several high-profile investigations into sex scandals. One of his witch-hunts resulted in two Vestal Virgins being buried alive when it was found that they had not lived up to their vows of purity. Yet, like many self-appointed guardians of public morality, Domitian's own conduct was far from being beyond reproach.

'Titus had such winning ways ... that he became an object of universal love and admiration.'

SUETONIUS, LIVES OF THE TWELVE CAESARS.

THE ERUPTION OF VESUVIUS

The volcano Mount Vesuvius dominates the Bay of Naples. By the first century AD, the fertility of the surrounding region had attracted many people to settle and farm there, and major towns like Pompeii (population *c.* 15,000) and Herculaneum (*c.* 5000) had grown up around the mountain's lower slopes. On the afternoon of 24 August, AD 79, after four days of minor foreshocks, the volcano exploded. For 19 hours, Vesuvius rained lava, rubble and volcanic ash over the surrounding region, completely burying Pompeii and Herculaneum and killing an unknown number of their inhabitants. One of the most prominent victims was the author and naval commander Pliny the Elder, who was then in command of the Roman fleet at nearby Misenum and who went to investigate the eruption at close hand. He was killed by what volcanologists now call 'pyroclastic flow', a cloud of superheated, choking gas. His nephew, Pliny the Younger, provided a detailed account of his death:

Pliny the Younger and his mother viewing the eruption of Vesuvius. Pliny's later description of the events of that day, in a letter to the historian Tacitus, gives a vivid account of the disaster.

'My uncle perished in a catastrophe which destroyed the loveliest regions of the earth, a fate shared by whole cities and their people. On 24 August, my mother drew his attention to a cloud of unusual size and appearance ... He changed his plan and what he had begun in a spirit of enquiry he completed as a hero ... the dense fumes choked his breathing by blocking his windpipe ... When daylight returned on the 26th, his body was found intact and uninjured, still fully clothed and looking more like sleep than death.'

Many of the citizens of the towns destroyed by the eruption – which were abandoned and never rebuilt – were found in the same state as Pliny the Elder when the settlements were rediscovered in the 1740s. The ash fall deposits that covered Pompeii preserved the people, houses and artifacts in remarkable condition. The two sites have yielded a wealth of information to geologists and historians on how the Romans of the first century AD lived.

Despite his personal shortcomings, Domitian retained the loyalty of the military, both in Rome and the provinces, while his dependence upon men who had risen to prominence under Vespasian protected entrenched interests. The army soon found itself busy along the northern borders of the empire, as Domitian annexed fresh territory north of the Rhine and embarked on a series of wars against the powerful Dacian kingdom (occupying roughly the area of modern Romania) that dragged on for almost 20 years. By the end of the AD 80s, however, discontent with his reign was beginning to translate into practical action, including an unsuccessful assassination attempt and a major revolt by the governor of lower Germany. The revolt was rapidly and brutally put down, but Domitian now grew ever more suspicious of people outside his immediate circle. These problems were compounded in AD 92 when two legions were routed by the Dacians, a crushing defeat that left the Danubian provinces open to invasion until a new expeditionary force restored order.

NERVA

BORN
8 November, AD 30

FATHER
M. Cocceius Nerva

MOTHER
Sergia Plautilla

PREDECESSOR
Domitian

BEGINNING OF REIGN
24 June, AD 79

DYNASTY
Nervo-Trajanic

DIED
27 January, AD 98

SUCCESSOR
Trajan

During this crisis, Domitian ordered the execution of several critics of his regime, both real and perceived. His high-handed actions outraged many in the senate who, along with palace functionaries, plotted his removal. On 18 September, AD 96, the chief of the palace domestic staff stabbed the emperor to death.

A sense of relief

The death of Domitian was greeted with unbridled joy by the senate, which immediately expunged his name from all the public monuments he had built. The Praetorian Guard was less than ecstatic, however, and it was only the intervention of its commanders and the senate's promise of a generous *donativum* that ensured the troops' support for the accession of the next emperor, Marcus Cocceius Nerva (AD 30–98). An elderly and well-respected senator, Nerva was the senate's candidate for the position and seems, like Galba before him, to have mainly owed his elevation to emperor to his age and childless state. Yet unlike Galba, he was alive to the necessity of maintaining the goodwill of the military, and promptly acceded to the praetorians' demands when they took to the streets, calling for the execution of Domitian's murderers.

Nerva was also aware that he had to choose a successor who would be acceptable to the army, and so named as his heir the commander of the legions in Upper Germany, the son of Vespasian's old marshal, Ulpius Traianus. His adoption of the younger Traianus – or Trajan as he is commonly known in English – brought a measure of stability to the political scene for the remaining year of Nerva's life. In addition to making an intelligent choice of successor, he endeared himself to the upper classes by discouraging prosecutions for treason, which had become something of a political game under Domitian, and granted amnesties to opponents of his predecessor who had been exiled. He died of a fever on 27 January, AD 98; his restrained use of power retrospectively earned him the accolade of being regarded as the first of the 'Five Good Emperors' who ruled Rome from AD 96 to 180.

Trajan proved a spectacularly good choice. Like Vespasian, he had worked his way up through the ranks, beginning with the minor official tasks that senators were given at the start of their careers and then holding subordinate commands in the legions before taking up more senior posts in Rome, where he was appointed consul in AD 91. Trajan's well-earned and growing reputation for efficiency constantly recommended him for higher office. Finally he commanded legions and governed provinces. By the time he became emperor, the 44-year-old Trajan knew the business of government inside-out.

A bust of Trajan, sculpted during his lifetime. One of the principal features of this emperor's reign was the good relations that he maintained with the Roman senate. This enabled him to carry out most of his ambitious plans without opposition.

At the time of Nerva's death, Trajan was in Lower Germany. News of his succession was brought to him by the future emperor Hadrian, then assigned to the army in Germany, but, ever the professional soldier, Trajan was in no hurry to return to Rome. In fact, he only arrived in the capital in AD 100, where he immediately set to work altering the cityscape. On land next to the Roman forum, a new forum began to take shape that would ultimately house a vast library and the ancient equivalent of a shopping mall. At the same time, Trajan also began an extensive reconstruction of the Circus Maximus, the great arena for chariot racing. Augustus had installed marble seating on the lower courses, and Trajan now extended this over the entire structure. In conjunction with the earlier Colosseum, these two new major public works projects now effectively surrounded the traditional heart of Rome with buildings put up solely for the benefit of the Roman people – a physical sign of continuity with Vespasian's regime and of the emperor's devotion to the welfare of his subjects.

Within the *domus*, Trajan's conduct seems largely to have coincided with the civic virtue that marked his public persona. Although the third-century historian Dio Cassius reports that he was given to excessive drinking and enjoyed the sexual company of boys, he was hard-working and imbued his staff with a sense that the 'spirit of his age' – a phrase that appears several times in the letters he exchanged with a governor in northwestern Turkey – required his officials to exercise wise government. These officials were charged with ensuring that rivalries between local politicians did not get out of hand, that town councils did not waste money on useless projects and that the administration of justice was honest. One of his appointments was that of the eminent senator and historian Tacitus to govern Asia in AD 112–113. Trajan also seems to have allowed those he trusted most a great deal of latitude, recalling Vespasian's treatment of his own father, and Augustus' management of the empire as a collective enterprise.

Within the palace, Trajan balanced the interests of senior officers with those of his family, which were dictated by Pompeia Plotina, the most powerful empress since Livia. Plotina was the power behind the throne,

TRAJAN

BORN
18 September, AD 53

FATHER
Marcus Ulpius Traianus

MOTHER
Marcia

MARRIED
Pompeia Plotina

CHILDREN
Hadrian (adopted)

PREDECESSOR
Nerva

BEGINNING OF REIGN
28 January, AD 98

DYNASTY
Nervo-Trajanic

DIED
9 August, AD 117

SUCCESSOR
Hadrian

TRAJAN'S FORUM AND TRAJAN'S COLUMN

The forum of Trajan near the Quirinal Hill in Rome took shape with great speed between AD 104 and 113, and stands in its entirety as a powerful symbolic expression of Trajan's values. The plan for the forum, designed by the Greek engineer and architect Apollodorus of Damascus, is thought to be based on that of a military camp. Five main elements comprise the forum: a 30-metre (100-ft) high column celebrating the conquest of Dacia, two libraries (one Greek, the other Latin), the massive Basilica Ulpia and the Temple of the Divine Trajan (possibly a later addition). The fact that the Temple of the Divine Trajan is situated not at the centre of the forum but behind the Basilica Ulpia suggests that it was not originally part of the plan, but may have been added later by Hadrian. These diverse structures all serve to emphasize the military virtues of Trajan, and his belief in Greco-Roman culture as the pinnacle of civilization.

With its spiral relief carvings telling the story of the emperor's two Dacian Wars in AD 101–102 and 105–106, Trajan's Column offers the most detailed

This section of Trajan's Column hints at the immense amount of detail on the spiral relief. These illustrations of the Roman army on campaign are an invaluable source of information to historians on ancient modes of warfare.

surviving picture of the Roman army on campaign, and of the central role played by the emperor. Trajan is shown no fewer than 59 times, engaged in various different activities: offering sacrifices, returning in triumph to Rome, addressing his army, rallying the troops in battle and rewarding them for their victories. Another notable feature of the column is the propagandistic picture it paints of the Roman army as a civilizing force – building bridges, cities and forts during its pacification of Dacia.

Some 2500 people are shown on the column's marble reliefs. Many of the depictions of people are remarkably detailed. For example, Trajan's legionary commanders all have distinctive facial features and were clearly meant to be recognizable as individuals. One of the most striking and gruesome portraits is that of the defeated Dacian king Decebalus slitting his own throat as Roman soldiers come to arrest him.

After Trajan's death in AD 117, the senate voted to have his ashes interred in an urn in the pedestal of the column.

cleverly forging close relationships with senior functionaries while maintaining the trust of her spouse. Like many other Roman imperial matriarchs before her, her principal aim was to secure dynastic preferment for a close relative. She ensured that Hadrian, Trajan's nephew and the husband of her niece, Sabina, gained enough experience in government that he would be fit to succeed as emperor if she failed to bear Trajan a son (which, given that she was already in her 40s when Trajan came to power, did indeed turn out to be the case).

Trajan's Dacian campaign

Trajan did not have an expansionist agenda at the outset, but found himself obliged to counter an immediate threat to the empire from north of the Danube. After Decebalus, king of the Dacians (reigned AD 87–106), attacked Roman territory in AD 101, he instantly found himself the target of a Roman punitive expedition. By the beginning of AD 103, his armies were so badly beaten that he reluctantly accepted peace terms making him a subject of Rome. But in AD 105 he broke the treaty, with devastating results both for himself and for his people. Within two years Dacia was made a province, and Decebalus committed suicide to avoid capture by a detachment of Roman cavalry. His severed head was later displayed in Rome on the steps leading up to the Capitol. The most striking account of the Dacian Wars is not a written record but a visual one – Trajan's Column, a 30-metre (100-ft) high marble pillar erected in AD 113 to commemorate the emperor's victorious campaign in Romania.

Meanwhile, in the east, the king of Arabia died and Trajan decided that it was time to absorb this longstanding Roman client state directly into the empire. Trajan's annexation of Arabia (roughly the area of modern Jordan) as a province in AD 106 completed a process begun by his father Marcus Ulpius Traianus, who had incorporated many of Rome's client states around Syria into the provincial structure of the empire under Vespasian. A century of contact with Roman administration in these regions had stimulated growing urbanization, which in turn made them more viable areas where direct Roman rule could be applied.

Yet if Trajan's Dacian Wars were motivated by a concern to preserve the security of the empire, it is hard to interpret his massive invasion of the Parthian empire in AD 113 as anything other than military adventurism. Following a plan of campaign likely inherited from the last days of Julius Caesar's reign, Trajan set out from Armenia and headed south into Mesopotamia (Iraq), capturing the western Parthian capital of Ctesiphon (near modern Baghdad) in AD 115. This was a major triumph, but it was to be shortlived. To the rear of Trajan's invasion force, the Jewish population of Cyrenaica (the North African coast west of Egypt),

Vibia Sabina (c. AD 86–136) was the wife of the emperor Hadrian. Theirs was an unhappy marriage, and her failure to bear him a son saw the succession pass to the Antonine dynasty. This statue is from the town of Vaison-la-Romaine in southern France.

HADRIAN

BORN
24 January, AD 76

FATHER
Publius Aelius Hadrianus
Afer

MOTHER
Domitia Paulina

MARRIED
Vibia Sabina

CHILDREN
Lucius Aelius, Antoninus
Pius (both adopted)

PREDECESSOR
Trajan

BEGINNING OF REIGN
10 August, AD 117

DYNASTY
Nervo-Trajanic

DIED
10 July, AD 138

SUCCESSOR
Antoninus Pius

Egypt, Palestine and other border regions suddenly rose up against their Roman overlords, apparently inspired by messianic visions of the world's end. In Mesopotamia itself, the eruption of fierce insurgencies a year after the Jewish revolt convinced Trajan that the best he could hope for was to install puppet governments in former satellite kingdoms of the Parthian empire, so that any regime filling the power vacuum in Ctespihon after Roman withdrawal would be too weak to pose a threat to Rome. He then began a fighting retreat, crushing rebel forces wherever he encountered them, and sending large detachments west to smash the Jewish revolts, a task they carried out with extreme brutality.

A legitimate successor?

As Trajan returned to the west in AD 117 he suddenly fell ill on the southern coast of Turkey and died on 9 August. Hadrian (AD 76–138), then governor of Syria, succeeded to the throne. While he was the only possible heir from within the imperial household, it appears that Trajan may have toyed with the idea of appointing someone else as his successor. Significantly, perhaps, Hadrian may only have been adopted as Trajan's son – thus putting his claim beyond all dispute – as Trajan lay dying. Or possibly not; there were whispers that Pompeia Plotina had slipped a servant into Trajan's deathbed to impersonate the emperor and make the announcement after the real Trajan had passed away without naming a successor. The rumour reflects serious tensions that were on the verge of erupting between senior generals and the royal household. Within months, even before Hadrian returned to Rome, four of Trajan's leading generals who were suspected of conspiring against Hadrian had been executed.

The executions shocked the political establishment, but effectively drove home the message that the new emperor would not tolerate dissent in any shape or form. A man of powerful intellect, Hadrian viewed officials as lackeys rather than colleagues and dealt firmly with anything he perceived as insubordination. The palace staff received warning of his imperious attitude when he fired two senior officials, a praetorian prefect and the biographer Suetonius (c. AD 69–c.140), then his chief secretary for correspondence in Latin, for excessive familiarity with his wife Vibia Sabina. Since these dismissals occurred in AD 122, while Hadrian was in Britain, it may be that he suspected his wife of trying to assume a similar role to that played by Plotina in Trajan's court. Sabina herself was publicly embarrassed by this event, when Hadrian declared that he would have divorced her if he had had the freedom permitted to private individuals. Similarly, when a poet recited

THE VILLA ADRIANA

The Villa Adriana in Tibur (modern Tivoli), some 20 miles (32 km) from Rome, was designed not simply as a splendid country retreat where Hadrian could enjoy nature, but also as a working palace from which to govern the empire. An inscription from Delphi in Greece makes it clear that he was already receiving foreign ambassadors there as early as AD 125, and the grand hall was plainly intended to host official receptions.

Construction of the villa, on the site of an earlier villa that may have been owned by Hadrian's father, began as soon as Hadrian became emperor in AD 117, and the first phase was largely complete by AD 125. The whole complex, covering some 100 hectares (250 acres), comprised 30 separate buildings. Chief among these

The Greek-inspired structure known as the Maritime Theatre in the Villa Adriana. Hadrian used a small house set on an island in the middle of the pool here as a place of relaxation.

were the throne room, library, theatre, stadium and several elaborate porticoes. Reflecting the emperor's deep love of Greek culture, the villa's architecture was heavily Greek-influenced. The second phase of construction, which lasted from AD 125 to 133, added further embellishments, including pavilions and further porticoes, many named for famous sites throughout the empire – especially from Athens, such as the Lyceum, Academy, Painted Stoa, and Prytaneion – as well as a pool named after Canopus, a city near Alexandria in Egypt.

some lines suggesting that he was thankful that he wasn't following the emperor on what he portrayed as lice-ridden journeys around the empire, Hadrian responded with a poem of his own lambasting the poet as a lazy wastrel.

Another sign of Hadrian's impatience with the political establishment was his desire to be absent from Rome as much as possible; more than half of his reign was spent outside Italy. Even when he was in Italy, he preferred to stay not in the capital but in the massive villa that he built for himself at Tivoli. His overt intellectualism and dislike of senatorial life are somewhat reminiscent of Tiberius, a parallel reinforced by his intense interest in astrology. Like Tiberius, he was also concerned to consolidate and develop the empire's existing holdings rather than wage new wars of conquest.

HADRIAN'S WALL

Hadrian's Wall, built between AD 122 and 128, covers a distance of 73 miles, or 80 Roman miles (117 kilometres) from Wallsend-on-Tyne on Britain's east coast to Bowness-on-Solway in the west. Many sections of it are still standing. It is likely that Hadrian himself surveyed the line of the wall during his visit to northern Britain in AD 122. For a distance of 42 miles (67 kilometres), the eastern end of the wall was constructed in stone, 3 metres (10 ft) thick and 4.1 metres (13.5 ft) high; the western portion was made of turf, roughly 6 metres (20 ft) wide at the base and 3.2 metres (10.5 ft) high. Small castles were set in the wall at each Roman mile (hence their name, 'milecastles'), while watchtowers were erected every third of a mile.

The Second, Sixth, and Twentieth Legions were all involved in construction of the wall, and the design of each milecastle varies according to which legion built it. Some 5.8 metres (19 ft) north of the wall was a forward defensive ditch,

the *vallum*; in most places, this measured 3 metres (10 ft) deep by 8 metres (26.5 ft) wide. A further series of 12 full-sized forts – the number was later increased to 17 – was built south of the wall, as was a second, slightly less extensive *vallum*. The total garrison of the wall and its supporting forts typically comprised some 9000 men.

Many of the troops who guarded this most northerly frontier of the Roman empire were auxiliaries from Belgium and Germany, along with local recruits. The wall, which was conceived as a protective cordon rather than as a major military barrier, was a potent symbol of Hadrian's determination to set limits to Rome's age of expansion.

A section of Hadrian's Wall near the fort at Housesteads (Vercovicium). The wall was an impressive feat of engineering, and utilized natural escarpments along its route. Construction proceeded from east to west, with three Roman legions involved in the work.

The great wall that Hadrian ordered built across northern Britain from AD 122 onwards was as much a sign to his own people that the province's borders were set as it was to the Caledonian tribes north of the wall (the Picts and Scots) that he had no interest in forcibly bringing them under the aegis of Roman rule. Other similar walls, made of wood and turf rather than stone, were also constructed along the frontiers of Rome's German provinces, and it was during Hadrian's reign that the familiar image of the empire as a fortress was first promulgated, protecting civilization from the barbarian hordes beyond its frontiers.

Judea erupts once more

During his extensive travels in the provinces, Hadrian became involved in the most intense personal relationship of his mature years, with a youth from Bithynia named Antinous. Historical sources do not say precisely when Hadrian met his young paramour, but he is estimated to have been around 13 or 14 years of age at their first encounter. In AD 130 the relationship came to a sudden and tragic end when Antinous drowned in the Nile. In his grief, Hadrian spared nothing in commemorating his beloved, including renaming the town closest to the place where he had died Antinopolis, and granting several cities permission to offer divine honours to his lover.

It is testament to Hadrian's firm grip on the empire that his authority was not impaired by what would have seemed a major domestic scandal in the case of a ruler who commanded less respect. His subjects' forbearance was doubtless also mingled with self-interest; Hadrian's willingness to promote outsiders to the imperial ruling class began to change the senate from a predominantly Italian and western body into one that more closely reflected the population of the empire as a whole. This was perhaps Hadrian's single greatest contribution to the continued success of the empire.

While generally humanist in his outlook and fair in his dealings with his subjects, Hadrian had a serious blind spot for the sensibilities of one particular group: the Jews. With no regard for their traditions, he may seriously have expected them to rejoice at the 'honour' he bestowed on Judea when he refounded Jerusalem as the Roman city of Aelia Capitolina. The outcome was quite the opposite. Inspired by the Rabbi Achiva, and led by Simeon ben Kosiba (who assumed the name Bar Kochba, or 'Son of the Star' in response to a prophecy by Achiva), the countryside of Judea took up arms against the Romans. Hatred of the Roman occupation was compounded when Hadrian toured his eastern provinces in AD 129–30 and proscribed the practice of circumcision. The Bar Kochba revolt lasted for three and a half years, from AD 132 to 135, and was quelled only by massive and merciless military intervention.

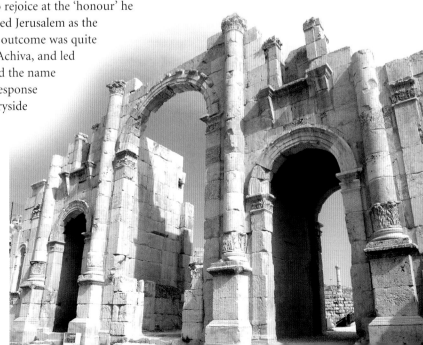

This magnificent, ornate gateway was built at the city of Gerasa (Jerash in present-day Jordan) to honour the visit by Hadrian to the region in AD 129. Gerasa was one of ten important cities on the eastern frontier known collectively as the Decapolis.

ANTONINUS PIUS

BORN
19 September, AD 86

FATHER
Titus Aurelius Fulvius

MOTHER
daughter of Arriua Antoninus (name unknown)

MARRIED
Faustina the Elder

CHILDREN
Faustina (natural); Marcus Aurelius; Lucius Verus (both adopted)

PREDECESSOR
Hadrian

BEGINNING OF REIGN
1 July, AD 138

DYNASTY
Antonine

DIED
10 July, AD 161

SUCCESSORS
Marcus Aurelius, Lucius Verus

By the early AD 130s it was clear that Hadrian was not going to have a son. The obvious successor would have been Pedanius Fuscus, the son of Hadrian's uncle, the venerable Julius Severianus, but Hadrian, who appears to have had a very difficult relationship with Severianus, would have none of it. In AD 136 he ordered them both to commit suicide and adopted Lucius Ceionius Commodus, whose name was changed to Lucius Aelius Verus. Aelius was the stepson of one of the men whom Hadrian had executed after Trajan's death, and his sudden adoption may have been out of remorse for this earlier injustice. It also had the advantage of ensuring that the throne would fall to a mature man with children of his own; Aelius had a young son, and one of his daughters was betrothed to a youth, Marcus Annius Verus, whom Hadrian also favoured. Then disaster struck – Aelius died on 1 January, AD 138, within months of his adoption, and Hadrian cast about for an heir whom he could trust to look after the interests of Aelius' children. In February AD 138 he adopted Aurelius Antoninus, the elderly uncle of Annius Verus, on condition that he would in turn adopt Verus and the son of Aelius. On 10 July of that year Hadrian died peacefully in a villa in the resort town of Baiae on the Bay of Naples.

Enter the Antonines

Aurelius Antoninus, who would become known to history as the emperor Antoninus Pius (AD 86–161), could not have been more different from his predecessor. He earned the name 'Pius' through his strict adherence to the wishes of Hadrian; indeed, his filial piety towards his adoptive father even extended to coercing an unwilling senate to proclaim Hadrian a god. However, in marked contrast to the much-travelled Hadrian, for the entire 23 years of his reign, Pius never left Italy. Instead, he remained in Rome and – as might have been expected of a man who had enjoyed a extremely successful senatorial career – was content to entrust the

Lucius Verus, co-ruler with Marcus Aurelius, led a flamboyant lifestyle, enjoying the theatre and the games of the circus, especially chariot racing. However, his achievements as a commander on the Parthian front confirmed that he was more than just a playboy.

An agate cameo showing the profiles of the emperor Marcus Aurelius and his wife Faustina the Younger. (c. AD 125–175). During their 30-year marriage, she bore her husband 13 children. Some later historians spread scurrilous rumours about Faustina, suggesting that Commodus was the illegitimate son of a gladiator.

day-to day business of government to experienced administrators. He also placed full confidence in provincial governors to suppress outbreaks of unrest during his reign, in Judea, Mauretania (North Africa) and Britain. Marcus Aurelius, as Marcus Annius Verus became known after his adoption, would later refer to Antoninus Pius as the model emperor: kind, diligent, polite to subordinates, unwilling to decide in haste and always putting the good of the community before anything else. Aside from Marcus Aurelius' personal recollections, little else is known of the man who ruled Rome at the height of its prosperity. During his reign – the longest since that of Augustus – there were no major wars, no scandals and no executions of prominent men, save one who had openly and unsuccessfully tried to incite a rebellion in Spain.

Long before Pius died, Marcus Aurelius had been marked out as the heir apparent, while the emperor permitted Lucius Aelius Verus' son Lucius to live in the palace only 'as a private citizen'. However, it had been Hadrian's express wish that Lucius and Marcus should eventually rule jointly, and, despite feeling no great affection for Hadrian, Marcus Aurelius felt honour-bound to obey his wishes. And so, when the senate met to vote him the few powers of an emperor that he did not already have, he refused to accept them unless the senate voted the same powers to Lucius. So began the joint reign of Marcus Aurelius (AD 121–180) and Lucius Verus (AD 130–169), an event unparalleled in Roman history.

LUCIUS VERUS

BORN
15 December, AD 130

FATHER
Lucius Aelius Verus

MOTHER
Avidia

MARRIED
Lucilla

CHILDREN
3 (names unknown)

PREDECESSOR
Antoninus Pius

BEGINNING OF REIGN
8 March, AD 161

DYNASTY
Antonine

DIED
AD 169

SUCCESSOR
Marcus Aurelius (alone)

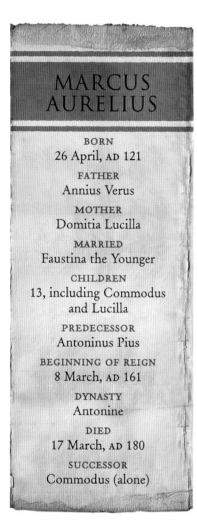

MARCUS AURELIUS

BORN
26 April, AD 121

FATHER
Annius Verus

MOTHER
Domitia Lucilla

MARRIED
Faustina the Younger

CHILDREN
13, including Commodus
and Lucilla

PREDECESSOR
Antoninus Pius

BEGINNING OF REIGN
8 March, AD 161

DYNASTY
Antonine

DIED
17 March, AD 180

SUCCESSOR
Commodus (alone)

Although the simultaneous election of two emperors might seem a radical break with the past, it was actually the logical extension of a time-honoured practice stretching back as far as the early years of Augustus' reign. For nearly 20 years after Actium, Agrippa had been his co-emperor in all but name, while in the last years of Augustus' life so too had Tiberius. Likewise, before their deaths, Germanicus and Drusus had performed a similar role for Tiberius and Titus had been virtual co-ruler with Vespasian, as had Trajan in the few months between his adoption by Nerva and the latter's death. It is also notable that, with the exception of Tiberius, all the emperors who had openly ruled in concert with one or more close confederates in their administration were regarded as very good rulers. Conversely, Domitian had alienated people by insisting on his sole prerogatives, and Hadrian's tight personal hold on the reins of power did not endear him to his subjects. Thus, while they had at times been forced to suffer the whims of autocratic rulers, Rome's governing classes far preferred regimes that were essentially collaborative. In any event, the mettle of the system of joint rule would soon be tested to its limits.

Vologaeses throws down the gauntlet

Even before Lucius Verus and Marcus Aurelius came to power, major changes were afoot on the empire's northern and eastern frontiers. Menacing new tribal groupings began to encroach on the areas adjoining Trajan's province of Dacia, which occupied an extremely exposed position north of the Danube. Meanwhile in Iraq, a new Parthian regime had come to power in the late AD 140s under King Vologaeses IV (r. AD 147–191), who was determined to reverse the political effects of Trajan's victories. His timely withdrawal of Roman troops before they became bogged down fighting endless insurgencies had left Rome with considerable influence in the former Parthian client kingdom of Characene in southern Iraq. This region was especially important because it was a vital transshipment point midway along a major trade route to India and east Asia. Goods unloaded at the port of Mesene, near modern Basra, were carried up the River Tigris and across the desert to Syria by a network of traders based at the desert city of Palmyra, which was formally incorporated within the Roman provincial system. In AD 157, Vologaeses seized control of Characene and, even as Pius lay dying, prepared a massive invasion of the eastern Roman provinces. Pius' decision not to react militarily to the Parthian invasion of Characene was, with hindsight, probably correct; the region was no more amenable to Roman rule than it had been under Trajan, while Vologaeses would ultimately do himself more harm than good by launching an offensive into Roman territory.

However, at the time Rome's decision not to nip Vologaeses' aggression in the bud looked like a monumental error of judgement, as the Parthian king's forces swept inexorably westward. In AD 161 his armies defeated a badly led provincial garrison in Commagene, north of Syria, and moved into Syria itself. Marcus responded by dispatching a huge army and several highly competent generals to Syria, with Lucius in titular control of the operation. While Lucius remained at Antioch – lacking experience of direct command, his function must largely have been to chair meetings of people who knew what they were doing – the newly arrived forces drove the Parthians back into their own territory.

In AD 163, under the command of the gifted young general Avidius Cassius (c. AD 130–175), these armies began to retrace the expedition of Trajan, and, two years later, destroyed the city of Seleucia on the Tigris and sacked the Persian capital at Ctesiphon. Rome's forces advanced as far as Medea (modern Iran). At this point Vologaeses IV fled, and the Romans proceeded to consolidate their grip on the border regions by installing new, more loyal client rulers there. Stability was thus restored and, following one further Roman campaign in northern Iraq, the armies withdrew to the west in AD 166. Lucius Verus was awarded a triumph, but died of a stroke three years later.

The city of Palmyra, sited at an oasis in the Syrian desert, came under Roman control during the reign of Tiberius. In the second century AD it attained great prosperity as a key trading city on the route from the Persian Gulf to central Asia. As an independent client state, it was to become a thorn in the side of later Roman rulers.

THE MEDITATIONS OF MARCUS AURELIUS

A cultured, contemplative man who never aspired to become emperor, Marcus Aurelius nevertheless was strongly imbued with a sense of the obligations that came with the imperial office once he had attained it. To help him gain perspective on his imperial duties and responsibilities, he evolved an individual form of Stoic philosophy. He jotted his thoughts down (in Greek) in a series of musings that have since become known as the *Meditations*. This personal diary, which he wrote while on campaign in the Northern Wars between AD 170 and 180 and was never intended for publication, contains reflections on the meaning of life and the transient nature of all things on earth, including imperial power. Although the tone of the *Meditations* is often melancholic, Marcus Aurelius never renounces his belief in an organizing principle guiding the universe. The *Meditations* have been much admired by later commentators, and even compared to Christ's Sermon on the Mount.

The Antonine plague

The Roman withdrawal took place against the backdrop of a sudden and devastating natural disaster. A pandemic illness took hold in Mesopotamia while the Romans were mopping up there. As they returned to their posts around the empire, the legions brought the disease with them. The result was catastrophic, with some 10 per cent of the empire's population – as many as six or seven million people – falling victim to the illness, which subsequently became known as the Antonine Plague. Ancient medicine had no cure; the famous Greek physician Galen (*c.* AD 129–199) described its symptoms as diarrhoea, high fever, and the appearance of pustules on the skin after nine days. Galen's brief account has led later experts to speculate that the disease was most likely smallpox.

In keeping with the common practice of his age, Marcus turned to the gods. Apollo, speaking from his oracle at Claros in western Turkey, is said to have prescribed certain rites to dispel the demons that were held responsible for the outbreak. Marcus circulated the news throughout the empire. Nor was this the only oracle he consulted. In the reign of Antoninus, a Greek prophet named Alexander had set up a new oracle at Abonuteichos in northwestern Turkey. Alexander had a snake named Glycon, who answered questions posed by the faithful. Marcus duly asked Glycon's advice not only about the plague, but also about a new threat looming over the empire; the tribes north of the Danube were poised to overrun the frontier.

The early years of the Northern Wars, as the conflict against the Danubian tribes is known, were grim for Rome. Acting on the advice of his oracles, Marcus had tossed two lions into the Danube as a votive offering to the river gods to thwart the barbarians' crossing. This attempted sacrifice failed on all counts. The lions simply swam the river, and in AD 170 the tribes penetrated as far south as Aquileia in northern Italy, where Marcus himself came under siege, while at least one Roman army was routed in the central Balkans. Once again, Marcus invoked the gods' help, and claims that this time they heard his prayers. In one case he is reported to have summoned a thunderbolt from heaven to destroy a siege engine; in another, the emperor's prayers (or the intervention of a favoured Egyptian magician) supposedly brought a thunderstorm to the aid of a hard-pressed legion. In AD 175 Marcus declared his only surviving son, the 14-year-old Commodus (AD 161–192), his co-emperor and began to groom him as his heir, while at the same time relying on experienced generals for day-to-day control. Not all of them welcomed Commodus' promotion. As soon the news became known, Avidius Cassius, hero of the Parthian campaign and supreme commander of the eastern provinces, declared himself emperor. This was a rash act that garnered little support; Cassius was declared a public enemy by the senate and killed by one of his own men.

The final years of Marcus Aurelius' reign saw incessant fighting on the northern border. But by now Rome's forces were in the ascendant, and a series of treaties mentioned by the historian Cassius Dio (*c.* AD 155–229) indicate that Marcus had begun to reestablish a system of client states north of the border when he suddenly fell ill and died at Sirmium in Pannonia on 17 March, AD 180. Commodus succeeded to the throne, the first teenaged emperor since Nero. The new emperor lacked any experience of government, but was surrounded by advisors steeped in the principle of collaborative rule, and so the people of Rome expected continued stability. Their confidence turned out to be badly misplaced; it is not without good cause that Edward Gibbon began his tale of the decline and fall of the Roman empire with the accession of Commodus.

A frieze panel showing Marcus Aurelius granting his pardon to the barbarian tribes he defeated in the Northern Wars. This conflict began badly for Rome, but after five years' hard fighting, the Romans turned the tide by AD 175.

The contrast between the reign of the so-called 'Five Good Emperors' and that of Commodus may have been overplayed by later generations; certainly the tyro emperor's portrayal in the 2000 Hollywood movie *Gladiator* has more than a touch of exaggerated *Grand Guignol* about it. Even Gibbon tacitly admitted that, since Rome's decline took 300 years to unfold, it would be unwise to place too much emphasis on Commodus' accession alone. But what he and later commentators were right to stress was that this event did mark the beginning of the terminal erosion of Rome's effective traditions of government.

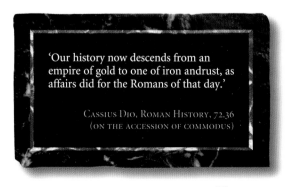

'Our history now descends from an empire of gold to one of iron andrust, as affairs did for the Romans of that day.'

CASSIUS DIO, ROMAN HISTORY, 72.36
(ON THE ACCESSION OF COMMODUS)

Running the Empire: Emperors and Administrators (AD 68–180)

Marcus Aurelius surrounded by his advisors. Marcus was renowned as a conscientious administrator who appointed highly capable officials, whatever their background. For example, he promoted the low-born Publius Helvius Pertinax to high office in recognition of his military skill.

Even Rome's most autocratic rulers had to rely upon a large and complex network of officials to conduct the business of empire. Military prowess was a key aptitude in ensuring a person's advancement but a head for finance was also an invaluable skill. The transition from Imperial Rome's turbulent early years to the long *pax Romana* of the second century AD was marked by a pronounced change in the style of governance.

Alongside the general dicta on humanity that Marcus Aurelius offers in his *Meditations*, he also makes a number of observations about people he knows and regularly encounters. These tell us a great deal about the circles in which a Roman emperor moved and the day-to-day considerations that motivated his actions. The people Marcus mentions fall broadly into two categories: members of the political élite and slaves in the imperial household. The ruler's daily concerns focus on life in the palace, and the best way to treat subordinates. For instance, Marcus notes that his station in life obliges him not to show anger, not to display signs of boredom and always to act fairly. Dealings with officials defined the parameters of Marcus Aurelius' existence and were central to his profound sense of duty; Cassius Dio says that he would routinely burn the midnight oil in order to finish his day's work. His responsibilities included hearing petitions from his subjects, reading reports from his officials, managing state finances, reviewing the dispositions of the army and appointing reliable people to run his empire. But who were these officials and what qualities did they need to perform their duties successfully?

The emperor's advisors

The officials who surrounded a Roman emperor at court were a microcosm of the government as a whole. There were members of the senate who had held various traditional magistracies, equestrians and freedmen. Each group had its particular sphere of influence. Generally speaking, senators were employed in areas relating to the command of armies and the government of provinces. Members of the equestrian order usually occupied posts that were connected with the finances of the state or in domains that were under the direct control of the emperor – notably, the extensive network of estates throughout Italy and the provinces that formed the *patrimonium* (the portfolio of property holdings bequeathed from one emperor to the next).

'For we are made for co-operation, like feet, like hands, like eyelids, like the rows of the upper and lower teeth.'

MARCUS AURELIUS, MEDITATIONS, 2.1

A favoured few equestrians obtained positions close to the emperor as secretaries, legal advisors or overseers of the grain supply of Rome. The importance of this latter post cannot be overstated: some 400,000 tonnes of grain were shipped into the city annually, and another 100,000 were required every year by the Roman army. Being appointed overseer of grain supplies was often a prerequisite for holding one of the city's two praetorian prefectures. Finally, freedmen tended to be entrusted with fiscal positions in the household and a variety of tasks connected with special matters of imperial concern such as the quality of entertainment in the palace, or public spectacles for the people of Rome.

The common denominator of all three groups of officials was their proven aptitude in financial affairs. With the exception of a few senior imperial secretaries who were recruited directly into their positions on the basis of their rhetorical or juristic skills, all those who were elevated into the upper echelons of the imperial service had shown that they could be trusted with money. This fact alone meant that officials tended largely to be recruited from the landholding classes, where it was an integral part of a young man's education to learn from his parents how to manage estates and large households. However, men whose fiscal competence had helped them earn their freedom could also win promotion.

A less obvious, but equally important, quality shared by members of all three groups was their ability to work within a hierarchical structure. Almost all senators and equestrians who entered the imperial service were required to spend at least one or two years as middle-ranking army officers. During their military service, these men were transferred rapidly from unit to unit, the primary aim being for them to gain experience in dealing with subordinates rather than necessarily acquire expertise in military tactics or fighting skills.

Winning friends and influencing people

Good people skills and a head for finance may have been preconditions for getting ahead in the emperor's service, but they were not the sole factors that determined the success or failure of a person's career. Fewer than one-third of the men who embarked on a senatorial career ever reached its pinnacle – the consulship. A similar proportion of equestrians attained the highest-paid jobs at the top of the ladder.

Rather – to quote an adage that still holds good even in more meritocratic modern societies – in Imperial Rome it was not just what you knew but who you knew. A key to success was the ability to make and exploit useful connections. Clearly, a person's chances of advancement were boosted if he had family members who had the emperor's ear. Yet this could only propel a person so far – a notable feature of the recommendations that have survived in the collections of Pliny the Younger and Fronto, Marcus' tutor, is that they are overwhelmingly for people who are just setting foot on the first few rungs on the promotion ladder. To advance further, a record of actual accomplishment and a proven ability to mix well in society were vital. When Pliny writes that a praetor named Larcius Macedo, forgetting that his own father was a freedman, treated his slaves harshly, his clear implication is that this man lacked the personal qualities expected of a senior official (elsewhere, Pliny makes it plain that he himself is deeply solicitous of his servants' welfare). Aside from this, Pliny seems also to have had a great gift for rhetoric. He made many appearances in the law courts, as did Tacitus, who was renowned as one of the finest orators of his age. Each legal case was a test not only of an orator's persuasive advocacy but also of their good judgement in picking the right person to defend or prosecute.

Likewise, the senate house was the venue for demonstrating political acumen. Here, aspiring statesmen vied to earn the respect of their peers: drawing out the business of the senate by arguing minor points merely irritated one's colleagues, whereas offering sensible suggestions on how to improve a proposal from the emperor helped establish

THE EMPEROR'S ESTATES

The wealth of the Roman empire was based almost exclusively on land, and naturally the emperor was the largest landowner in the empire. Over time, the imperial holdings grew ever larger, either through seizure of land from political enemies or through donations by well-wishers keen to curry favour with the emperor of the day. By the late second century AD there were imperial estates in almost every province, in some cases making up almost one-fifth of the entire territory.

'You see how busy and significant were the days, which extraordinarily pleasant evenings followed. We were invited to dinner every night, which were simple affairs when you consider that he is the emperor. Sometimes we listened to recitations, and sometimes we just talked. On the last day (such is his diligent generosity) we were given gifts.'

PLINY THE YOUNGER (ON WORKING WITH TRAJAN. LETTER 6.31.13-14).

a person's reputation for wisdom and independent thought. Great finesse was called for in political machinations; senators could only be arraigned by their peers, but if an individual began proceedings against a fellow senator who had behaved badly in the hope of winning the emperor's favour, he was at risk of alienating his colleagues. The wise man knew how to balance the interests of his class against the interests of the emperor, showing independence without arrogance.

By the latter stages of a career a man would have chosen a path that suited his abilities. Some men displayed genuine leadership qualities, moving effortlessly from one senior position of command to the next in different armies. Such skills were especially sought after during Rome's long-running and arduous struggles against the Danubian tribes and the resurgent Parthians in the reign of Marcus Aurelius. During this period, martial ability was at such a premium that commanders who already had a proven track record of success were constantly on the lookout for others whose skills could support their own. For example, Claudius Pompeianus, Marcus' brother-in-law,

A senator delivering his peroration in a legal hearing before the Roman senate. Character witness played a major role in such proceedings. Ultimately, high-profile Roman court cases had as much to do with showcasing a rising advocate's skill at presenting himself as a champion of justice as with establishing the defendant's innocence or guilt.

championed the cause of one Publius Helvius Pertinax (AD 126–193), the son of a freedman, who showed exceptional talent in war, and defended him against critics who claimed that his lowly birth disqualified him for the highest offices. Marcus heeded Pompeianus' advice, and Pertinax gained both the consulship and the governorship of an important province. Later, he was to win the ultimate prize by becoming emperor, albeit only for three months.

Grace and favour

For their part, emperors had their own ways of deciding whom to trust. One tried and tested method was to invite a prospective appointee to dinner, or to join the ruler for a few days to help him decide legal cases (Trajan did this, once, with Pliny). In a letter preserved by Suetonius, Augustus revealed to Tiberius that he had been dining and playing dice with a couple of senior generals. Augustus also maintained a council of senators that changed every six months so that he could get to know the men who served him. Nor were these occasions reserved for senators alone; letters from several emperors include reference to notable men of the equestrian orders who sat with them to deliberate on official business.

A frieze showing Roman government officials. From the late first century onwards, the collaborative system of government worked extremely effectively, as Rome's rulers consulted their advisors at informal meeetings. For example, Pliny the Younger recounts that his uncle, a famous writer and senior equestrian official, routinely visited Vespasian at home.

Many later rulers – notably the 'Five Good Emperors' – followed Augustus' example by revolving invitations to participate so that they could take the measure of as many members of the upper classes as possible. These sessions served a number of purposes, affording the emperor an opportunity to form his own impression of a person's judgement, giving potential appointees an insight into the emperor's approach to various issues, and (not least) performing a 'public relations' function of allowing the ruler to demonstrate his decency. As the younger Pliny put it after his audience with Trajan, 'what could be more pleasant than to witness the justice, wisdom and grace of the emperor in a quiet place where these qualities were easily revealed'. The extent to which Trajan relied on these meetings as training sessions is reflected in his later communication to Pliny as governor of Bithynia, reminding him that he knew 'very well that it is my fixed position that reverence for my name may never be sought from fear or terror or through charges of treason'. Trajan, who had himself spent many thankless years governing provinces under the notoriously nit-picking Domitian, set great store by giving governors free rein to exercise their own initiative. Instead of bombarding his subordinates with rules and regulations for every occasion, Trajan expected them to improvise in accordance with what they could reasonably intuit would be his wishes.

Changing imperial styles

The writings of the historian Tacitus chart the shift that took place in styles of governance between Augustus and Vespasian. In his *Annals*, Tacitus exonerates certain provincial governors from former times of the charge that their profligate lifestyles compromised their ability to do their job effectively. But the very fact that he feels it necessary to highlight their sybaritic excesses is eloquent testimony that things had changed by the time he was writing. All the men whom Tacitus cites advanced under Nero, an emperor who was a byword for self-indulgence, and for Tacitus their career histories are axiomatic of two general rules regarding the ruler and his officials: first, that the ambitious man must be able to read the mood of the emperor, and second that each emperor's habits are reflected in the behaviour of his subordinates.

Ephesus in the province of Asia was a major Roman city. Asia was considered a jewel in the crown of the Roman empire, and Trajan bestowed a great honour on the historian Tacitus when he appointed him governor of the region in AD 112.

PLINY THE YOUNGER

Pliny the Younger (AD 63–*c*.113) was born the son of a landowner in Comum (modern Como, Lombardy, Italy). His father died when he was young and he went to Rome to complete his education. He learned rhetoric and took part in the trials of a number of provincial governors. Readily absorbed into the senatorial class, he rose through a series of civil and military offices. Under Trajan, he was appointed governor of the combined provinces of Bithynia and Pontus (on the southern Black Sea Coast) between AD 103 and 105, where he remained until his death; though a senior position, this could not match the post later attained by his friend Tacitus in Asia – a fine but important distinction in the competitive world of the senior Roman senator. Nevertheless, he amassed great wealth; it is estimated that his estates were worth some 20 million sesterces (a labourer's daily wage was four sesterces). Pliny's life, encompassing most of the main public offices open to a Roman citizen, is often taken as the quintessential model of a successful career under the imperial system. His *Letters*, written between AD 97 and 110, provide a unique record of Roman administration and everyday life in the first century AD.

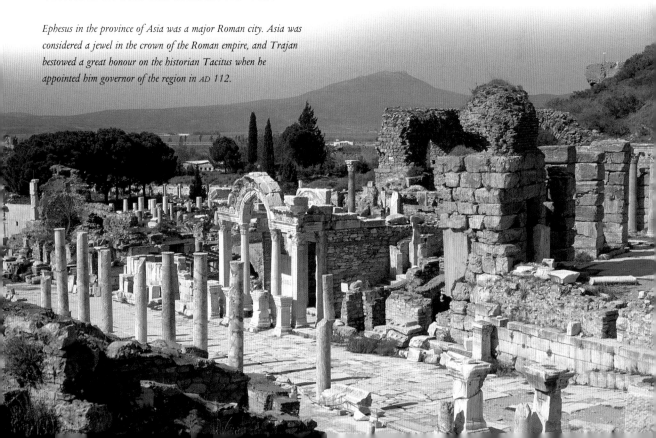

Certainly, Pliny, Tacitus, and others who made their way in the second century AD seem to have been genuinely moderate in their personal habits. In this, they took their cue from the emperors of the day, especially Vespasian, Trajan and Marcus Aurelius. Even Hadrian, who had a penchant for all things Greek (often synonymous with decadence) shunned outright debauchery.

The role of freedmen

The conduct of the emperors from Vespasian to Marcus was a reaction against the inward looking, *domus*-dominated administrative style of the Julio-Claudians. Imperial freedmen who occupied publicly prominent positions under Claudius and Nero were not so evident in the second century AD, but they had not vanished entirely. Vespasian, after all, lived with a freedwoman who had grown up in the palace, while the man who stabbed Domitian was Stephanus, the freedman in charge of intimate access to the emperor, or *cubicularius*. One of the cases that Pliny heard with Trajan concerned one Ulpius Eurythemus, an imperial freedman who held a procuratorship. He was charged with helping an equestrian procurator named Sempronius Senecio forge the will of a senator. Having laid the charge, the heirs then claimed they were afraid to appear, leading Trajan to exclaim that just as he was not Nero, neither was Eurythemus a Polyclitus. Even so, the case was still postponed and eventually dropped. The link between Senecio and Eurythemus reveals that influential freedmen socialized with equestrians, while the *cubicularius* was effectively on a level with the praetorian prefects, the most senior equestrian officials in the realm.

Where did such people come from? There is some evidence to suggest that 'imperial freedman' could be a voluntary career choice for people outside the élite. A papyrus letter from Egypt mentions a man who decided to go to Rome to become a freedman of Caesar, while a *cubicularius* of Hadrian named Aelius Alcibiades was honoured by his home city in western Turkey as a benefactor. At the end of the second century, the immensely powerful freedwoman, Marcia, mistress of Marcus' son Commodus, and one of the effective heads of government in his last years, also gave substantial sums to her homeland. She had begun her career as a freedwoman of Marcus Aurelius' daughter. Strictly speaking, to become a freedman or freedwoman a person had first to be a slave, and thus should not have a 'home city' at all (being

An unknown imperial household, depicted on a mosaic from a Roman villa in Sicily. To be emperor in the second century meant being able to rule in concert with various different groups of officials, to set clear boundaries between them, and to recognize that each group could make a valuable contribution to running the empire. The household of the second-century emperor was very much a corporate entity.

A SEASONED COMMENTATOR

One of the most important historians of Ancient Rome – and the source of much of our knowledge about the empire under the Julio-Claudians and the Flavians – was Cornelius Tacitus (*c.* AD 56–117). He began his ultimately distinguished senatorial career in the final years of Vespasian's reign. Occupying various provincial administrative posts, he even flourished under Domitian, but the experience left him with a pronounced loathing of autocracy that emerges clearly from his writings. His renown as a public orator grew under Nerva and Trajan and he was made consul in AD 97 and governor of Asia in AD 112–13.

Tacitus' most famous historical treatises – the *Annals* and the *Histories* – were written in the latter years of his life. The first of these works treats the reign of the Julio-Claudian dynasty, from AD 14–68: their abiding theme is human dignity warped by the perverse characters of Rome's early emperors. The *Histories*, which treat the period AD 69–96, open with civil war, insurrection and disaster but end with an acknowledgment of Vespasian's qualities. The works are notable for their scrupulous attention to historical sources, their perceptive observations on the mainsprings of power and their acute analysis of people's motivations. In general, the author's tone is one of world-weariness and deep suspicion of imperial rule and its potential for abuse. Yet for all this, behind Tacitus' account of the bloody early years of Roman imperial history is his keen awareness that he is enjoying the freedom to write in conditions of far greater security than in the period he describes:

'It is the rare fortune of these days that a man may think what he likes and say what he thinks.'

TACITUS, HISTORIES, I.I

regarded merely as a chattel of their master). Yet the persistent suggestion from the time of Augustus onwards is that some freedmen and women had actually endured only very short periods of slavery, and that, in some cases, they had willingly taken that condition upon themselves, as palace staff recruited servants with the necessary skills to participate in government. These aptitudes may have been sexual, cultural or fiscal. The key point was that freedmen brought to Roman government an indispensable range of experiences and skills quite different from those of senators or equestrians.

Even Pliny had to admit that it was right for Trajan to have influential freedmen so long as they shared the essential values of the governing class: a frugal lifestyle and a willingness to work hard. Yet behind this praise of hard work lies a veiled but potent threat. The emperor who shared the values of his subjects would live long and prosper. The emperor who did not would inevitably fall victim to those around him.

'In these two ways you must always be prepared: the one, only to act as the principle of the royal and lawgiving art prescribes for the benefit of mankind; the second, to change your purpose, if some one is there to correct and guide you away from some fancy of yours.'

MARCUS AURELIUS, MEDITATIONS, 3.12

Civic Pride:
Caesars and their Cities
(AD 68–180)

'When were there so many cities on land or throughout the sea, and when have they been so adorned?' So asked Aelius Aristides (AD 117–181), a prominent Greek orator from western Turkey in a eulogy on Rome delivered in the reign of Antoninus Pius. Aristides' praise of cities as markers of prosperity reflects not only his decidedly urban outlook, but also that of the Roman government. Another Greek writing at the same time, the historian Appian of Alexandria (c. AD 95–c.165), obliquely made the same point when noting that the emperor was wont to refuse applications by barbarians to be taken under Roman rule on the grounds that they would not be viable to govern. By definition, barbarians were people who did not live in cities.

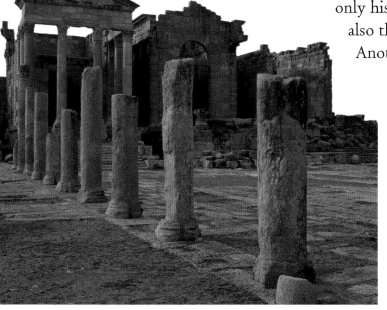

In common with many cities in North Africa, Sufetula (modern Sbeitla, in Tunisia) attained great prosperity in the second century AD – the source of Sufetula's wealth was olives. A sign of any Roman settlement's prominence was the presence of temples; these imposing ruins in Sufetula are the temples of Jupiter, Juno and Minerva.

At first glance, this emphasis on cities might seem odd in an empire in which more than three-quarters of the population lived on the land. Yet almost all the land farmed by these people – if not owned by the emperor or the *res publica* – was attached to cities. From an administrative point of view, then, a Roman province was a collection of civic territories interspersed with tracts of imperial or public land.

Cities and civilization

The cities in a province fell, broadly speaking, into two categories: stipendiary and free. Stipendiary cities were liable to tribute, while free cities had an independent relationship with the Roman state. The

CITIZENSHIP AND FOREIGN POLICY

Rome used citizenship as a key instrument of its imperial policy. After an area had been conquered or had voluntarily allied itself with Rome, communities that showed themselves amenable to becoming stable political confederates were granted 'minor' forms of Roman citizenship. There were several gradations of citizenship and the legal rights associated with them varied. For example, a community at a transitional phase between provincial status (with no citizens' rights) and full citizenship would be granted *ius Latii*, or the 'Latin Right' which entitled its people to protection under Roman law but did not give them the right to stand for public office.

As a full Roman citizen, an individual had the following fundamental legal entitlements:

- The right to stand for civil or public office
- The right to make legal contracts
- The right to have a lawful marriage
- The right to sue (and be sued) in the courts
- The right to appeal the decisions of magistrates
- The right to appear before a properly constituted court and to defend oneself
- The right not to be tortured or scourged
- The right of immunity from some taxes and other obligations

The granting of citizenship was a vital part of the process of Romanization; Rome's strategy of formally incorporating as many conquered peoples as possible into its system of government rather than treating them as vassals goes a long way to explaining the success of the Roman empire.

precise nature of this relationship varied according to the history of the region; some free cities had stood by Rome during a past crisis and been rewarded with a special treaty, while others had been settled by Roman citizens. As *coloniae* of Rome, these latter cities were exempt from tribute payments. The vast majority of such colonies had arisen through the resettlement of veterans from the civil wars of the first century BC. The intention was that they would serve as centres of Latin culture and as sources of manpower when it was necessary to recall former soldiers to active service in times of emergency.

In Rome's western provinces there also existed many urban centres known as *municipia*; these were places that had been granted civic constitutions from Rome, and whose typical inhabitants, though of provincial descent, enjoyed partial Roman citizenship. Moreover, if elected to a civic magistracy, provincial people were granted full rights of citizenship. Though inferior in status to the *coloniae*, the *municipia* demonstrated the Roman state's interest in rewarding provincials who abandoned 'barbarism' for the ideals of Roman civilization. In the eastern holdings of the empire, where the Romans were willing to accept that the values of Greek civic life were sufficiently like their own, there was no such deliberate attempt to transplant Latin culture. It remains one of the unique features of the Roman imperial system that the culture of a conquered people could be so thoroughly assimilated into that of the conqueror.

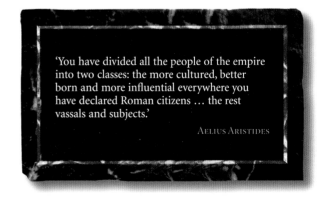

'You have divided all the people of the empire into two classes: the more cultured, better born and more influential everywhere you have declared Roman citizens … the rest vassals and subjects.'

AELIUS ARISTIDES

The job of the governor was to make annual tours of his province in order to settle legal disputes and ensure that the cities were being properly administered. Since it was usually impractical for him to visit every city, provinces were divided into judicial districts, or conventus, each containing a principal city where the governor conducted his business for a few weeks each year. There was considerable profit to be made from a governor's visit, with people coming from far and wide for an audience with him, and consequently cities vied fiercely with one another for the honour of being recognized as a provincial centre.

'If he [the governor] arrives at some famous city, or the leading city of the province, he should tolerate the city's commendation of itself to him and ought not to look bored when hearing its praise of itself since provincials hold that as a point of honour for themselves.'

ULPIAN, THE DIGEST 1.7.1

This competition ordinarily took the form of expenditure on civic amenities such as theatres, market places, fountains and – in the western provinces – amphitheatres for staging gladiatorial combat. Prior to the reign of Hadrian, and only in the eastern provinces, a single city would be recognized as the metropolis – literally 'mother city' – of the province. After Hadrian, other cities were also granted the same status, thus generating further competition between the larger cities.

The imperial cult

Many further privileges accrued to a city once it had been given the status of metropolis. For example, such cities automatically became the site of the provincial assembly, an organ of local government that was independent of the governor. In this capacity, the metropolis was the place to which all the stipendiary cities of the province sent representatives to celebrate the annual festival of the emperor. Thus, to honour a city by designating it a metropolis was to make it the regional centre of the imperial cult.

The imperial cult acted as the focal point for direct expressions of loyalty to the emperor. In the eastern provinces, the cult developed out of earlier votive traditions that became widespread around the time of the death of Alexander the Great in 323 BC. At first, these devotions were merely a way of expressing gratitude to individuals – not just rulers – who had rendered extraordinary services. However, over time, between the death of Alexander and the rise of Roman hegemony in the region, the use of divine honours became restricted to kings. Yet with the advent of Roman rule in the eastern Mediterranean and Asia Minor, the use of divine honours once more expanded to encompass private individuals, including a number of Roman governors.

CRADLES OF CIVILIZATION

In the Roman mindset, civilization was synonymous with urban life; any conquered territory aspiring to take on the culture of Rome advanced by developing cities. The typical Roman city was built to a standard layout, with a grid system of streets, a colonnaded forum and public baths. The design sometimes also incorporated a theatre. As provincial cities vied with one another to improve their facilities and status, they all adopted this pattern. A further feature of the urban landscape, which demonstrated that a city had 'arrived', was an officially sanctioned temple in honour of the emperor. The fact that such temples were taken as a sign of genuine development as a 'Roman' city is underscored by the temple that

Claudius dedicated to himself at Camulodunum (Colchester), the principal city in Roman Britain. The area was scarcely Romanized, and the temple was torn down at the outbreak of Boudicca's revolt. Looking back, Tacitus took a very dim view of this presumptuous edifice.

'... [at Camulodunum] the temple raised to the deified Claudius continually met the view, like the citadel of an eternal tyranny; while the priests, chosen for its service, were bound under the pretext of religion to pour out their fortunes like water ...'

TACITUS, ANNALS XIV.31.

The first-century BC Maison Carrée in Nîmes, southern France, is one of the best preserved temples in the Roman world.

Romans had a very ambivalent attitude attitude towards ruler cult. Although, like the Greeks, they were quite at ease with rhetorical comparisons of mortals to gods, they strongly resisted the notion that any living Roman should be revered as a god by his peers. In philosophical terms, while most Romans believed that certain gods had once been mortal, they were adamant that they only assumed divine form after their deaths. This is why the divine honours that the senate voted Julius Caesar during his lifetime caused such grave offence, whereas the erection of a temple for the divine Julius in the wake of the comet that appeared after his death was completely uncontroversial.

The top tier of this exquisite onyx cameo gem – the Gemma Augustea – shows Augustus (left of centre) surrounded by various gods. To his right is seated Roma, the patron goddess of the capital city, while behind the emperor, and crowning him with a laurel wreath, stands Oikoumene, the personification of the inhabited world. Augustus himself was only deified after his death.

Augustus was largely instrumental in creating the cult of the divine Julius, yet he understood clearly that, no matter how many temples were erected or festivals founded in his own honour in the provinces, no ruler cult would exist for him in Rome while he was still alive. But at the same time he realized that the ruler cult was a useful tool for provincial organization, and therefore agreed that the assembly of the three provinces of Gaul could offer sacrifices on his behalf (this observance was standard in all ruler cults, and distinguished the rites for rulers from those of the immortal gods, to whom the sacrifices were offered). Later, he permitted the culturally Greek cities of Asia Minor to set up temples to him.

When Augustus died, the symbolic ascent of his soul to the heavens was staged at his funeral. The decision to create a cult in his honour was widely regarded as an act of approbation, a popular way of passing favourable judgement on his reign. Thus, the imperial cult and power politics became inextricably intertwined; when Tiberius, for example, refused to allow a cult to be established for himself in Spain, Tacitus commented that this showed a lack of ambition on his part. Likewise, Hadrian's deification was not a foregone conclusion; the senate and the people evidently regarded it as a subject of legitimate political debate. Finally, Antoninus Pius forced the decision through. Romans took the view that the emperor should be aware that his posthumous reputation depended upon the goodwill of his subjects.

The understanding of the imperial cult at Rome was quite distinct from the way it operated in the provinces. In Rome, the formulae of deification were retrospective, whereas in the provinces they tended to be prospective. There, emperors received divine honours as soon as they ascended the throne, and every year without fail provincial assemblies would send a delegation to the emperor to inform him of the honours they had bestowed upon him. However, these delegations were far from being sycophantic acts of obeisance. Rather, the imperial cult provided a highly practical opportunity for provincials to engage with the distant power that controlled their lives. While in the capital, provincial delegates could forge useful political contacts, advance their careers and even air complaints against the governor.

The city and the countryside

The imperial cult bound the cities of the provinces together, and in turn bound the provinces to the emperor. As tangible proof of the positive effect of government and the cultural benefits of civilization, cities also played a vital role in conveying such values to the vast mass of people who lived in the countryside. Even in the most rural areas, peasants who did not live directly on estates owned by the emperor or aristocrats – and even many who did – congregated in villages that tried, to the best of their ability, to equip themselves with all the amenities of urban life. These villages put up public baths, assembly buildings, fountains and market places, in the hope that they might one day attain civic status. Settlements arose on the fringes of the Arabian desert calling themselves 'mother villages' to distinguish themselves from lesser spots by imitating the titulature of cities.

'I think I am becoming a god.'

VESPASIAN'S LAST WORDS, ACCORDING TO SUETONIUS, LIVES OF THE TWELVE CAESARS, VESPASIAN, 23

THE ROMAN COUNTRYSIDE, IMAGINED AND REAL

Writers of the Latin Golden Age, notably Horace and Virgil, painted an idyllic picture of life on the land. For example, in his *Eclogues* (42–37 BC) Virgil describes an idealized pastoral landscape, though his later *Georgics* (36–29 BC) focus on more practical aspects of agriculture. Around the same time, Horace invokes a romantic image of the farmer, free of the city dweller's cares:

A mosaic showing a naked cowherd playing a flute while tending his cattle. The pastoral idyll, a far cry from reality, was a favourite theme of Roman poets.

born Roman writer Lucius Moderatus Columella (AD 4–70), who wrote a 12-book treatise on agriculture, *De Re Rustica*, along with a smaller work on trees, *De Arboribus*. These works treat the vital but mundane matters of farming, dispensing practical advice on everything from animal husbandry, viticulture and the best arrangement for a threshing-floor to choosing one's farmhands wisely:

'Happy the man, who, remote
from business, after the manner
of the ancient race of mortals,
cultivates his paternal lands
with his own oxen, disengaged from every kind of usury.'
EPODES 2 (30 BC)

In truth, rural life in Roman times was extremely harsh. Farmers had to contend with scant rainfall and crop failure, not to mention the constant need to pay rent as a tenant to the owner of the estate. We know most about the realities of farming from the first-century Spanish-

'So my advice at the start is not
to appoint an overseer from that
sort of slaves who are physically
attractive, and certainly not from that class which has
busied itself with the voluptuous occupations of the city.
The lazy and sleepy-headed class of servants, accustomed
to idling, to the Campus, the Circus, and the theatres, to
gambling, to cookshops, to bawdy-houses, never ceases to
dream of these follies; and when they carry them over into
their farming, the master suffers not so much loss in the
slave himself as in his whole estate.'

In a number of settlements, some inhabitants attained a level of personal prosperity well above that of subsistence farmers – so great, in fact, that it could sometimes put their lives in danger. Some wealthy villagers only appear in the historical record because they were kidnapped and held to ransom. Their abductors were Roman soldiers working for imperial procurators who were seeking to feather their own nests by stealing from people whose oppression they reckoned the emperor would never notice. In many cases they may well have been right; but in other instances we know that the villagers were able to organize themselves, find a patron and persuade the emperor to address their grievances.

Pontius Pilate symbolically washing his hands of the blood of Christ, in a painting by the 19th-century French artist James Tissot. The partisan mob that called for Jesus' execution invoked the popular myth of the sovereign emperor who took a personal interest in every legal case throughout the empire.

To his rural-dwelling subjects, the emperor was not a hated figure of oppression who was deemed responsible for imposing the rents or taxes that they had to pay, appointing the officials who tormented them or commanding the army whose soldiers terrorized them. On the contrary, he was an abstract symbol of justice who was commonly supposed to listen to even the most lowly plaintiff. Cassius Dio relates a famous incident in which Hadrian rebuffed an old woman who had come to him to complain of an injustice. To his claim that he did not have time to listen to her, she tartly responded 'then cease to be ruler'. Suitably chastened, the emperor reportedly stopped in his tracks and asked her to present her complaint. This story, which recurs in different forms throughout Classical Antiquity, is probably apocryphal, but it does eloquently bear out Plutarch's observation that 'nothing so befits a ruler as the work of justice'.

Other popular tales attest to how widespread the notion was of the emperor as a beneficent figure who could right all wrongs. For example, two Roman authors tell the story of a man who was magically transformed into an ass by a slave-girl with whom he was having an affair. When he is goaded and beaten, he cries out to Caesar to help him. Though clearly intended for comic effect, this story still reflects an attitude towards the imperial office that was widely held. And so, when a Jew named Paul of Tarsus – the future St. Paul – who had been arrested in Jerusalem for preaching Christianity, protested that he should have his case heard by the emperor in person rather than by his representative in Judea, nobody found this at all preposterous, and he was duly packed off to Rome. The story of Paul as St Luke tells it in the Acts of the Apostles stresses the point that no matter was so insignificant that the emperor might not find out about it.

The crowd who gathered at the headquarters of the procurator of Judea in Jerusalem during the Passover season of AD 36 were voicing the same idea when they goaded Pontius Pilate into executing Jesus of Galilee on a charge of treason; the mob called out to Pilate that he would be no 'friend of Caesar' if he did not carry out the sentence. It evidently struck the author of the Gospel of St John as wholly plausible for a Roman magistrate to be swayed by the threat that a complaint of official misconduct involving a person of no significance whatsoever to the emperor – Jesus was not a Roman citizen – might lead to censure.

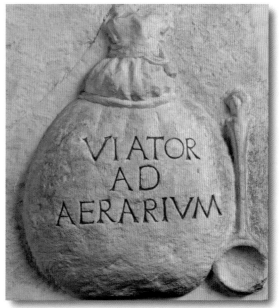

A relief showing a sack of money belonging to a 'Viator ad Aerarium', an attaché to the state treasury. Over time, the Roman empire employed an increasing number of bureaucrats who were charged with collecting taxes. Many officials became over-zealous in carrying out their duties, and disputes were frequent.

The imperial taxation system

The quaint notion that the emperor cared about every matter, however trivial, may well have its origins in the omnipresence of certain institutions of imperial rule. Foremost among these was the all-embracing Roman system of taxation, which made its presence felt in everyone's lives. All the inhabitants of the empire who were not Roman citizens were subject to a tax on their persons and a tax on their property, known as the tribute. On the other hand, citizenship made a person liable to certain taxes from which non-citizens were exempt, such as an inheritance tax that Augustus instituted in 6 BC to fund the resettlement of demobilized legionaries.

The imperial tax system was the single most obvious symbol of Roman control. The instrument that officials charged with tax collection used to assess how the tax burden should fall was the census. This exercise required every man to declare the number of people in his household, including the slaves he kept, and his riches. The most famous census in Roman history was that conducted by the Roman governor of Syria and Judea, Publius Sulpicius Quirinius in AD 6, which the Gospel of St Luke in the New Testament associates with the birth of Christ ('...a decree went out from Caesar Augustus that all the world should be taxed'). New acquisitions of territory were always accompanied by a census, and the process was repeated on various schedules throughout the empire. In most of the empire these reassessments fell once a decade, in Syria once every 12 years, while in Egypt, they recurred every 14 years.

Once the assessment was complete, collection in the provinces was delegated to local officials – municipal councillors known as *curiales*. This cut the cost of administration even if it did not eliminate controversy. The registers of people's liabilities were not always regarded as fair, and disputes were frequent. To assist them in their collection duties, the *curiales* maintained gangs of enforcers, and if these thugs failed to persuade recalcitrant taxpayers to pay up, the officials were empowered to second troops from the governor. It was a system that depended on the threat of violence, a threat that loomed large over the great majority of the empire's population. Little wonder, then, that they were given to imagining that somewhere above it all there resided a beneficent emperor who could intervene to save them.

Ultimately, however, the Roman tax system was self-regulating; peasants who were too harshly treated would simply flee the land, thereby reducing the revenue stream to the empire. Moreover, local officials whose enforcement methods were excessively high-handed were precisely those who were likely to be embezzling potential income from the state. This is why it was so important for senior officials to develop an understanding of what went on at the local level, and to have first-hand knowledge of the conflicts that could, if unchecked, tear a community apart. The key role that they performed was to balance the interests of the local administrative class upon which they depended for day-to-day government and the interests of the governed.

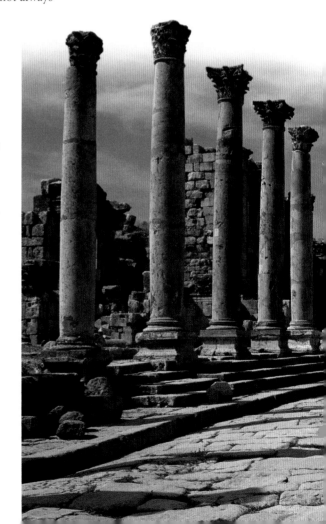

All roads do not lead to Rome

As the tax system provided the basic forum of interaction between government and the governed, so it also helped shape the empire. In economic terms, the empire created a superstructure made up of a number of relatively autonomous zones, each of which centred either on a major city or on a large military garrison. In the west, these zones included the two main areas of military occupation along the Rhine and Danube rivers, each with a garrison of around 80,000 men, and Rome. In the east, the principal zones were the highly urbanized region of western Turkey (Asia Minor), which included Ephesus, Pergamon and Smyrna, as well as a host of smaller places, plus the area around Antioch in Syria. In all cases, the zones' hinterlands supplied the major cities or garrisons with revenue, goods and services. Rome, for instance, with a population of around one million people, required the excess agricultural resources of North Africa, Spain and Egypt to support its existence.

The fact that Rome needed food from abroad to survive did not mean that the economic traffic was all in one direction. Continuing consumer demand in Rome directly benefited the regions that supplied it. For example, the infrastructure required to ship North Africa's agricultural surplus to Rome was directly responsible for regenerating Carthage as a major city. Similarly, in Egypt, the supply chain that led from the fertile Nile Valley confirmed the status of Alexandria as a major city as a major city; in addition to handling large quantities of home-grown agricultural produce, the city was also a key entrepôt for the lucrative trade in luxury goods – chiefly spices – from Asia. On a smaller scale, the same process generated wealth throughout the empire. The garrisons on the Rhine were supported by the excess production of France, while the army on the Danube stimulated the growth of agriculture throughout the Balkans. In both areas, which had no significant urban settlement prior to the Roman conquest, a number of major

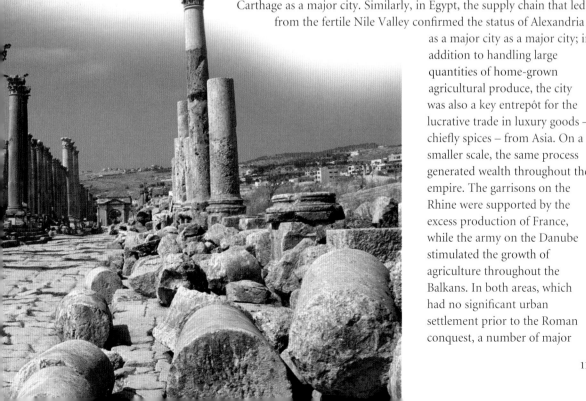

Grand columns line the 'Cardus Maximus' in the city of Gerasa in Jordan. The cardus, or cardo, was the name given to the principal street in a Roman city in which economic activity took place. Such streets were lined with the shops of merchants.

cities grew up along or near rivers. In Germany, these cities included Bonn (Bonna), Trier (Augusta Treverorum), Mainz (Moguntiacum) and Cologne (Colonia Agrippina), with significant further development along the Rhône at Lyons (Lugdunum) and in the ancient city of Marseilles (Massilia). Along the Danube, large conurbations arose at Aquincum and Sirmium, as well as Siscia on the major east–west road to the south and Thessalonika. In Britain, London grew into a major trading city, while Córdoba (Corduba) in Spain emerged as the centre of the highly productive Guadalquivir valley.

A print depicting a quaestor wearing his robe and surrounded by official insignia. The office of quaestor was originally instituted in the days of the republic; holders of the title were responsible for supervising the treasury and the state's financial affairs.

By establishing a redistribution network for excess production, and creating a stable market for goods from far and wide, the Roman empire brought a hitherto unknown level of prosperity to the territories under its control. The system also enabled Roman emperors to alleviate periods of hardship in particular areas by diverting surpluses from regions that were thriving.

The striking feature of the imperial redistribution system is that all roads did not lead to Rome. While massive grain fleets did indeed sail there every year from North Africa and Alexandria, the rest of the trade flowed away from the capital. There were no ancient equivalents of the bullion fleets of early modern Spain sailing into the harbours of Italy, having despoiled the resources of the empire. Most of the tax revenue that was collected, either in agricultural produce (required for the land tax) or hard currency (deriving from the poll tax and various taxes on the transshipment of goods) was used to support the administration in the areas where it was collected, or in the areas serviced by the local redistribution network.

Fiscal flaws

The decentralization of the Roman system was its greatest strength, for it meant that if disaster struck in one area, the rest of the empire could remain relatively free of disruption. On the other hand, the fact that most tax revenue supported local needs also meant that emperors were often chronically short of cash. In response, over the course of the first two centuries, the emperors began gradually to reduce the quantity of pure silver in the basic silver coin, the denarius, to roughly 60 per cent,

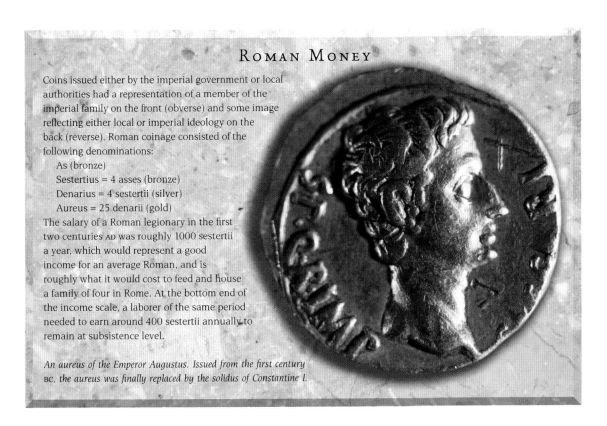

ROMAN MONEY

Coins issued either by the imperial government or local authorities had a representation of a member of the imperial family on the front (obverse) and some image reflecting either local or imperial ideology on the back (reverse). Roman coinage consisted of the following denominations:

As (bronze)
Sestertius = 4 asses (bronze)
Denarius = 4 sestertii (silver)
Aureus = 25 denarii (gold)

The salary of a Roman legionary in the first two centuries AD was roughly 1000 sestertii a year, which would represent a good income for an average Roman, and is roughly what it would cost to feed and house a family of four in Rome. At the bottom end of the income scale, a laborer of the same period needed to earn around 400 sestertii annually to remain at subsistence level.

An aureus of the Emperor Augustus. Issued from the first century BC, *the aureus was finally replaced by the solidus of Constantine I.*

avoiding rampant inflation by tariffing the denarius against the basic gold coin, or aureus, at a rate of 25:1. The result was that inflation in the course of the two centuries after Augustus remained relatively stable, at around 0.25 per cent annually.

Although the emperors could control inflation by supporting the gold standard, and alleviate shortages by redirecting surpluses, their fiscal condition remained parlous. The tax system, based as it was on the relatively inelastic system of 10- to 14-year censuses, could not be counted on to generate massive new revenues when they were needed. Shortfalls in the budget had to be made up by emperors who, from the time of Augustus onwards, diverted surpluses from their own income to the state treasury (*aerarium*). However, the transfer of imperial funds was not always enough. In the crisis of the Danubian wars, Marcus Aurelius was actually forced to auction off palace furniture to meet his expenses. Nor was it just wartime that depleted the coffers; despite the fact that the empire enjoyed a long period of peace in the reign of Antoninus Pius, he still found it necessary to impose a luxury tax on the upper classes in the form of a 25–33 per cent surcharge on the sale of gladiators. By the time Marcus, in a magnanimous gesture celebrating his military victories, finally repealed the gladiator tax it had yielded between five and seven million denarii a year, the equivalent of about 7.5 per cent of the base cost of the entire Roman army.

The Imperial Melting Pot: Roman Culture
(AD 68–180)

The Roman empire embraced many different cultures, yet still managed to instil in the peoples under its protection a sense of being Roman. Not that this task was at all straightforward; ultimately, the authority of the Roman state depended upon the willing acquiescence of its subjects. If the terrible tale of the Jewish revolts of the first and second centuries reveal nothing else about Roman administration, it was that popular insurrection in just a small province had the capacity to stretch the resources of the empire to their limit. What, then, were the methods by which hearts and minds were won?

Rome's key policy of sharing power with local élites meant that it could not simply prescribe what it meant to be Roman and expect people to follow unquestioningly. Broadly speaking, the empire was divided between the Greek-speaking east and the Latin-speaking west, but this crude distinction conceals radical differences in the way that Latin or Greek culture were assimilated by the vast mass of people for whom neither language was indigenous. In Britain, Germany and Gaul, Latin was often a second language to either local Celtic or Germanic dialects.

A funerary sculpture of a married couple of Etruscan origin from the Temple of Scasato in the town of Falerii (modern Civita Castellana, Tuscany). From its earliest history, Rome conquered and assimilated other Italian peoples such as the Etruscans. In the imperial period, ever more diverse ethnicities were brought under the Roman aegis.

E Pluribus Unum

Roman Africa – the province centred on Carthage – was a particularly interesting case. Though a Roman province since the end of the Third Punic War (146 BC), it retained a distinct linguistic and cultural identity. The first language of an African aristocrat might well be Punic (the dialect of ancient Carthage, which developed from the language of the Phoenician traders who founded the city) or some other local tongue. Even North Africans who attained high office in Roman service maintained a strong connection to their roots. For example,

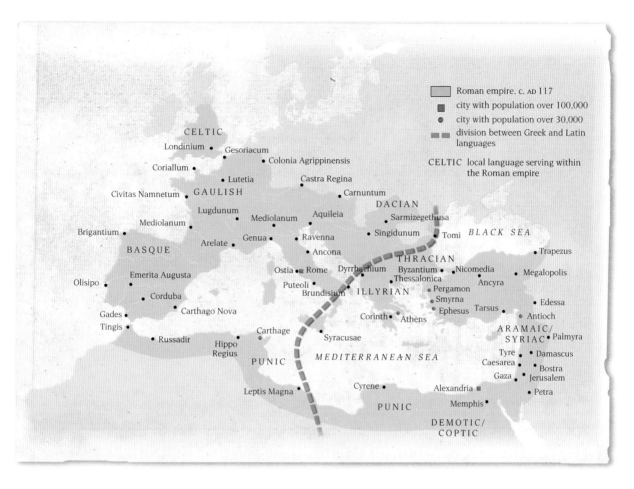

Map showing the broad cultural and linguistic divisions with the Roman empire during the first century AD. It is testament to Roman organizational skill that the empire successfully embraced such a diverse mix of peoples over several centuries.

Lusius Quietus, one of the four leading generals executed by Hadrian at the start of his reign was the son of a North African tribal chieftain, and probably spoke a Berber dialect. Likewise, the Historia Augusta (a late-Roman collection of biographies of emperors from AD 117 to 284) recounts that Septimius Severus (AD 146–211), the future emperor who entered the senate under Marcus, spoke Latin with such a heavy Punic accent that he pronounced his own name 'Sheptimiush Shervush'.

In Egypt, many local officials had a very poor command of Greek – we know of one village administrator there, Petaus the son of Petaus, who could barely spell his own name in Greek – because their first language was a form of Egyptian known as Demotic. In Syria, the dominant language was Aramaic, while in Asia Minor a hodgepodge of ancient languages continued to be spoken in preference to Greek; the Acts of the Apostles relate that when Paul of Tarsus performed a miracle in the city of Lystra in Asia Minor on his first missionary journey in AD 47, those who witnessed it cried out in Lycaonian. As late as the third century AD, the Roman jurist Ulpian (d. 223) noted that a governor had to be able to accommodate people speaking Phoenician and Aramaic, as well as Latin and Greek, in his court. Ulpian himself came from Tyre, a Roman *colonia* in the eastern Mediterranean that was an enclave of Latin culture in a district where otherwise Phoenician and Aramaic were far more common than Greek or Latin. One suspects that if Ulpian had been from Gaul, he would have included Celtic; it is certainly clear from the comments of two Christian commentators of the second century that the original languages of that region continued to be spoken, if not written, long after the start of the Roman occupation. Conversely, a Gaul named Favorinus (*c.* AD 80–150, whose other claim to fame was an undescended testicle) mastered the Greek language so perfectly that he became one of the foremost Greek orators in Rome during the reign of Hadrian.

A world of entertainment

Roman emperors promoted various practices that were designed to inculcate the values of Roman culture into the peoples of the wider empire. The incentive was that favours would be granted by Rome to those willing to assimilate. These initiatives included encouraging people to learn Greek and Latin well enough to be able to participate in government, to construct cities on a Greek or Latin model and to adopt Greek or Roman dress. Roman values were transmitted not only through the periodic appearances of senior magistrates, but also through various forms of public announcements – missives from the emperor were always read out in a public ceremony and then posted in a public place – or public spectacles.

'Two things only the Roman people desire – bread and the games of the circus.'

JUVENAL, SATIRES X, 80

Secular public spectacles came in three basic forms: theatrical events, athletic contests and public combats. Theatrical events might take the form of full productions of plays – usually, but not exclusively, works that were part of the standard canon of didactic works. However, they might also include solo performances of excerpts of 'greatest hits' from famous plays, sometimes set to musical accompaniment; poetic recitations, musical performances and choral acts; mimes (a generic term for 'low-brow' performances that ranged from situational comedies and clown routines to dancing displays); and pantomime, a form of tragedy involving a dancer, accompanied by a singer and percussion band, who performed a routine on a mythological theme. On some occasions, these events would be supplemented with performances illustrating an important event in the history of the empire – for instance, a papyrus has survived containing part of the script for a depiction of Trajan's ascent to the gods, which was staged in an Egyptian town after his death.

Athletic contests were based on the festivals of pre-Roman Greece, in which naked athletes competed in a series of races and track-and-field events such as the pentathlon. Another popular attraction was the triumvirate of combat sports: boxing, wrestling, and pancration, a brutal combination of the two. Athletic contests might also involve equestrian events. These included both horse races as we know them and races with chariots drawn by two- or four-horse teams. Such chariot races were run on courses of varying dimensions, which could accommodate a large number of contestants – as many as 48 chariots at the hippodrome at Olympia in Greece.

By contrast, circus chariot races, which evolved in Rome's valley of the *circus maximus*, were run on a track of set dimensions. A maximum of 12 teams took part in such races, completing seven laps around a central barrier with tight turns at each end. These spectacles were fast and furious and extremely dangerous for the participants, with

An actor (left) playing the role of a king, from a fresco in the city of Herculaneum. Heavily influenced by Greek drama, theatrical performances of various kinds were a very popular form of entertainment in the Roman world. The first purpose-built theatre in Rome was erected by Pompey in 55–54 BC.

THE ROMAN WILD ANIMAL TRADE

As entertainments in the Colosseum in Rome and other amphitheatres throughout the empire grew increasingly popular, there arose a huge demand for wild animals for use in these lavish public spectacles. All parts of the empire were scoured for wildlife in what became a highly profitable trade. After they had been transported to Italy, the animals were kept in special zoos before being transferred to pens below the wooden floor of the Colosseum. From there, they were winched up to the arena, either to be killed by huntsmen or to be goaded into attacking one another. Augustus had 3500 animals from Africa slaughtered in 26 wild-beast baitings, and 9000 animals perished in the 100 days of games that were celebrated when Titus opened the Colosseum. The animals used in these grotesque and cruel spectacles included lions, bears, tigers, wolves, and even crocodiles and rhinoceroses. So great was the Romans' bloodlust that several species were depleted almost to extinction by hunting for the wildlife trade; the Barbary lion from the provinces of Numidia and Mauretania, for example, came close to being wiped out in this period.

A beautifully detailed mosaic from the North African city of Leptis Magna shows hunters killing deer and a wild boar, and a prisoner being mauled by a leopard.

accidents a frequent occurrence. Another feature that distinguished chariot races within the circus from those elsewhere was that circus races were dominated by four professional factions – known from the colours worn by their drivers as the Blues, Greens, Reds and Whites. These factions had been responsible for organizing the circus races from as early as the fourth century BC.

Public combat had existed as a form of entertainment since Republican times, but was only expanded into a major spectacle throughout the empire after the Battle of Actium. It appeared in several guises, the most common of which were gladiatorial bouts between two or more men, variously armed. Other types of public blood sports were those in which professional hunters stalked and killed wild animals, and, most notoriously, the execution of criminals in combat. Such gruesome charades might involve the men being tortured in ways that recalled the mythological punishments of famous offenders against the gods.

Alternatively, in a form of punishment known as 'exposure to the beasts', they were sent unprotected into the arena to be mauled to death by lions, tigers, bears or wolves. Another variant was to force condemned men to fight one another to the death in duels.

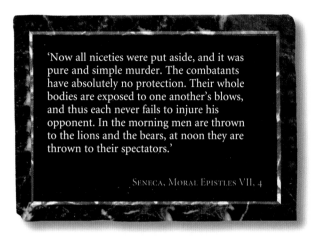

'Now all niceties were put aside, and it was pure and simple murder. The combatants have absolutely no protection. Their whole bodies are exposed to one another's blows, and thus each never fails to injure his opponent. In the morning men are thrown to the lions and the bears, at noon they are thrown to their spectators.'

SENECA, MORAL EPISTLES VII, 4

Unlike modern spectators, who avidly follow championship events that last for weeks or even months, the ancient audience required instant gratification. When people gathered to watch a sporting event, be it athletic, gladiatorial or equestrian, they expected to see close contests, thrilled to rapid changes of fortune and found it an added bonus if one or more of the contestants failed to make it out of the arena in one piece. In combat sports, for instance, all the contests would be crammed into a single day so that the spectators did not have to wait for the outcome. This meant that the eventual winner needed to record a gruelling series of decisive victories on the way to securing the championship, with almost no time between bouts. Since, in a sport like boxing, the victor had to win by an equivalent of a technical knockout each time, the final would be as much a test of stamina as it was of technical skill. Endurance, and the ability to withstand pain, were traits that were deeply admired by Romans.

The Roman psyche

But what did it mean, in essence, to be a Roman? Difficult though it is to divine the collective psyche of a former age – and a distant one at that – certain leitmotifs emerge clearly from looking at diverse aspects of Roman culture. One of these is a fascination with pain and suffering. For example, aside from their sheer entertainment value, gladiators struck such a resonant chord with the Roman public because they were powerful symbols of fortitude, putting life and limb at risk in bouts that almost invariably ended with some sort of injury.

This is not to say that the Roman attitude towards gladiators was unambiguous; on the one hand, they were reviled for being as low as slaves in the social hierarchy, but on the other they were greatly admired for their bravery, with some even being accorded celebrity status. A similar equivocal attitude attached to the question of suffering on the part of the fighters. A certain amount of bloodshed added to the spectacle, but mass deaths were neither inevitable (the fatality rate was only around 5 per cent in any given set of games) nor especially desirable. Gladiatorial contests were less about slaking a crowd's bloodlust than about providing a protracted display of fighting skill. It is for this reason, and not out of any solicitude for the gladiators' welfare, that fights to the death were banned everywhere except Rome after the Julio-Claudian period. Even there, they were rare occurrences, being staged only when the emperor was in attendance. Interestingly, by the time of Marcus Aurelius, combat with steel swords and tridents was often supplanted by the use of wooden weapons. This innovation was presumably designed to prolong the entertainment.

The motif of fortitude recurs in the epic tales that emerged as the one original literary genre of the imperial period. The heroes of these stories, such as Aeneas, were redoubtable wanderers who endured great hardship to achieve their ultimate goal of finding a home. Often they had to confront the threat or actuality of intense suffering during their journey. Both in the works of contemporaries like Virgil and Ovid and in those of the earlier Greek writers Homer and Sophocles, the Roman audience found itself captivated by lurid examples of suffering, such as that undergone by the character Philoctetes. The greatest archer to accompany the Greeks to the siege of Troy, Philoctetes was bitten by a serpent and, in intense pain from the suppurating wound that developed, was abandoned on the island of Lemnos by his companions when they could no longer bear to hear his cries of agony or smell the stench from his wound.

On stage, preferred themes also ran to the more extreme episodes from mythology: Medea, who murdered her children, was a great favourite with Romans – the young Augustus even wrote a play on the theme – as was the banquet at which Atreus fed his brother Thyestes the stewed bodies of his children, the madness of Hercules or the bizarre sexual encounter between a Spartan woman, Leda, and the god Zeus, who had disguised himself as a swan.

The counterpoint to this fascination with pain was the Romans' admiration for outward displays of intense calm. The ideal Roman man was a person who stoically kept his passions to himself, comporting himself in life with every bit as much serenity as the graceful stone statue that every prominent citizen aspired

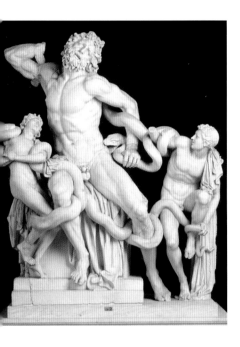

A popular tale from Troy that captured Romans' imagination was that of the priest Laocöon, who tried to prevent his fellow citizens from dragging the wooden horse into the city. For this, he was subjected to a ghastly fate by the gods, being crushed to death by two huge serpents. Laocöon's story was vividly recounted in Virgil's Aeneid.

'There came over the calm water from Tenedos two snakes, forging through the sea in great coils and making side by side for the shore … Their eyes were blazing and bloodshot, and they hissed as they licked their lips with darting tongues…they made straight for Laocöon and seized him and bound him in their huge and scaly coils…He struggled frantically to wrench open the knots, his priestly bands drenched with filth and black venom, and his terrible cries rose to the sky …'

VIRGIL, AENEID BOOK 2

to have his native city erect in his honour. Yet behind this façade he might, like Marcus Aurelius, write letters to friends detailing the illnesses he suffered and the pain that he overcame. The orator Aelius Aristides, whose medical conditions strike modern readers as deeply psychosomatic, spent years seeking treatments from the priest of the god Asclepius and regarded his ailments almost as a religious devotion that brought him closer to God.

Religion and culture

Lacking the scientific and medical knowledge we now use to understand – and in some cases avert or alleviate – natural catastrophes, the Romans had only the gods to turn to when plague, earthquakes, storms or famine struck. Thus Marcus Aurelius consulted the mystic Alexander of Abonuteichos and his oracular snake Glycon when the barbarians threatened, and appealed to the god Apollo when the empire was blighted by the Antonine Plague. His conviction that the gods would speak through oracles and respond to his prayers derived from the Stoic philosophy that lay behind all his thoughts and actions. It was a basic tenet of Stoicism that the seamless nexus of events – Fate, in other words – was indistinguishable from the divine will of Zeus. This belief in a form of providential design entailed understanding the laws of Nature as the material presence of the divine in the universe. To exist in harmony with these laws was therefore Marcus' main aim:

Detail of a fresco painting preserved in the ruins of Pompeii after the city was buried by the eruption of Vesuvius in AD 79. It shows Medea holding a sword and contemplating the murder of her own children as a terrible act of revenge against her errant husband Jason (left).

'*So far as concerns the gods, the messages sent from them, their aids and revelations, nothing prevents me from living according to Nature, even though I slip from this at times, through my own fault, by not observing the reminders and virtual instructions from the gods.*'
(MEDITATIONS 1.17.6)

What distinguished Marcus' Stoic belief in fate and the gods (as well as that of other leading philosophical movements of the age such as Platonism and Pythagoreanism) was the idea that the many gods in the Roman pantheon all acted in accordance with the will of a single divine organizing principle. This was a highly sophisticated, intellectual viewpoint, however. For many others in the empire, the gods who were the focus of their devotions were considerably less well organized. The Roman empire was filled with shrines and temples to gods of all sizes and shapes, many of distinctly local origin, and people sought out the ones who could respond to their specific concerns. The highly undogmatic Roman approach to faith, which did not attempt to impose any official, authorized religion on diverse peoples, was one of the most significant stabilizing factors in the empire.

Belief in the gods was hallowed by tradition, and was often backed up by extensive anecdotal evidence of divine intervention. For instance, temples dedicated to Asclepius, the god of healing, kept records of the ways in which he had cured the sick within their walls. In addition, oracular shrines documented the responses that the gods had given there, while cities recorded moments when the gods had averted disaster or revealed new rites to them to heal rifts in their relationship. People were in no doubt that the gods existed because they could see the results of their actions all around them. Moreover, they knew how to worship the gods because the gods themselves had instructed them how to do so. They were also aware that the gods gave different instructions to different people.

The most commonplace form of religious observance in the Roman empire was the act of sacrifice. People brought whatever offerings they could afford, either burning them on an altar if they were trying to reach a god thought to dwell in the heavens, or pouring them on the ground if they were trying to petition one of the deities that lived beneath the earth. The rich were expected to make greater sacrifices than the poor, for the order of worship ideally reflected the order of society. In the Roman mind, there was no separation of the political and religious spheres because the maintenance of the social order depended upon the happiness of the gods. Thus the Roman

The most important oracle in the classical world, at Delphi on the slopes of Mount Parnassus in Greece, was dedicated to the god Apollo. For centuries, the Pythia (priestess) there dispensed prophesies. This Roman sculpture shows Apollo beside the oracle.

emperor was also a priest – from the time of Augustus onwards he held a variety of priestly offices in the state, chief among which was that of pontifex maximus. The leaders of communities throughout the empire would also usually hold some sort of priesthood in their lifetimes.

A marble relief from the Temple of Vespasian in the Roman Forum, depicting a priest leading a sacrificial bull to the altar. The act of sacrifice was a key element in Roman religious rites.

Oracles, charlatans and visionaries

The inseparability of politics and traditional cult was another manifestation of the key role that religion played as a force for social cohesion. For some, however, traditional devotions did not go far enough. Such was the importance of the gods that many sought more direct ways to appeal to them outside the established limits of cult, which they regarded as an essentially passive religious activity. One such mechanism used to establish a more immediate relationship with the gods was divination.

Modes of divination were immensely varied. One way was to pay a visit to oracles, where the gods were thought to speak through inspired prophets. In the main, at established shrines, the gods only spoke directly to people of a high enough social standing to merit direct communication. A more indirect method of approaching a god was to consult an oracle that worked by a system of lot. A classic form of this type of divination in Egypt involved putting two notes, each containing an identical query and an alternative response, into an urn and taking the one that was drawn out as the god's answer. Other methods involved rolling dice and matching the number rolled against a list of predetermined responses, or observing fish feeding in a sacred pool, the eating habits of sacred chickens, or the way that a cheese floated. At sacrifices the slaughtered beast would be inspected after it had been killed to see if some sign was evident in its entrails, the behaviour of the animal would be closely watched to make sure that it comported itself properly on the way to its death, and, in the Roman tradition, a close eye was kept upon the weather and the flight of birds.

Where these activities began to overstep the boundaries of acceptable behaviour was when people solicited the wisdom of the gods from clairvoyants, magicians or seers who claimed to possess sacred writing from the sages of the distant past. Worse still, they could be employed to cast a spell on enemies: another common form of ancient religious text that has been unearthed by archaeologists is the *defixio*, usually a lead tablet with a curse upon it that was buried in some place where it was hoped that a demonic spirit would be called forth. The second-century Greek satirist Lucian (AD 120–*c*.180) lampooned such all-purpose charlatans in his essay *Alexander The Oracle-Monger* (an attack on the prophet consulted by Marcus Aurelius, Alexander of Abonuteichos) as 'those who advertise enchantments, miraculous incantations, charms for your love-affairs, visitations for your enemies, disclosures of buried treasure, and successions to estates.'

The Roman mystic Apollonius of Tyana. One of Apollonius' most celebrated acts was to have supposedly brought back a Roman senator's daughter from the dead. He was also said to have had a vision of the murder of Domitian as it was taking place, and described it in lurid detail. Edward Gibbon says of Apollonius: 'we are at a loss to discover whether he was a sage, an imposter or a fanatic'.

For all its tolerance of local religious practices, the Roman state took a very dim view of prophets who operated outside the parameters of the state, especially magicians who claimed to be able to invoke supernatural visitations. Such people were potentially very dangerous – visionary prophets were responsible for fomenting the Jewish revolt in the time of Trajan, and the German rebellion that raged after Vespasian ascended the throne was fuelled by the visions of a woman named Veleda. Every emperor from Augustus onwards issued edicts against all manner of unauthorized contact with the divine. People who dabbled in magic to jinx their neighbours, along with the magicians who advised them how to do so, were liable to be sentenced to death. Even so, people who felt driven to desperate measures could not be prevented from appealing to them, and even emperors were known to consult independent experts. Hadrian, for example, showered gifts on an Egyptian magician named Pancrates, while Marcus let it be known that the miraculous downpour that saved his soldiers during the Northern Wars was the work of another Egyptian magician named Harnouphis. Hadrian also published the horoscope of one of the senators whom he executed as a way of proving that he had done the right thing: conveniently, it showed that the man was destined to be a traitor. The huge gulf between what the law demanded and popular practice in consulting such practitioners attests to the abiding Roman fascination with divine revelation.

One especially famous visionary of the Roman world was a long-lived man by the name of Apollonius of Tyana (*c.* AD 1–100). Apollonius was credited with having saved the city of Ephesus from a plague demon and with curing the sick through faith-healing. When he died, many people believed that he had ascended to heaven, and sacred objects that he was thought to have used to ward off demons were widespread throughout the Eastern empire centuries after his death.

MITHRAISM

The rites of Mithras were based on a complex mixture of astrology and myth. Members of this all-male cult were arranged into a hierarchy of seven grades, with the highest grade usually reserved for the individual who had the highest social standing in the world at large. The seven grades, which corresponded to the seven planets known to ancient astronomy, were the Father (Saturn), Heliodromos or 'Sun Runner' (the Sun), Persian (Moon), Lion (Jupiter), Soldier (Mars), Nymphus (Venus) and the Raven (Mercury). Rituals of Mithraism included an initiation banquet commemorating the meal that Mithras took with the Sun after he had created the world by killing a cosmic bull. The flowing blood of the slain bull was supposedly the source of all life and vegetation on Earth. During this ceremony, the

Mithras slaying the cosmic bull. All Mithraea contained a sculpture like this; occasionally, a bull would even be sacrificed during the ceremonies.

Father pointed a bow at a naked initiate, recalling Mithras' firing of an arrow at a stone, bringing forth water. Another rite, the procession of the Heliodromos, mimicked the journey of the sun through the equinoxes and symbolized the journey taken by the human soul.

The appeal of Mithraism was enhanced by the stress that its powerful liturgy placed on secrecy; because Mithras had killed the cosmic bull in a cave, the cult's temples, or Mithraea (singular: Mithraeum), were all located underground. There was also a great emphasis on loyalty and discipline, making Mithraism highly attractive to soldiers. Mithraea were especially common where legions were stationed – one such ritual chamber has even been found under Hadrian's Wall.

Eastern cults

The Romans also had the sense that Graeco-Roman culture was relatively young compared with the ancient cultures of Egypt and Mesopotamia. Tourists – including the emperor Hadrian – travelled to Egypt to marvel at ancient books of wisdom and sit at the feet of members of obscure cults. Egyptian temples were repositories of texts that dated back to the time of the Pharaohs, and Egyptians were more than happy to supply this tourist market with purported 'translations' of books of ancient wisdom into Greek (usually the ideas were deeply Hellenized to suit the buyers' tastes and bore only a passing resemblance to the original text). Another powerful Eastern influence on Roman religious thought was the ancient Persian sage Zoroaster; again, however, as with the learning of Egypt, Romans' understanding of Zoroastrianism was not primarily based on scholarly study of the core texts, but rather on debased, mediated forms of the religion. This somewhat dilettantish interest in the wisdom of the East was part and parcel of educated Romans' unquenchable sense of cultural superiority. Their fascination derived less from a desire to learn from other cultures than from a smug satisfaction that the world under Rome's control embraced the collected wisdom of sages from all eras and all places.

Judas Iscariot hanging himself from the 'Judas tree' in shame at having betrayed Christ (from a column capital in the Romanesque cathedral of Autun, France). One of the texts produced by an early Christian splinter group – the Gnostics – was the so-called 'Gospel of Judas', found in Egypt. This document purports to be a personal revelation of Jesus to Judas, and is highly critical of emerging Christian orthodoxy based on the four gospels. Controversially, it presents Judas' betrayal as being in accordance with Jesus' wishes.

The fascination with new religious understanding from outside the Graeco-Roman tradition lies behind the adoption of a number of Eastern cults in the first century AD, whose popularity continued to expand over following centuries. One of these was the cult of Isis and Serapis, originally invented, it seems, by the first Ptolemaic king of Egypt in the early fourth century BC. Supported by an extensive mythology and a large body of religious texts – especially hymns in praise of Isis – the cult took hold throughout the Roman empire. Another cult that gained a huge following was that of the Persian sun-god Mithras, which came to prominence in the later first century AD. The Roman form of Mithraism came via a sect in the area of eastern Turkey known as Commagene, who adopted traditions of Persian worship that had existed there since the days of Alexander the Great.

The rise of Christianity

Aspects of both the cults of Isis and Mithras, which promised salvation in an afterlife to devoted acolytes, were reflected in yet another Eastern cult that emerged in the course of the first century AD. Unlike the other two, however, this cult was far less readily absorbed into the bounds of conventional society. True, the cult of Isis had on occasion been officially suppressed – even being outlawed altogether for a while in Rome during the reign of Tiberius after its priests facilitated a notorious sex scandal involving people of senatorial status – but it never fundamentally challenged the norms of Roman society. Still less the cult of Mithras, which could even be construed as being openly supportive of the status quo. The same could not be said, however, of the cult whose central tenet was that a Jewish prophet executed in AD 36 by the Roman governor of Judea was the son of God and the saviour of mankind.

The fervent belief of the first followers of Jesus in the corruption of the world around them, and the rejection by many of any deity other than the One God of Jewish scripture, set the new movement at odds with all its neighbours. Christianity, as it emerged from the teachings of the first generation of preachers after the execution of Jesus, appealed to people as a genuine alternative to current religious practices. To be sure, other religious groups – notably the Celtic Druids – had found themselves at variance with the Roman state, but none of these other movements had texts in a language – Greek – that was universally understood.

Christianity appealed especially to people seeking an alternative to conventional morality. Unlike the Isis or Mithras cults, it turned not on the marvellous actions of a god, but rather on the suffering of a human being who had dared to defy established authority. Within a couple of generations, Christians had begun to produce a literature unequalled in its complexity and modernity, addressing as it did not some mythic past, but the conditions of life in the here and now. Even though splinter groups produced their own books of revelation that made the message of Jesus far more arcane than its expression in the four gospels and the letters of the early teachers, they still adhered to a core narrative that was firmly established by the reign of Domitian.

'My dear Pliny, you have done as you ought in examining the cases of those people who were charged with being Christians. It is impossible to lay down a general rule which will dictate a specific course of action. They must not be hunted down; if they are brought before you and the case is proven they must be punished; if, however someone should deny that he is a Christian, and make it clear that he is not by making sacrifice to our gods, although that person may have been suspect in the past, he should be pardoned for repentance. Pamphlets posted without the name of an author must play no part in any accusation. They create the worst sort of precedent and are out of keeping with the spirit of our age.'

VIRGIL, AENEID BOOK 2

People were drawn to the new faith both because it was wholly independent of the power structure of the state, and by its insistence on a strict moral code. The often brutal response of the Roman government only served to increase Christianity's popular appeal and publicize its message. Nero blamed Christians for the great fire of Rome in AD 64, and later emperors came to regard the new faith as so subversive that it ought to be banned. But just as outlawing magic did not quell interest in it, neither did the proscription of Christianity, which was only enforced erratically. The rise of Christianity in the first two centuries AD was not unparalleled as a sociological phenomenon, but it was unique in providing an alternative model for approaching the divine in a world where divine action was profoundly important.

REINVENTING
CAESAR

*A mosaic showing a scene of idyllic domesticity at
a Roman villa. While many areas under Roman
control remained peaceful and prosperous in the third
century AD, governance of the empire was blighted
by decades of indecision and upheaval.*

The Slippery Slope:
The Beginnings of Rome's Decline
(AD 180–211)

One thing that emerges very clearly from the works of Tacitus is that he was no purblind admirer of every aspect of Roman culture or of Rome's military might per se. He knew that Roman armies were often poorly drilled and inept and that grave defeats could result from these shortcomings. He also recognized the tendency of Romans to rest on the cultural laurels of the distant past. Finally, he was all too keenly aware that, beyond the empire's northern frontiers, there dwelt many unconquered (and unconquerable) peoples who might, in time, be impossible to contain. Yet, despite his critical acumen, even Tacitus failed to pinpoint what we, with the benefit of hindsight, can identify as the empire's greatest weakness – the highly traditional nature of Roman thought.

A bust of the Roman Emperor Commodus in his preferred guise as the god Hercules, dressed in a lion skin and wielding a club. Commodus was a homicidal sociopath, even killing his practice opponents while preparing for his gladiatorial appearances.

Nowhere is this traditionalism more painfully evident than in the attitude that Romans of the second century AD took to their army. Two short books of this period that treat military matters have come down to us, written by a historian and philosopher of Greek descent called Arrian of Nicomedia (c. AD 92–175). Arrian not only had a practical knowledge of contemporary warfare – as governor of the Roman province of Cappadocia from AD 130 to 138, he commanded an army that repelled an invasion by the Alan tribes from the steppes of central Asia – he was also a learned scholar of ancient history. In particular, he admired Alexander the Great, and his account of the campaigns of the Macedonian king remains the foundation for modern study of that era. Yet therein lay the problem; for all his undoubted accomplishments on the battlefield, when formulating tactics, Arrian recommends infantry formations that are adaptations of the fourth-century BC phalanx used by his military hero. In writing on cavalry tactics, Arrian is marginally more up-to-date, but even then he commends innovations borrowed from the Gallic and Spanish tribes in the first century BC.

Hidebound by tradition

Another surviving text from the same period on fighting tactics comes from North Africa. It is in the form of an inscription recording a series of speeches that Arrian's patron Hadrian gave when visiting the area, praising the drills performed by various auxiliary units. Tellingly, one of these formations is precisely the same Spanish cavalry drill described by Arrian. Apart from providing clear evidence that the two men were well versed in military affairs, the coincidence of this identical tactic being recommended in two different parts of the Roman world also smacks of the dead hand of tradition. The troops that Hadrian was inspecting were the garrison that patrolled the northern boundaries of the Sahara, yet there is nothing in his speech to suggest that he took into account the very special requirements of desert warfare.

Certainly, there was no centralized drill manual, and Roman armies had been known since the days of the republic for adopting the fighting and campaigning skills of their adversaries. (For example, the ploy of troops using inflated animal skins to swim across rivers had been learned from the Batavian tribes of northern Belgium.) However, these days lay far in the past, and for a long time no new strategic or tactical thinking had been evolved to cope with changed circumstances.

This same complacent attitude is still in evidence during the reign of Marcus Aurelius. In a manual on generalship entitled *The Stratagems of War*, a Macedonian writer named Polyaenus gathered together the successful stratagems of famous commanders of the past. He dedicated his book to Marcus and Verus, who at the time (AD 162–165) were campaigning against the Parthians. The sweeping, anecdotal approach taken in Polyaenus' book to the art of war stood in a long and honourable tradition of learning from the past. Nor were such writings the only source that an aspiring Roman general could consult; at the other end of the spectrum stood the kind of detailed treatise on practical aspects of warfare exemplified by Apollodorus of Damascus' work on siege engines. In this, Trajan's chief military engineer during the Dacian Wars urged his successor Hadrian to heed the vital importance of technical data in the construction of such machines.

TIMELINE

AD 180 Commodus succeeds Marcus Aurelius as emperor

192 Assassination of Commodus by a group of conspirators

193 Year of three emperors, as Pertinax, Didius Julianus and Septimius Severus take control in quick succession

194 Septimius Severus embarks on a war against the Parthians (to 195)

195 Severus conquers Byzantium, held by followers of Pescennius Niger. Clodius Albinus is proclaimed emperor by the legions in Britain

197 Clodius Albinus' defeat by Severus at the Battle of Lugdunum brings the civil war to an end

199 Peace between Rome and the Parthian empire is concluded with the foundation of the Roman province of Mesopotamia

c. **200** The road system is largely complete throughout the empire

205 Execution of Plautianus

211 Severus dies at York while on campaign in Britain. He is succeeded by his sons Caracalla and Geta

Romans and barbarians join battle, in a detail from a painting by the Roman Mannerist artist Giuseppe Cesari (1568–1640). The first-century AD pro-Roman Jewish historian Josephus was full of praise for the Roman army's discipline: 'Absolute obedience to the officers creates an army which is well-behaved in peacetime and which moves as a single body in battle.' However, by the second century, its tactics had become ossified and predictable.

Yet, for all their ostensible differences, these two works both focus on minutiae of tactics in preference to analyzing more fundamental strategic problems. Senior Roman officers were trained, first and foremost, in the arts of administration. And this, in a nutshell, was the Achilles' heel of the Roman army in the second century AD. Rome had no war college, and Roman commanders' understanding of warfare seems primarily to have been based upon the analysis of examples of past success rather than a wider appreciation of the factors that underlay that success. The most renowned generals of history – Alexander, Hannibal and Caesar – had all had the ability to adjust rapidly to changing circumstances. The generals who served under Marcus, though perfectly competent, seem rather to have favoured tradition over experimentation. Ironically, in learning by rote the career details of their illustrious predecessors, they failed to take on board precisely those essential, spontaneous qualities – innovation and flexibility – that made them truly great. And so, notwithstanding its initial success, Marcus' invasion of Persia in AD 163 was based on a plan devised by Julius Caesar in 44 BC, while the northern wars fought during his reign dragged on interminably because the enemy steadfastly refused to offer battle under conditions that Roman commanders had been schooled to deal with.

The issues that Tacitus highlighted – cultural complacency and the vast expanse of the non-Roman world to the north – would come to dominate the 80 years following Marcus' death. Beginning with internal upheaval, the empire's problems were later compounded by the sudden emergence of a militarily competent Persian dynasty in the 220s. Persian successes would so weaken Rome's central government that its defences against the northern tribes crumbled. Consequently, for more than a decade after AD 260, the empire split into three parts. The catastrophes of the 250s and 260s ushered in an era of radical reform rivalling that which saw the emergence of the imperial office in the time of Augustus. By AD 337, the Roman emperor was a Christian and Rome had ceased to be the centre of imperial government.

Theatre of blood

The reign of Commodus was hallmarked by moments of extraordinary theatricality and brutality. Throughout his 12 years in power, Commodus showed a marked aversion to hands-on governance. Instead, he devoted his time to pleasure, and, ultimately, to learning the arts of an amphitheatrical entertainer. Meanwhile, those of his lieutenants to whom he entrusted the reins of government did their best to upset the fragile balance achieved by the emperors of the previous century. In the end, the scales tipped over into civil war, heralding the rise of a new regime in which the tensions unleashed at the end of Commodus' reign would never be fully reconciled.

The basic problem with Commodus was simply that he wasn't very bright. Naturally inclined to sloth, he left the business of government to a series of favourites. They, in turn, alienated those who wished for a continuation of the Antonine style of collaborative rule, even though they were often unwilling to make the concessions necessary for that system to work. The first crisis of Commodus' reign, two years after his accession, arose from nothing more serious than his crass insensitivity to the feelings of his elder sister Lucilla, who felt that the emperor's wife was threatening the prerogatives due to her, as the widow of Lucius Verus. Her response to the slights that she perceived was to gather about her a group of discontented younger senators and hatch a plot to assassinate her brother. The conspiracy might even have succeeded, if the chosen assassin had not shouted 'the senate sends you this' as he drew a dagger on the emperor, whereupon he was

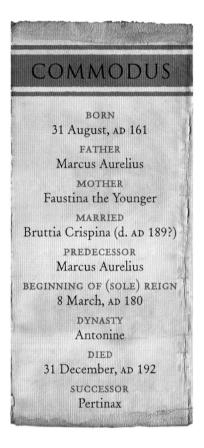

COMMODUS

BORN
31 August, AD 161
FATHER
Marcus Aurelius
MOTHER
Faustina the Younger
MARRIED
Bruttia Crispina (d. AD 189?)
PREDECESSOR
Marcus Aurelius
BEGINNING OF (SOLE) REIGN
8 March, AD 180
DYNASTY
Antonine
DIED
31 December, AD 192
SUCCESSOR
Pertinax

overpowered and disarmed. What emerged from this bungled assassination was far from the conspirators' intentions. One of the praetorian prefects, a man named Tigidius Perennis, noticed the emperor's abject terror during the incident and decided to turn it to his advantage. Inveigling himself into a position of trust by exploiting Commodus' fears, Perennis dominated the government for the next five years.

Perennis was the most powerful official since Sejanus, and just as brutal and efficient in eliminating his political rivals. He took control of organizing the security of the empire, a task in which he acquitted himself well. The generals that Perennis appointed successfully maintained order on the frontiers, and so the image of Commodus that was projected to the provinces was largely positive, in marked contrast to his appalling reputation in Rome. Yet Perennis had made many powerful enemies in Rome, especially in Commodus' inner circle, and before long Commodus' chief *cubicularius*, Marcus Aurelius Cleander, conspired to remove him. When a delegation of soldiers from mutinous legions in Britain arrived in Rome to warn Commodus of an alleged plot against him by Perennis, Cleander corroborated their claims and secured the emperor's agreement in having the legionaries murder the praetorian prefect. Cleander, whose background as a former slave made it impossible for him to claim a position that was formally outside the palace bureaucracy, now managed the state under the title of *pugione*, which may be translated as 'dagger bearer' or, perhaps more accurately, 'emperor's bodyguard'.

> 'This man was not naturally evil, but was as simple as any person that ever lived. His stupidity, together with his cowardice, enslaved him to his companions, and it was through them, at first, that he missed out on the better life and was then led into cruel and lustful ways.'
>
> CASSIUS DIO, HISTORY OF ROME, 72.1

Cleander's influence remained unchecked for a number of years until AD 189, when the prefect of the grain supply, in collusion with other figures in the court – including Commodus' sister Fadilla and his mistress, Marcia – arranged for a riot to take place in the Circus Maximus. The plan was to discredit Cleander in the emperor's eyes, and it worked brilliantly. The trouble began when a gigantic mime actress entered the arena and told the crowd that Cleander was planning to starve them; when the mob took to the streets, Commodus ordered Cleander's immediate execution. Effective government now devolved to Marcia, Eclectus (the new *cubicularius*, with whom she had a longstanding romantic liaison) and the new praetorian prefect.

COMMODUS THE SHOWMAN

Unlike his father Marcus Aurelius, Commodus had no ambition to conduct military campaigns, and spent most of his reign in Rome. A man of extravagant and wanton tastes, Commodus was fond of both gladiators and the god Hercules. So great was his affection for both that he wanted to emulate them. He was also extremely vain, and so had Rome renamed *colonia Commodiana* in his own honour. Rome's renaming took place in AD 190, the same year that Commodus added the name Hercules to his own after displaying his skill as a beast hunter in the amphitheatre at Lanuvium.

At the *ludi Romani* in AD 192, Commodus appeared in the Colosseum as both a beast hunter and gladiator in a series of performances that were intended to evoke the 12 labours of Hercules. The events included Commodus fighting gladiators (who were armed with wooden weapons) and a wide range of other events. Among these were displays of archery – including, we are told, the decapitation of ostriches with specially designed arrows – and the massacre of physically disabled people who were dressed as mythological monsters to recall Hercules' role in the battle between the Gods and Giants. At one point Cassius Dio says that he even held up the head of an ostrich in front of the seats where the senators sat, suggesting that he could do the same to them. Clearly absurd though this spectacle must have been, the senators dared not be seen laughing at the emperor. By the time of Commodus' assassination, the senate hated him so profoundly that it ordered statues depicting him to be torn down and his name to be chiselled off public inscriptions.

Commodus entering the Colosseum at the head of a band of gladiators. Cassius Dio says that his feats of archery included killing a panther in the arena.

The biggest problem facing the new governing coalition was that Commodus was growing ever more unbridled in his debauchery. He began to present himself as the god Hercules and ordered that Rome be renamed in his honour. In the autumn of AD 192 he took to the floor of the amphitheatre. Having trained extensively as a public combatant – he may even have moved into a gladiatorial dormitory for

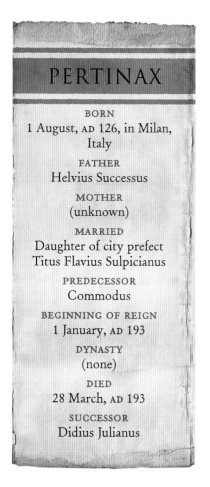

PERTINAX

BORN
1 August, AD 126, in Milan, Italy

FATHER
Helvius Successus

MOTHER
(unknown)

MARRIED
Daughter of city prefect Titus Flavius Sulpicianus

PREDECESSOR
Commodus

BEGINNING OF REIGN
1 January, AD 193

DYNASTY
(none)

DIED
28 March, AD 193

SUCCESSOR
Didius Julianus

a spell – he treated the Roman people to displays of his fighting prowess. In one of these extravaganzas, he staged a sickening entertainment that involved him slaughtering physically handicapped people whom he had forced to dress up as mythological enemies of the gods. This grotesque spectacle proved to be the final straw. On the last day of AD 192, Marcia fed Commodus some poisoned beef; when it appeared that he might recover, she ordered a professional wrestler, Narcissus, to finish the job by strangling the emperor.

Sold to the highest bidder

The plot to assassinate Commodus had been organized in such an impromptu and secretive manner that the conspirators had not even had time to arrange the succession in advance. So it was that in the middle of the night, the elderly Helvius Pertinax (AD 126–193), twice consul of Rome and one of Marcus' best generals, was approached by the assassins and offered the job. He duly became emperor on New Year's Day, AD 193. The appointment was a disaster, with Pertinax turning out to be a harsh and unpopular disciplinarian. In particular, the praetorian guard resented the fact that the palace staff had conspired to murder an emperor whose eccentricities had worked in its favour, and was instantly restive when presented with a *fait accompli*. In March, a group of 300 praetorians left their camp and stormed the palace. When Pertinax tried to face them down, he was killed. He had reigned for just 86 days.

The day and night after the death of Pertinax witnessed one of the most bizarre events in the long history of Rome. The praetorian guard was adamant that no man could be made emperor without its prior approval, but on this occasion had no candidate in mind. One of the praetorian prefects had gone to the camp to negotiate on his own behalf when there suddenly appeared outside the walls a wealthy senator named Didius Julianus (AD 133–193). Accompanied by a crowd of followers chanting slogans in favour of Commodus, he gained admission to the camp and, having promised to pay a much larger accession *donativum*, or gift, than his rival, won the guards' support. Accession gifts had a long history going back to the time of Tiberius, and the amount offered by Julianus was not much more than the sum Marcus Aurelius had paid when he became emperor. Yet the circumstances were far more nakedly corrupt when

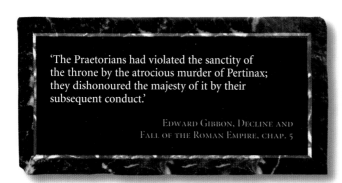

'The Praetorians had violated the sanctity of the throne by the atrocious murder of Pertinax; they dishonoured the majesty of it by their subsequent conduct.'

EDWARD GIBBON, DECLINE AND FALL OF THE ROMAN EMPIRE, CHAP. 5

A revolt of the Praetorian Guard. This force, which first came to prominence under Tiberius, overplayed its hand as power-broker in the murder of Pertinax and the installation of Didius Julianus. When Septimius Severus took control, he disbanded the Praetorians and replaced them with an élite guard drawn from his own trusted Pannonian legions.

Julianus took office. In encouraging this public auction of the throne, Julianus colluded in the notion that the army held the whip hand in appointing a new emperor. This lesson was immediately taken to heart outside Rome.

Out of Africa

Long before AD 193, Tacitus had written in his account of the civil wars of AD 69 that the dread secret of empire was that it was possible to make an emperor elsewhere than in Rome. No sooner had the events surrounding Julianus' succession became known in the provinces than three provincial governors were immediately proclaimed emperor by their armies: Clodius Albinus (c. AD 145–197) in Britain, Pescennius Niger (c. AD 145–194) in Syria and Septimius Severus (AD 146–211) on the Danube. It is entirely likely that all three men, aware that Pertinax was in a weak position, had already planned some sort of intervention; his murder simply provided the excuse they needed.

Of the three new claimants to the throne, Severus was in the strongest position. The descendant of a wealthy North African family of Phoenician ancestry in the city of Leptis Magna, he had risen through the ranks of the senate to become commander of Roman forces in Pannonia by AD 191. The central European armies, totalling ten legions, were the most powerful in the empire. Moreover, Severus had taken care to forge an alliance with the other governors in the region – one of whom was his elder brother – and they were all at his disposal. And, last but not least, of all the pretenders to the throne, he was physically closest to Rome. Proclaimed emperor at Carnuntum (on the Danube, now in Lower Austria) on 9 April, Severus was in Rome by mid-June. As Severus approached the city, Julianus realized that

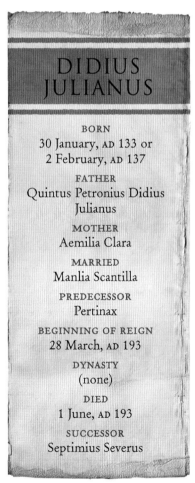

DIDIUS JULIANUS

BORN
30 January, AD 133 or
2 February, AD 137

FATHER
Quintus Petronius Didius
Julianus

MOTHER
Aemilia Clara

MARRIED
Manlia Scantilla

PREDECESSOR
Pertinax

BEGINNING OF REIGN
28 March, AD 193

DYNASTY
(none)

DIED
1 June, AD 193

SUCCESSOR
Septimius Severus

The son of a wealthy family of the equestrian class in North Africa, Septimius Severus took his first step towards power when he was elected a senator in AD 172. His firm rule, if at times brutal, helped put the empire back on course after the wasted years of Commodus' reign.

resistance would be futile; he was soon dispatched by a member of the praetorian guard. His pathetic last words were reportedly 'But what evil have I done. Whom have I killed?' The betrayal of Julianus did the guard no good – Severus dismissed them and appointed members of his army in their place. He then departed to attack Niger and struck a deal with Albinus, trading the position of heir apparent, or Caesar, in return for his loyalty. This alliance was merely a temporary expedient.

Meanwhile, Pescennius Niger's actions in the east had already precipitated civil war. Heavily outnumbered, he knew that his only hope of success lay in quickly invading territory held by Severus and winning swift victories before his rival could concentrate his forces. For his part, Severus had needed few men to take Rome and so had lost no time in dispatching a large part of his army to face Niger. Before long, he had managed to displace the theatre of war eastward through Turkey into Syria. Winning the final battle in May AD 194 at a place called Issus – previously famous as the site of a great victory by Alexander the Great – Severus spent the rest of the year hunting down supporters of Niger, rewarding those who had switched allegiance and launching an expedition against the western provinces of the Persian empire. The immediate pretext for this act of aggression was that the Persian king had aided Niger. Even before returning to Rome, Severus

THE BATTLE OF LUGDUNUM

This engagement between Septimius Severus and the usurper Clodius Albinus, governor of Britain, was one of the bloodiest and fiercely contested battles ever fought between Roman forces. Historical records of the clash are scanty, but it is estimated that a total of around 100,000 troops were involved. In the autumn of AD 196, Albinus crossed over to Gaul with a some 40,000 men from the British garrison to confront his rival claimant to the Roman throne. There, he won an initial skirmish against Severus' legate Virius Lupus, but he could not hope to prevail against Severus' vastly superior forces, and was presently joined by forces from Spain (Hispania Tarraconensis). Meanwhile, Severus marched on Gaul at the head of his powerful Danubian and German legions.

On 19 February, AD 197, the two sides met at Lugdunum, the modern French city of Lyons on the River Rhône. The battle raged for two days, with the fortunes of both sides ebbing and flowing. Eventually, however, Severus' superiority in cavalry turned the tide of battle in his favour. It is not known whether Albinus was killed during the fighting or committed suicide. In a foretaste of his later bloodthirsty vindictiveness, Septimius Severus had his enemy's body beheaded and rode over the headless corpse in his chariot, before sending Albinus' head back to Rome as a warning to potential opponents there. The body itself, along with those of Albinus' immediate family members and senatorial supporters, was thrown into the Rhône.

elevated Caracalla, the elder of his two sons, to the rank of Caesar. This amounted to a declaration of war on Albinus, who was crushed after fierce fighting in February AD 197 at the Battle of Lugdunum (Lyons).

Rome's new dictator

Between his return to Rome in AD 195 and his departure to fight against Albinus, Severus took the remarkable step of retroactively having himself adopted into the family of Marcus Aurelius. This attempt to validate his claim to authority was backed by the specious assertion that Commodus was his brother. It could have been interpreted as a salute to the traditions of an earlier age, but Severus eschewed the merciful moderation of his new-found Antonine ancestors. Rather, his avowed role-model was the dictator Sulla, a fact he made plain in a thinly veiled threat to senators when they protested at his deification of Commodus. His large-scale executions of men who were suspected of sympathizing with his rivals certainly recalled Sulla's proscriptions.

Although Severus filled Rome with monuments to his regime, he clearly did not feel at ease in the capital. Immediately after defeating Albinus, he took off for a further campaign in the east, sacking the Persian capital at Ctesiphon, and adding new provinces between the Euphrates and Tigris rivers in what is now southeastern Turkey. This was the first significant addition of new territory to the empire since the time of Trajan, and it soon proved to be a source of serious trouble. The new province, known as Mesopotamia, was a constant provocation and *casus belli* to later Persian kings, who saw Roman control of the region as a threat to their security.

In the years following his invasion of Persia, Severus continued to traverse the provinces, visiting first Egypt and then his North African homeland, where he rebuilt his home city of Leptis Magna to make it appear a suitable place of origin for an emperor. While he was engaged on his extensive travels, Severus turned over much of the day-to-day administration of the empire to his kinsman and fellow North African Gaius Fulvius Plautianus (d. AD 205). Plautianus had performed invaluable services for Severus in the perilous year of AD 193 – including ensuring that his wife and children were spirited out of Rome before Julianus could do them harm – and was now sole praetorian prefect. He further strengthened his bond to the emperor by marrying off his daughter Fulvia Plautilla to Severus' son Caracalla. Plautianus enjoyed such favour at this time that statues of him were erected alongside those of close members of the imperial household.

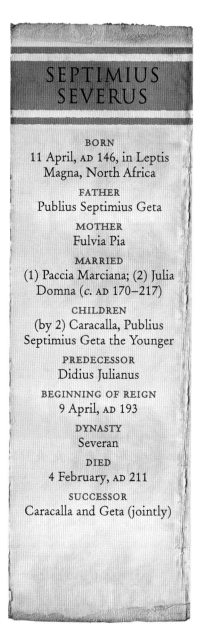

SEPTIMIUS SEVERUS

BORN
11 April, AD 146, in Leptis Magna, North Africa

FATHER
Publius Septimius Geta

MOTHER
Fulvia Pia

MARRIED
(1) Paccia Marciana; (2) Julia Domna (c. AD 170–217)

CHILDREN
(by 2) Caracalla, Publius Septimius Geta the Younger

PREDECESSOR
Didius Julianus

BEGINNING OF REIGN
9 April, AD 193

DYNASTY
Severan

DIED
4 February, AD 211

SUCCESSOR
Caracalla and Geta (jointly)

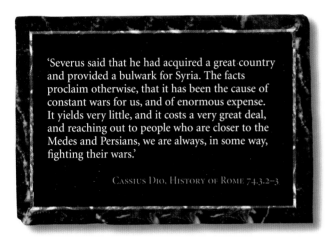

'Severus said that he had acquired a great country and provided a bulwark for Syria. The facts proclaim otherwise, that it has been the cause of constant wars for us, and of enormous expense. It yields very little, and it costs a very great deal, and reaching out to people who are closer to the Medes and Persians, we are always, in some way, fighting their wars.'

CASSIUS DIO, HISTORY OF ROME 74.3.2–3

Cassius Dio claims that when unfounded rumours of Plautianus' demise swept the empire, civic officials tore down these statues and were subsequently executed for treason.

A troubled succession

In the course of AD 205 the relationship between Severus and Plautianus cooled dramatically. The agent of the change may have been Caracalla, who hated both his wife Fulvia Plautilla and his father-in-law. Accused of organizing a conspiracy, Plautianus was summoned to the palace and summarily executed.

Effective control of the state now passed to a group of Severus' most trusted confederates, including Papinian (AD 142–212), the greatest jurist of the age. Another key member of the charmed circle was Severus' wife, Julia Domna (c. AD 170–217). Julia was related to the formerly royal house of the Syrian city of Emesa (Homs), whose members now held the priesthood of the sky god; Severus – like many emperors before him spellbound by astrology – is reputed to have married her after he learned that her horoscope predicted she would marry a king. Their marriage was a happy one, and she bore Severus two sons in quick succession – Caracalla in AD 186 and Publius Septimius Geta in AD 189. The two boys were quarrelsome from the outset; tensions between them were not eased by the fact that their mother made it quite clear that Geta was her favourite. In his final years, their father made several fruitless attempts to reconcile his warring sons.

Ever ambivalent about Rome, Septimius Severus took personal command of a campaign in northern Britain in AD 209 to push back tribes that had broken through the Antonine Wall. Operations went well, but the emperor fell severely ill and died at Eboracum (York) in February AD 211. Prior to his death, Severus probably recognized that neither of his sons – both of whom accompanied him on his British campaign – was yet capable of ruling on his own. He therefore decreed that they should ascend the throne jointly; accordingly, in AD 211, Caracalla and Geta became co-emperors of Rome, an arrangement that had not been witnessed for 50 years since the joint rule of Marcus Aurelius and Lucius Verus. The sibling rivalry between Severus' two sons was driven by intense hatred and, before the year was through, their turbulent relationship was to end in bloodshed.

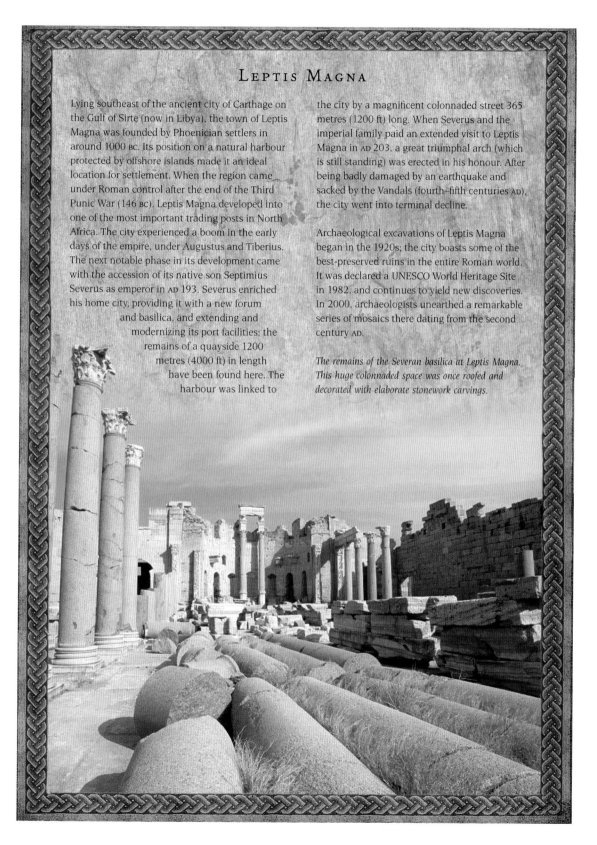

LEPTIS MAGNA

Lying southeast of the ancient city of Carthage on the Gulf of Sirte (now in Libya), the town of Leptis Magna was founded by Phoenician settlers in around 1000 BC. Its position on a natural harbour protected by offshore islands made it an ideal location for settlement. When the region came under Roman control after the end of the Third Punic War (146 BC), Leptis Magna developed into one of the most important trading posts in North Africa. The city experienced a boom in the early days of the empire, under Augustus and Tiberius. The next notable phase in its development came with the accession of its native son Septimius Severus as emperor in AD 193. Severus enriched his home city, providing it with a new forum and basilica, and extending and modernizing its port facilities; the remains of a quayside 1200 metres (4000 ft) in length have been found here. The harbour was linked to the city by a magnificent colonnaded street 365 metres (1200 ft) long. When Severus and the imperial family paid an extended visit to Leptis Magna in AD 203, a great triumphal arch (which is still standing) was erected in his honour. After being badly damaged by an earthquake and sacked by the Vandals (fourth–fifth centuries AD), the city went into terminal decline.

Archaeological excavations of Leptis Magna began in the 1920s; the city boasts some of the best-preserved ruins in the entire Roman world. It was declared a UNESCO World Heritage Site in 1982, and continues to yield new discoveries. In 2000, archaeologists unearthed a remarkable series of mosaics there dating from the second century AD.

The remains of the Severan basilica at Leptis Magna. This huge colonnaded space was once roofed and decorated with elaborate stonework carvings.

143

Inadequates and Misfits: Emperors of the Early Third Century (AD 211–238)

Severus' reported deathbed advice to his sons was that they should 'live in harmony with one another, enrich the soldiers, and despise everyone else'. The second and final elements of this edict represent a radical break with the policies of the Antonine age. While careful to maintain good relations with the military, rulers from Tiberius onwards had always been wary of identifying too closely with it. It was a problematic new departure that the emperor's authority should now be seen to depend solely on the wishes of the army.

Septimius Severus' son, the emperor Caracalla. One upshot of the army's growing influence as power-broker in this period was that it was now virtually impossible for emperors to entrust significant commands to others, lest they found their authority usurped. The reigns of Severus' successors saw rulers with little military aptitude accompanying armies on campaign, with often catastrophic results.

If Severus had hoped that his sons would learn to get along, he would have been seriously disappointed at the outcome. By the time they returned to Rome, the new joint rulers had ceased speaking to each other, and set about dividing the imperial palace between them, walling off direct access points between the two zones. The administration was hopelessly split between advisers such as Papinian, who were devoted to trying to make dual government work, and partisans of either side. In this power struggle, Geta was at a severe disadvantage. He was younger, possibly less ruthless, and certainly less well connected than his brother. By 25 December, AD 211, Caracalla felt that he had gained enough of an upper hand to summon Geta to a private meeting. It was a trap; centurions of the guard concealed in the room butchered him as he sought the protection of his mother, who had come to mediate the encounter. A wholesale massacre then ensued of anyone, including Papinian, who was deemed potentially disloyal to Caracalla. It is alleged that this round of bloodletting claimed up to 12,000 lives.

A coin with the portrait of the joint emperor Geta, brother of Caracalla. Their lifelong sibling rivalry came to a deadly end when Geta was assassinated after just a few months in power.

The unpopular populist

For all his calculated brutality, Caracalla seems to have craved popular acclaim. He spent a great deal of time at the circus, gave private exhibitions of his skill as a hunter and was a competent enough athlete to master driving a racing chariot, albeit not in public. In styling himself a man of the people, his intention may have been to let the populace of Rome know that he shared their pleasures, while expressly avoiding the excessive showmanship of Commodus.

Early in AD 212, Caracalla also took the remarkable step of inviting the empire to share in his joy at having escaped unscathed the alleged plots of his brother by issuing an edict (the so-called *Constitutio Antoniniana*) that conferred citizenship upon all free-born inhabitants of the empire:

> '*Imperator Caesar Marcus Aurelius Augustus Antoninus Pius herewith decrees the following: After having received numerous requests and petitions enquiring above all how I propose to give thanks to the immortal gods for saving me by granting me victory over my enemies, I now deem it prudent to announce that I am minded to undertake in gratitude an act of great magnanimity and piety, as befits the gods' great majesty … Accordingly, I am granting to all those non-citizens who dwell within the borders of the Empire the rights of Roman citizenship, including all those who live in cities of whatever kind but with the exception of the* dediticii *[prisoners of war settled in Roman territory]. It is meet and proper that the general populace should also henceforth share in the joy of my victory. This edict shall redound to the greater glory of the Roman people.*'

(FROM A PAPYRUS FOUND IN EGYPT IN 1901 – N.B. INCLUDES EDITORIAL INTERPOLATIONS TO MAKE SENSE OF THE BADLY DAMAGED GREEK TEXT)

Most of Rome's imperial subjects had not been citizens prior to the promulgation of this edict. However, even taking Caracalla's professed motivation for this decree at face value, the impact of the *Constitutio* was more symbolic than real; people were still attached to the empire

TIMELINE

AD 211 Caracalla has his brother Geta murdered

212 The *Constitutio Antoniniana* is promulgated, making most freemen in the empire Roman citizens

215 The Antoninianus, a high-denomination silver coin, is issued

216 Rome conducts another war against the Parthians (to 217); the Baths of Caracalla are completed

217 Caracalla's murder near Carrhae precipitates a severe crisis for the empire

218 Elagabalus ascends the throne, and institutes worship of the sun deity in Rome

222 Severus Alexander becomes Roman emperor

225 Ardashir I topples the Parthian empire and founds the Sassanid dynasty

230 Sassanid forces attack the Roman province of Mesopotamia

235 Alexander Severus is murdered by his troops in Moguntiacum (Mainz)

238 The Year of Six Emperors. Goths invade the lower Danube region for the first time, devastating Moesia (Bulgaria) and Thrace

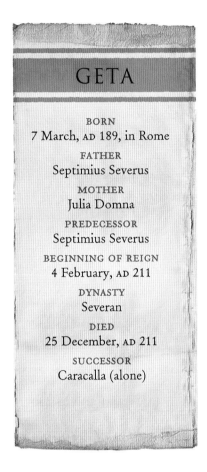

GETA

BORN
7 March, AD 189, in Rome

FATHER
Septimius Severus

MOTHER
Julia Domna

PREDECESSOR
Septimius Severus

BEGINNING OF REIGN
4 February, AD 211

DYNASTY
Severan

DIED
25 December, AD 211

SUCCESSOR
Caracalla (alone)

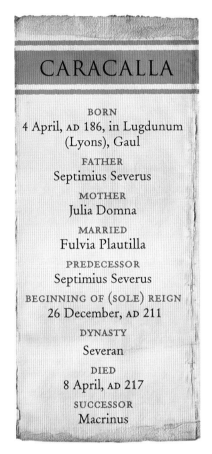

CARACALLA

BORN
4 April, AD 186, in Lugdunum
(Lyons), Gaul

FATHER
Septimius Severus

MOTHER
Julia Domna

MARRIED
Fulvia Plautilla

PREDECESSOR
Septimius Severus

BEGINNING OF (SOLE) REIGN
26 December, AD 211

DYNASTY
Severan

DIED
8 April, AD 217

SUCCESSOR
Macrinus

through the mechanisms of local government, meaning that it mattered little whether they were formally designated citizens or not. More significantly, the age-old protections that Roman citizens had enjoyed from cruel and unusual punishments, such as exposure to the beasts and crucifixion, had long since been eroded, so that only people who were both citizens and locally important people were now spared the horrors of those modes of execution. By the early third century, even high social status was not always adequate protection if the charge against a person was sufficiently serious.

Cassius Dio, for one, took a highly sceptical view of Caracalla's supposed magnanimity when he claimed that the *Constitutio Antoniniana* was a cynical move aimed solely at increasing taxes that were raised in hard currency. One result of the edict was indeed that more people now became liable to inheritance taxes. The decree ultimately derived its name from Septimius Severus' forced attempt to cover his own dynasty in some of the reflected glory of the Antonines. However, the spirit of the age of these 'new' Antonines was very different from that of their illustrious second-century predecessors.

Caracalla plainly failed in his objective of winning over the Roman people, despite ordering lavish public works such as the extensive Baths of Caracalla in AD 212. Instead, he took off for the provinces, journeying from the Rhine to the Danube before proceeding further east. As he spent more and more time in the company of his troops, he followed the dying words of his father by shamelessly currying favour with the army. He increased soldiers' pay substantially (to 1250 denarii

THE BATHS OF CARACALLA

Built between AD 212 and 216, the Baths of Caracalla was an extensive leisure complex containing not only *thermae* (public baths) with their hot, warm and cold rooms and other facilities but also gardens, gymnasia and a well-stocked library. Around the edge of the complex were several rooms used as shops, bars and brothels. Water was piped to the baths via an aqueduct that supplied Rome with fresh rainwater from hills 56 miles (90 kilometres) away. The dome of the circular hot bath was higher than that of the Pantheon, and in all over 1600 bathers could be accommodated. Elaborately decorated mosaic floors were laid throughout the building, which covered a total area of about 13 hectares (32 acres).

The Baths of Caracalla are a fine example of Roman expertise in hydraulic engineering: water flowed into a cistern and was then piped to hot and cold rooms.

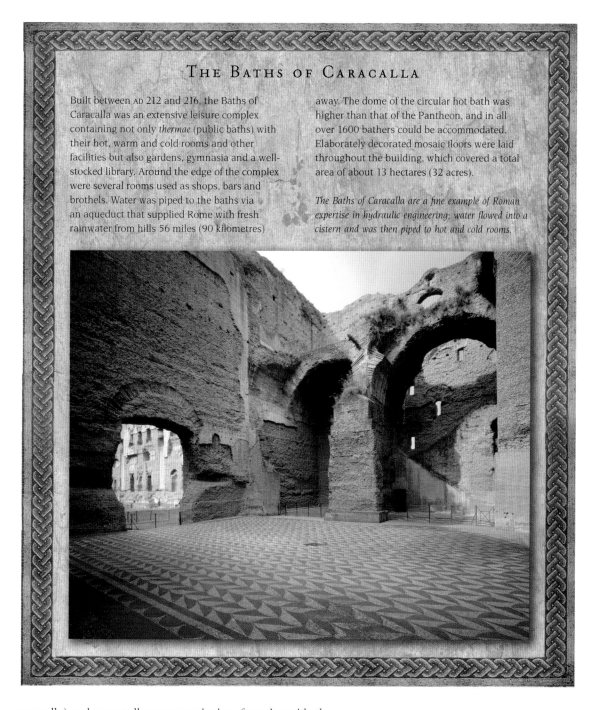

annually) and reportedly even marched on foot alongside the legionaries. The unashamed favouritism he displayed towards the military was only matched by his callous disregard towards civilian populations. In AD 215, Caracalla's response to insulting chants (regarding the death of his brother) from a hostile crowd that had assembled as he entered the city of Alexandria in Egypt was to unleash a wholesale massacre of his tormentors.

Taunted by a mob about the circumstances of his brother Geta's death, when Caracalla rode into Alexandria in AD 215, his patience snapped and he set his troops on the crowd. The governor of the city was executed for allowing the riot to take place, and thousands of protestors were killed.

MACRINUS

BORN
c. AD 185, in Mauretania, North Africa

FATHER
(unknown)

MOTHER
(unknown)

MARRIED
(unknown)

CHILDREN
Diadumenianus

PREDECESSOR
Caracalla

BEGINNING OF REIGN
8 April, AD 217

DYNASTY
None

DIED
June, AD 218

SUCCESSOR
Elagabalus

In the course of his travels Caracalla became fascinated with Alexander the Great, presenting himself as a new version of the great conqueror and even rearming some legions in the style of the ancient Macedonians. In AD 216, he resolved to undertake a serious military adventure, and emulate his hero Alexander by invading the Persian empire. By the end of that year, he stood on the plain of Gaugamela (near Mosul in northern Iraq), where Alexander had won one of his greatest victories, before withdrawing to overwinter with the army in Roman territory.

Caracalla had long fancied himself something of an antiquarian, with a particular interest in artifacts relating to the mythological past or to the gods. As he waited to launch his Parthian campaign, he decided to spend the first week of April AD 217 viewing ancient ruins around Carrhae – modern Harran in southern Turkey – one of the oldest inhabited sites on earth. Venturing out from the city one day to visit a nearby temple dedicated to the moon goddess Luna, he dismounted from his horse to relieve himself. As he did so, a man who had been suborned by Marcus Opellius Macrinus (AD 165–218), one of the praetorian prefects, ran him through with his sword. This undignified end was not unfitting for such a nefarious and disliked ruler.

A short interregnum

After several days of intense negotiation, the general staff agreed to make Macrinus emperor. Despite being implicated in the conspiracy against Caracalla, it was not a job that Macrinus sought with any great eagerness, as the situation confronting him was extremely dangerous. The king of Persia was advancing on Roman territory at the head of a substantial force, while discontent was rife among the rank and file of the Roman army. After an indecisive encounter with the Persians, who agreed to make peace in return for an enormous indemnity payment, Macrinus withdrew the army to spend the winter in Syria. He would have been better advised to return to Rome.

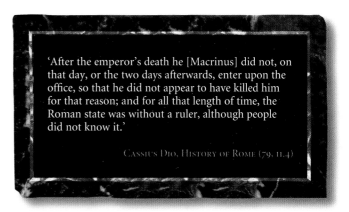

'After the emperor's death he [Macrinus] did not, on that day, or the two days afterwards, enter upon the office, so that he did not appear to have killed him for that reason; and for all that length of time, the Roman state was without a ruler, although people did not know it.'

CASSIUS DIO, HISTORY OF ROME (79, 11.4)

Never popular with the army, Macrinus made the situation worse when he declared his intention of rescinding the additional pay granted by Caracalla to new recruits. Although existing soldiers kept their new pay packages, they felt threatened by the move. Another cloud was also looming on Macrinus' horizon; Caracalla's mother Julia Domna, who had accompanied her son to the east, died in the early months of his reign, but her sister, Julia Maesa began to plot against the new emperor. Fearful that she would lose the prerogatives that went with being an imperial aunt, she withdrew to the family homeland of Emesa in Syria. There she encountered her teenaged nephew Varius Avitus Bassianus, who was the chief priest of the local sun-god Elagabal. Because he somewhat resembled Caracalla, she was able to convince soldiers of the legion stationed near the city that Bassianus was in fact his illegitimate son. The soldiers were already unhappy with Macrinus, and with the additional sweetener of a substantial bribe, promptly proclaimed the boy emperor when he was brought to their camp. Macrinus bungled an attempt to nip the revolt in the bud, but finally managed to muster a force to confront his rivals. The battle was evenly matched until Macrinus lost his nerve and fled the field. He got as far as Asia Minor before a centurion who had been sent in pursuit caught up with him and cut off his head.

The most eccentric emperor

Although his formal name as emperor was Marcus Aurelius Antoninus (reinforcing his spurious claim to be related to Caracalla), the young man from Emesa is generally known by a Latinized form of the name of his patron deity: Elagabalus (c. AD 203–222). His reign is one of the most controversial in Roman history, despite the best efforts of the effective palace staff that he inherited from Caracalla to rein in his excesses. The civil war that brought Elagabalus to the throne was essentially a struggle for control between members of the government

Julia Maesa (AD 165–224), the aunt of Caracalla, successfully plotted to overthrow Macrinus and install her grandson Elagabalus as emperor. She and her daughter Julia Soaemias corroborated his claim by falsely maintaining that the boy was Caracalla's illegitimate son.

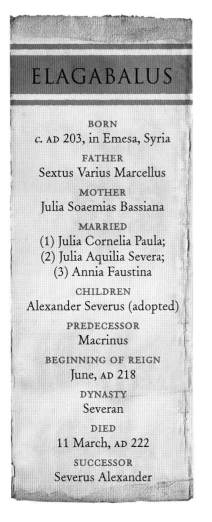

ELAGABALUS

BORN
c. AD 203, in Emesa, Syria

FATHER
Sextus Varius Marcellus

MOTHER
Julia Soaemias Bassiana

MARRIED
(1) Julia Cornelia Paula;
(2) Julia Aquilia Severa;
(3) Annia Faustina

CHILDREN
Alexander Severus (adopted)

PREDECESSOR
Macrinus

BEGINNING OF REIGN
June, AD 218

DYNASTY
Severan

DIED
11 March, AD 222

SUCCESSOR
Severus Alexander

who were closely associated with the palace and the more bureaucratic elements that had supported Macrinus. The ascendant palace group made genuine efforts to include members of the senate and senior equestrian bureaucracy in the regime.

Contemporary commentators such as Cassius Dio and Marius Maximus would later castigate the palace faction as a collection of worthless sexual deviants. This is probably a piece of retrospective self-justification, for both men were comfortably employed under this discredited regime. Marius continued to hold the prefecture of Rome that Macrinus had granted him, while Dio had a sinecure as overseer of financial affairs in his home province of Bithynia. The issue that would divide Dio and other decent provincial administrators from their patrons in Rome was the uncontrollably eccentric behaviour of the emperor.

Elagabalus believed passionately in the power of the sun-god and was intent on installing him as the principal deity in the Roman Pantheon. Giving Elagabal the Latin honorific *Deus Sol Invictus* ('God the Undefeated Sun'), Elagabalus dressed in elaborate priestly robes and led dances around the god's altar. However, the emperor's exotic form of piety struck more conventional Romans as nothing short of a transvestite charade, and Roman senators had limited tolerance for such expressions of cultural difference. As if all this were not enough, the emperor then announced that the gods of the Roman pantheon were henceforth all subservient to Elagabal. The pinnacle of Elagabalus' scandalous behaviour was reached when he married the Vestal Virgin Aquilia Severa, a blatant violation of one the most hallowed tenets of traditional Roman religious observance. The emperor claimed that 'godlike children' would result from their union.

While this religious controversy was raging, turmoil also reigned within the emperor's own *domus*. The imperial household was riven by factionalism, and relations between his mother Julia Soaemias and her sister Julia Mamaea were becoming increasingly strained. The matriarch of the clan, Julia Maesa, could do little to reconcile them. She may also have sensed that the emperor's very public eccentricities were becoming intolerable, that violent change was in the offing and that she should position herself so as to be able to exploit that change. In AD 221, she convinced Elagabalus to name his cousin, Severus Alexander (AD 208–235) as his heir. Too late, Elagabalus realized that by adopting a refreshingly conventional young man, he had effectively signed his own death warrant. At the beginning of AD 222 he went to

THE ELAGABALLIUM

The god Elagabal was originally a Semitic mountain god who was thought to inhabit a meteorite that stood in his temple at Emesa (Homs) in Syria. With the passage of time, understanding of the nature of this god changed, so that he came to be perceived as a sky god, and later still as the sun god. Because he was regarded as the supreme deity, the emperor Elagabalus decided to relocate him to a site on the Palatine Hill, taking over and enlarging a temple of Jupiter until a new purpose-built home could be constructed for him. While in Rome, the emperor attempted to find his god a wife, first taking the image of Vesta from her temple in the Forum (a move that was intended to parallel his own marriage to a Vestal Virgin). Later, after his own divorce from the Vestal, the emperor sought a new mate for his god, this

During his reign, Elagabalus rode roughshod over Roman sexual and religious mores. His eccentricities finally brought about his demise.

time the sky goddess Urania of Carthage, who also inhabited a meteorite, and was housed in a new temple on the Capitoline. In the final year of his reign, Elagabalus constructed an enormous new temple for the god, and held an elaborate ceremony in which the god 'drove' a chariot, with the emperor walking in front of it, to the new temple.

The emperor's actions appalled his Roman subjects, and, after his death, the first temple was re-dedicated to Jupiter, probably now under the title of *Jupiter Ultor* (Jupiter the Avenger). The fate of the second temple is unclear, but it is possible that, in the reign of Constantine (AD 307–337), it was incorporated into the church of Santa Croce in Gerusalemme.

the praetorian camp, and ordered them to murder Alexander. Although the precise details of what then occurred are confused, the praetorians (probably bribed by Maesa and Mamaea) ended up killing both Elagabalus and Julia Soaemias, dumping their bodies in the Tiber and proclaiming Severus Alexander emperor. The senate confirmed the decision of the guard banished the cult of the alien god Elagabal to Emesa. This would not, however, be the last time that a Roman emperor decided to favour a religion based upon the worship of what was originally a Semitic mountain god.

The power behind the throne

Severus Alexander, who was probably aged about 11 when he ascended the throne, was no more capable of running the empire than his cousin. What he did have, though, was a much smarter mother than his predecessor. Julia Mamaea moved quickly to secure the loyalty of members of the traditional aristocracy. Men who might reasonably have thought that their careers were over – including Cassius Dio – were brought back into positions of prominence, and the court ceased to be dominated by members of the royal household. In many ways, the new regime looked like a vision of the age of Marcus Aurelius, when experienced statesmen advised a young emperor, who then acted according

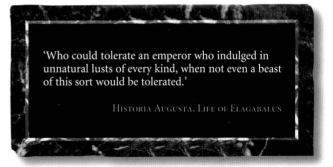

'Who could tolerate an emperor who indulged in unnatural lusts of every kind, when not even a beast of this sort would be tolerated.'

HISTORIA AUGUSTA, LIFE OF ELAGABALUS

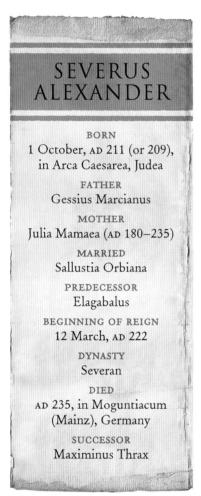

SEVERUS ALEXANDER

BORN
1 October, AD 211 (or 209),
in Arca Caesarea, Judea

FATHER
Gessius Marcianus

MOTHER
Julia Mamaea (AD 180–235)

MARRIED
Sallustia Orbiana

PREDECESSOR
Elagabalus

BEGINNING OF REIGN
12 March, AD 222

DYNASTY
Severan

DIED
AD 235, in Moguntiacum
(Mainz), Germany

SUCCESSOR
Maximinus Thrax

Severus Alexander survived his cousin Elagabalus' attempt to have him killed when he was still a young boy. Coming to the throne at the age of 11, Alexander was long under the thumb of his ambitious mother Julia Mamaea. When he lost the army's support, they were both murdered.

to this wise counsel. The problem was that appearances were deceptive in this case; Severus Alexander was in fact incapable of acting as a chief executive, and the government defaulted into a deeply conservative, reactive mentality. Under ordinary circumstances this might not have been fatal. But circumstances were far from ordinary.

In AD 225, Ardashir, ruler of a southern Iranian principality, overthrew the king of Parthia and founded a new dynasty – the Sassanids – which became renowned for its religious fundamentalism and military prowess. The Sassanid dynasty was to rule Persia for over 400 years until Muslim armies conquered the region in AD 651. Once again, Rome found itself under threat from a familiar quarter.

Rome dithered as Ardashir consolidated his power. The emperor and his advisors had no coherent strategy and crucially failed to appreciate that the powerful driving force behind the Iranian revolution was a strict adherence to the principles of Zoroastrianism. Ardashir believed that he was doing the will of Ahura Mazda, the god of Light and Truth, by destroying the servants of Ahriman, the god of the Lie and Darkness. Instead, Rome continued to back the discredited old regime. It was only when Ardashir launched raids against the province of Mesopotamia, and the garrison there mutinied, that the central government decided to act. Alexander himself journeyed east with his mother to oversee the operations.

The only positive thing that can be said about the Roman invasion of Parthia in AD 231 is that, unlike previous such ventures, it at least tried to show originality by not slavishly following Caesar's superannuated battle plan. That said – given the complete lack of decent intelligence about Ardashir's dispositions – it would have fared far better if it had. Caesar had been a past-master at bringing pressure to bear at decisive points against his enemy; by contrast, Severus' generals did just the opposite. Splitting the army into three parts, they sent one into northwestern Iran, where forces hostile to Ardashir still held out in the kingdom of Media, another on the familiar route towards Ctesiphon

NAQSH-I RUSTAM

The archaeological site of Naqsh-i Rustam ('picture of Rustam'), so called because later peoples interpreted the rock-cut reliefs there as images of the legendary Persian hero Rustam, is situated about eight miles (13 km) northwest of the ancient Persian capital of Persepolis. Its use prior to the sixth–fifth centuries BC remains obscure, but it was developed as a royal necropolis by Darius I of Persia (549–486 BC), who had his tomb built into the rock face. Six other kings from the ancient Achaemenid Persian empire were also laid to rest in tombs sunk into the cliffs. By the third century AD, Naqsh-i Rustam had developed into a site of great spiritual significance to Zoroastrianism, and it was this connection that drew Ardashir there. He

On this relief from Naqsh-i Rustam, Ardashir I, founder of the Sassanid dynasty, is shown receiving his crown from the supreme Zoroastrian god Ahura Mazda.

and several of his successors in the Sassanid empire had images of their victories carved into the cliffs. For example, some of the finest carvings at Naqsh-i Rustam are those from the reign of Ardashir's son Shapur I (r. AD 241–272) in the massive fire temple that was built there. These magnificently preserved reliefs show Shapur's triumph over the Roman emperors Gordian III, Philip the Arab and Valerian. The accompanying inscriptions, in Middle Persian, Parthian and Greek, provide key details about Shapur's wars against Rome and the structure of his kingdom.

The first of a series of shortlived 'soldier emperors' who ruled Rome in the mid-third century AD prior to the succession of Aurelian, Maximinus spent his entire three years in power on campaign, principally against the Germans and the Dacians. He came to be regarded by later historians as uncouth and cruel and was given the somewhat disparaging epithet 'Thrax' – 'the Thracian'.

from the north and a third down the River Euphrates in the direction of the kingdom of Mesene. These separate forces committed a cardinal military error by failing to advance in a coordinated fashion. No sooner had the southern column reached the vast marshlands that once extended north of the modern city of Basra than it was routed. The central column was stopped in its tracks, and only the northern expedition gained some measure of success.

These humiliations badly damaged Alexander's prestige, and he was desperate to try and recoup some success to offset the fiasco in Persia. Returning to Rome to celebrate a rather hollow triumph in AD 233, he departed the following year, again accompanied by his mother, for the German frontier. This effort to win back the loyalty of the army failed. In early March, AD 235 Alexander and Mamaea were murdered at Mainz in a mutiny led by a junior officer from Thrace called Julius Maximinus (*c.* AD 173–238).

Maximinus seized the throne for himself and immediately tried to secure his position by launching a series of attacks against the tribes north of the Rhine and Danube. He never set foot in Rome, and offended the populace by cutting back on subsidizing the grain supply. The traditional aristocracy plainly resented an upstart, and in February, AD 238 the senate lent its support to an elderly senator, Gordian (*c.* AD 159–238), who declared himself emperor in North Africa.

The year of the six emperors

The initial phases of the revolt of AD 238 were deeply depressing. Gordian I and his son Gordian II (*c.* AD 192–238), who had also been declared emperor, were killed by soldiers under the command of the governor of the neighbouring province of Numidia, a loyal supporter of Maximinus. Realizing that Maximinus was unlikely to be a merciful victor, the senate then elected a board of 20 men to uphold the defence of the realm against the emperor, whom it declared an enemy of the state. This action of the senate was eloquent testimony to the great store it set by the principle of collegial government. In accordance with this, not one but two men, Pupienus (*c.* AD 178–238) and Balbinus (d. AD 238), were promptly declared co-emperors. When friends of the deceased Gordians instigated a riot among the Roman people because that family had been cut out of the succession, Pupienus and Balbinus agreed to include the nephew of the younger Gordian, a youth of 13,

MAXIMINUS THRAX	GORDIAN I	GORDIAN II	PUPIENUS	BALBINUS	GORDIAN III
BORN *c.* AD 173, in Thrace	BORN *c.* AD 159	BORN *c.* AD 192	BORN *c.* AD 178	BORN (unknown)	BORN 20 January, AD 225
FATHER Gaius Julius Verus Maximus (AD 220–238)	FATHER (unknown)	FATHER (unknown)	FATHER (unknown)	FATHER (unknown)	FATHER (unknown)
MOTHER (unknown)	MOTHER (unknown)	MOTHER (unknown)	MOTHER (unknown)	MOTHER (unknown)	MOTHER Antonia Gordiana
PREDECESSOR Severus Alexander	CHILDREN Gordian II; Antonia Gordiana	CHILDREN (unknown)	CHILDREN (unknown)	CHILDREN (unknown)	MARRIED Sabina Tranquiliana
BEGINNING OF REIGN 20 March, AD 235	PREDECESSOR Maximinus Thrax	PREDECESSOR Maximinus Thrax	PREDECESSOR Gordian I and II	PREDECESSOR Gordian I and II	PREDECESSOR Pupienus and Balbinus
DYNASTY Severan	BEGINNING OF REIGN 22 March, AD 238	BEGINNING OF REIGN 22 March, AD 238	BEGINNING OF REIGN 22 April, AD 238	BEGINNING OF REIGN 22 April, AD 238	BEGINNING OF REIGN 22 April, AD 238
DIED April AD 238, in Aquileia, northern Italy	DYNASTY Gordianan	DYNASTY Gordianan	DYNASTY Gordianan	DYNASTY Gordianan	DYNASTY Gordianan
SUCCESSOR Gordian III	DIED 12 April, AD 238, in Carthage	DIED 12 April, AD 238, in Carthage	DIED 29 July, AD 238	DIED 29 July, AD 238	DIED 11 February, AD 244
	SUCCESSOR Pupienus and Balbinus	SUCCESSOR Pupienus and Balbinus	SUCCESSOR Gordian III	SUCCESSOR Gordian III	SUCCESSOR Philip the Arab

in their new imperial college as heir apparent. It is a sign of the deep discontent that was growing with Maximinus that declarations of loyalty to this unlikely coalition began to arrive from many parts of the empire even as the emperor led his battle-hardened army from the Balkans into Italy.

Even given this patent lack of enthusiasm for Maximinus, the events of the late winter and early spring of AD 238 must have astonished the contemporary world. When Maximinus entered Italy, his army came to a halt before the city of Aquileia, whose strong defences had once provided refuge for Marcus Aurelius in the early phase of his war against the northern tribes. Weeks passed while Maximinus tried unsuccessfully to capture the city. The army, which in all likelihood was not properly provisioned, grew restless, and, at the beginning of April, murdered its emperor.

Pupienus and Balbinus did not enjoy their triumph for long. The praetorian guard, which feared that it would be replaced in this highly volatile situation of shifting political allegiances, murdered the co-emperors and declared for Gordian III (AD 225–244). Since Maximinus had made his own son co-emperor when he invaded Italy, the young Gordian officially became the seventh person to hold the position of Augustus in the course of AD 238. His reign, which was dominated by members of the equestrian bureaucracy, would last for nearly six years before he fell victim to the new power that had arisen in the east.

Anarchy and Disorder:
The Crisis of the Third Century
(AD 239–270)

Rome was so inherently unstable that it was AD 241 before the empire was able to mount a truly robust response to the challenge posed by the Sassanid empire. Gordian III made his father-in-law, an equestrian named Timesitheus, praetorian prefect. Timesitheus took a long time to muster Rome's forces and get them into position to attack. Yet when the assault finally took place, in AD 243, the Persians under Ardashir's son Shapur I (r. AD 241–272) were roundly defeated, being pushed back over the Euphrates and routed at the Battle of Resaena.

A Sassanian relief sculpture from Naqsh-i Rustam shows Emperor Valerian (right) being forced to kneel and pay homage to the mounted figure of Shapur I. Valerian's capture in AD 260 marked an all-time low point in Roman military fortunes. Some later Roman sources even claimed that the emperor's body was skinned to provide a permanent trophy of Roman submission.

Timesitheus died suddenly, and his colleague as praetorian prefect, Julius Priscus, now the effective head of the government, elevated his own brother Marcus Julius Philippus (*c.* AD 204–249) to be his co-prefect. They remained in office as the army, now with Gordian in titular command, launched an ill-advised invasion of Iraq in the winter of AD 244. As the Romans established a bridgehead on the Euphrates from which to advance on Ctesiphon, Shapur struck. The Roman army was defeated and, shortly thereafter, Gordian was murdered in his camp. Philippus became emperor; he is known to history as Philip the Arab, since his family's origins lay in Syria.

*When Philip the Arab became emperor in AD 244, he transformed
his home town of Shahba (then in the Roman province of Syria,
now in Jordan) into a magnificent metropolis with modern
amenities. Renamed Philippopolis, it was protected with a new
defensive wall, and equipped with temples, baths, theatres, and
triumphal arches. Many of the new buildings had superb mosaics.*

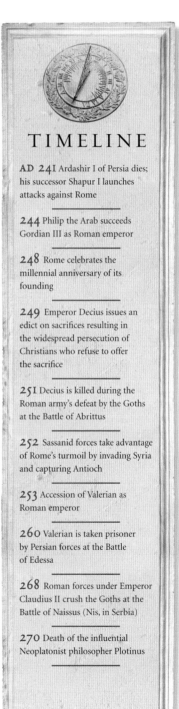

TIMELINE

AD 241 Ardashir I of Persia dies;
his successor Shapur I launches
attacks against Rome

244 Philip the Arab succeeds
Gordian III as Roman emperor

248 Rome celebrates the
millennial anniversary of its
founding

249 Emperor Decius issues an
edict on sacrifices resulting in
the widespread persecution of
Christians who refuse to offer
the sacrifice

251 Decius is killed during the
Roman army's defeat by the Goths
at the Battle of Abrittus

252 Sassanid forces take advantage
of Rome's turmoil by invading Syria
and capturing Antioch

253 Accession of Valerian as
Roman emperor

260 Valerian is taken prisoner
by Persian forces at the Battle
of Edessa

268 Roman forces under Emperor
Claudius II crush the Goths at the
Battle of Naissus (Nis, in Serbia)

270 Death of the influential
Neoplatonist philosopher Plotinus

A hands-on ruler

The reign of Philip marks an interesting turning point in the history
of the third century AD. He was the first equestrian emperor to govern
from Rome – neither Macrinus nor Maximinus had gone near the
capital – and he took a decidedly proactive approach to the empire's
more intractable problems. One of the major issues that he set out to
tackle was imperial finance. The ignominious peace settlement he was
forced to conclude with Persia after Gordian's defeat entailed large
reparations payments (and was soon violated anyway). A further huge
drain on the state's finances were the lavish celebrations held in AD 248
to mark the 1000th anniversary of the founding of Rome.

Despite his concern over the state of the imperial coffers, Philip would
have viewed the outlay on the millennial games as vital for proclaiming
his prestige. Another expensive but indispensable vanity project was
reconstruction of his native city of Shahba in modern Jordan. As an
outsider from a part of the empire that had not yet produced a ruler,
Philip would doubtless have felt the need to burnish his Roman
credentials by equipping his home town with magnificent edifices

THE MILLENNIAL GAMES

In either the fourth or third century BC the Romans initiated the practice of celebrating the end of a *saeculum* with sacrifices and games. The *saeculum*, which was theoretically the equivalent of the span of the lifetime of the longest-lived person on earth, was variously set at 100 or 110 years. The two methods of counting were both employed in the imperial period. Using the longer count, Augustus first reinstated the games in 17 BC, when the 700th anniversary of Rome was celebrated at the Parilia, the festival held on 21 April every year to commemorate the founding of the city in 753 BC. Claudius ordered games to be held in AD 48 to mark the 800th anniversary of the foundation of

Gladiators fighting a panther and a lion in the arena. Emperors spared no expense in staging major events to mark Rome's anniversaries.

the city, claiming that his count was more accurate, while Domitian celebrated games of his own in 88, six years early by the Augustan reckoning. Antoninus Pius celebrated the next games in AD 148 for the 900th anniversary of the city, while Alexander Severus reverted to the Augustan count and repeated the celebration in AD 204. Philip's games in AD 248 to mark the 1000th anniversary of Rome were the last to be held. The millenarian forebodings that this event unleashed may have been responsible for a rash of revolts that broke out later that year. The games were certainly spectacular, involving massive gladiatorial exhibitions and the destruction of a host of exotic animals.

befitting the birthplace of an emperor. Philippopolis – as the new city 56 miles (90 kilometres) south of Damascus was called – is remarkable for its many fine buildings, including temples, a theatre and bath houses, all in the Roman architectural style.

To pay for all of this, Philip increased the number of people in each community who were responsible for making up any shortfall in annual tax payments from their own pockets. Regarding the overall administration of the empire, he realized that the Severan centralization of authority around the person of the emperor was deeply flawed. He counteracted this trend by appointing men to effectively serve as deputy emperors in various regions. His first two such appointments were family members – Julius Priscus in the east, and a relative named Severianus in the Balkans.

Yet if this decentralization was at root a good idea, another of Philip's money-saving measures – cutting subsidies to the tribes north of the Danube – turned out to be not such a prudent move. Since the chiefs who were loyal depended upon these payments to maintain their status, the effect of Philip's cuts was either to undermine loyalists or turn them against Rome. Trouble flared almost immediately after he took office, and, in the wake of the millennial games, more serious revolts broke out in the regions of Moesia and Pannonia. Gaius Messius Quintus Decius (*c.* AD 201–251), a senator who had once served Maximinus in the civil war of AD 238, was sent to suppress the trouble on the Danube. However, no sooner had he succeeded in his mission than his troops persuaded him to proclaim himself emperor. He marched on Rome and defeated and killed Philip at Verona.

Attempts to revive past glories

Few emperors have left such a strong impression on the historical sources as Decius, who was passionately attached to a vision of the traditions of the imperial past, while utterly lacking the ability to secure those traditions. One of his most notable acts, almost as soon as he had defeated Philip, was to promulgate an edict ordering all citizens of the empire to sacrifice for the welfare of the state. Another was to issue coins commemorating the 'good emperors' of the past, as part of what appears to have been a concerted attempt to rewrite the history of the early third century. A third was to take for himself the name of Trajan, thus associating himself with a past golden age of imperial rule.

Unfortunately for both Decius and the empire as a whole, he lacked the qualities of his namesake. None of his initiatives addressed the fundamental causes of unrest along the northern frontiers or in the eastern provinces, where rebellions had been smouldering since the

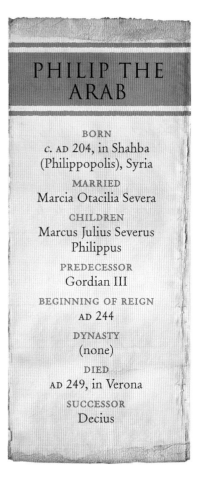

PHILIP THE ARAB

BORN
c. AD 204, in Shahba
(Philippopolis), Syria

MARRIED
Marcia Otacilia Severa

CHILDREN
Marcus Julius Severus
Philippus

PREDECESSOR
Gordian III

BEGINNING OF REIGN
AD 244

DYNASTY
(none)

DIED
AD 249, in Verona

SUCCESSOR
Decius

DECIUS' EDICT ON SACRIFICES

Shortly after he took the throne from Philip, Decius issued an edict requiring all his subjects to offer sacrifices to the gods for the well-being of the empire. The terms of the edict appear to have been quite detailed, ordering everyone to offer the sacrifice before the local authorities where they lived and to obtain a certificate testifying that they had done so. A number of these certificates have turned up on papyri from Egypt, of which the following text is a typical example:

'To those in charge of the sacrifice of the village of Theadelphia, from Aurelia Bellias, daughter of Peteres, and her daughter, Kapinis. We have always been constant in sacrificing to the gods, and now too, in your presence, in accordance with the regulations, I have poured libations and sacrificed and tasted the offerings, and I ask you to certify this below. May you continue to prosper.' (in a second hand) *'We, Aurelius Serenus and Aurelius Hermas, saw you sacrificing.'* (a third hand) *'I, Hermas, certify.'* (first hand once more) *'The first year of the Caesar Gaius Messius Quintus Traianus Decius Pius, Felix, Augustus, 21 June, 250.'*

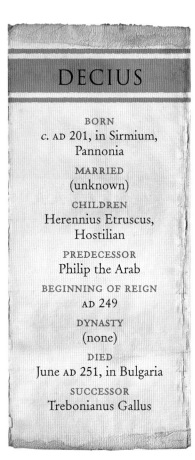

DECIUS

BORN
c. AD 201, in Sirmium, Pannonia

MARRIED
(unknown)

CHILDREN
Herennius Etruscus, Hostilian

PREDECESSOR
Philip the Arab

BEGINNING OF REIGN
AD 249

DYNASTY
(none)

DIED
June AD 251, in Bulgaria

SUCCESSOR
Trebonianus Gallus

later years of Philip's reign. Of the two threats, the one from the northern tribes – this time ancestors of the later Gothic peoples – was the more urgent. A large invading force of Goths swept across the Danube in AD 250, ambushing Decius and destroying a large part of his army before laying waste to the great city of Philippopolis (the settlement named after Philip of Macedon; now the city of Plovdiv in Bulgaria). Although Decius finally caught up with the raiders, his army was lured into swampy terrain and destroyed at the Battle of Abrittus in June AD 251. The emperor and his son both fell in this engagement. Trebonianus Gallus (*c.* AD 206–253), one of the governors of the Danubian provinces, succeeded to the throne.

Overwhelmed by enemies

In AD 252, Shapur I invaded the eastern provinces by moving up the Euphrates rather than across northern Mesopotamia, the expected route for a Persian attack. He crushed a Roman army at Barbalissos, before ravaging Syria and sacking Antioch. At the same time, a group of tribesmen from the Black Sea coast launched seaborne atttacks, bursting through the Dardanelles into the Aegean and sacking many cities there, including Ephesus, the greatest city of western Turkey.

The years AD 251–252 rank as the worst in Roman imperial history: three major cities were sacked, two armies were destroyed and the emperor was seemingly powerless to prevent the carnage. When the Danubian army won a victory in AD 253, it proclaimed its own general, Aemilianus (*c.* AD 207–253), emperor. Aemilianus defeated Gallus in central Italy before falling prey to Valerian (AD 200–260), an ally of Gallus who had arrived too late to help the former emperor.

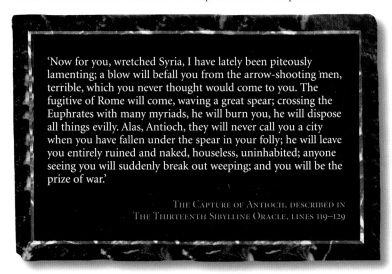

'Now for you, wretched Syria, I have lately been piteously lamenting; a blow will befall you from the arrow-shooting men, terrible, which you never thought would come to you. The fugitive of Rome will come, waving a great spear; crossing the Euphrates with many myriads, he will burn you, he will dispose all things evilly. Alas, Antioch, they will never call you a city when you have fallen under the spear in your folly; he will leave you entirely ruined and naked, houseless, uninhabited; anyone seeing you will suddenly break out weeping; and you will be the prize of war.'

THE CAPTURE OF ANTIOCH, DESCRIBED IN
THE THIRTEENTH SIBYLLINE ORACLE, LINES 119–129

Valerian, another deeply committed traditionalist, saw it as his task to defend the existing frontiers, while eliminating those who did not subscribe to the cultural unity of the empire. It was he who, in AD 257, issued the first empire-wide edict ordering active persecution of the Christian Church, the seizure of Christians' property and the execution of Christians who did not recant their beliefs. At the same time, he understood that he could not secure the empire on his own. As soon as he became emperor, Valerian elevated his son Gallienus (*c.* AD 218–268), then a man of mature years, to be his co-ruler, and appointed various sons of Gallienus to the rank of Caesar. The joint rule of Valerian and Gallienus with designated successors presaged more successful similar arrangements later in the century. By AD 260, however, this expedient probably signified no more than that the empire was now ungovernable by a single individual and on the brink of collapse.

A battle scene involving Romans and Germans on a sarcophagus made during the reign of Decius. The central figure on horseback is thought to be Decius' son Hostilian. Increasingly in the third century, Roman armies found themselves confronted by enemies who refused to engage in the kind of set-piece battles at which the Romans excelled. Instead, both the Persians and the Goths employed effective mobile, hit-and-run tactics against their adversary.

An emperor in chains

In AD 259, after failing to defend western Turkey from yet another naval assault from the Black Sea, Valerian found himself threatened by a new Persian invasion. Shapur crossed into the Roman province of Mesopotamia in the spring of AD 260 to find a Roman army weakened by disease and on the verge of mutiny. When, after suffering a defeat south of Edessa, Valerian sued for peace, Shapur threw him in chains

'A great battle took place between us and Caesar Valerian around Carrhae and Edessa and we took him prisoner with our own hand … and men of the Roman Empire, non-Aryans, we deported. We settled them in the empire of Iran in Persis, Parthia, Khuzistan, in Babylonia and in other lands where there were domains of our father, grandfathers, and our ancestors. We searched out for conquest many other lands, and we acquired fame for heroism.'

DEEDS OF THE DIVINE SHAPUR, 16

and sent him as a captive to Persia while his armies plundered the eastern provinces. He was the only Roman emperor ever to be taken prisoner. Later Roman tradition held that Shapur humiliated Valerian by using him as a human footstool when mounting his horse. Yet Persian sources claim that the ex-emperor ended his days in Bishapur, in eastern Iran, where he and some of his former troops were employed on engineering projects such as bridge-building.

The disgrace of Valerian's surrender precipitated a major crisis. In the east, as the Persian army overextended itself, the most senior official to survive the disaster, Fulvius Macrianus (d. AD 261), rallied what was left of the army and drove the Persians back. In this campaign, he was given invaluable military assistance by Septimius Odaenathus (d. AD 268), prince of Palmyra. The Palmyrenes had every reason to fear the rise of the Sassanian kingdom, as the Persians began to threaten Palmyra's traditional dominance over key trade routes in the Middle East. Odaenathus had initially tried to counter the Persian

TREBONIANUS GALLUS	AEMILIANUS	VALERIAN	GALLIENUS
BORN c. AD 206	BORN c. AD 207	BORN c. AD 200	BORN c. AD 218
MARRIED Afinia Gemina Baebiana	MARRIED Cornelia Supra	MARRIED Egnatia Mariniana	FATHER Valerian
CHILDREN Gaius Vibius Volusianus, Vibia Galla	PREDECESSOR Trebonianus Gallus	CHILDREN Gallienus, Valerianus Minor	MOTHER Egnatia Mariniana
PREDECESSOR Decius	BEGINNING OF REIGN AD 253	PREDECESSOR Aemilianus	MARRIED Cornelia Salonina
BEGINNING OF REIGN AD 251	DYNASTY Gordianan	BEGINNING OF REIGN AD 253	CHILDREN Valerianus, Saloninus, Egnatius, Marinianus
DIED August AD 253, at Terni, Umbria	DIED September AD 253, at Spoleto, Umbria	DYNASTY Gordianan	PREDECESSOR Aemilianus
SUCCESSOR Aemilianus	SUCCESSOR Valerian	DIED c. AD 260, at Bishapur, Iran	BEGINNING OF (SOLE) REIGN AD 260
		SUCCESSOR Gallienus	DIED AD 268, at Milan
			SUCCESSOR Claudius II

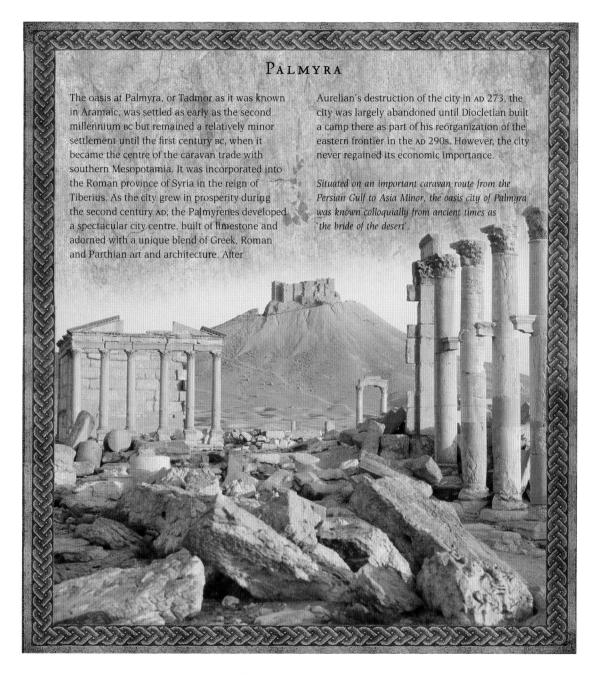

PALMYRA

The oasis at Palmyra, or Tadmor as it was known in Aramaic, was settled as early as the second millennium BC but remained a relatively minor settlement until the first century BC, when it became the centre of the caravan trade with southern Mesopotamia. It was incorporated into the Roman province of Syria in the reign of Tiberius. As the city grew in prosperity during the second century AD, the Palmyrenes developed a spectacular city centre, built of limestone and adorned with a unique blend of Greek, Roman and Parthian art and architecture. After

Aurelian's destruction of the city in AD 273, the city was largely abandoned until Diocletian built a camp there as part of his reorganization of the eastern frontier in the AD 290s. However, the city never regained its economic importance.

Situated on an important caravan route from the Persian Gulf to Asia Minor, the oasis city of Palmyra was known colloquially from ancient times as 'the bride of the desert'.

threat through diplomacy, sending gifts to Shapur I. However, when his overtures were rebuffed, Odaenathus renounced Palmyra's neutral stance, raised a large mounted army and threw in his lot with Rome.

After repulsing Shapur, Macrianus had his sons declared emperor and then invaded the Balkans, where two revolts had broken out at the news of Valerian's defeat. Gallienus defeated the uprisings and Macrianus' attempted invasion but, realizing that he could not restore order in the east without help, recognized Odaenathus as commander there.

A bust of the Emperor Gallienus. As well as scoring some important military successes during a difficult period for Rome, Gallienus was a pragmatic ruler who reversed his father Valerian's dogmatic policies against the Christians and reached an accommodation with this community. Freedom of worship was granted and some seized property restored.

Palmyrene armies enjoyed considerable success against Shapur, and Odaenathus proclaimed himself 'King of Kings', governing and dressing in a style more evocative of a Persian king than a Roman official. Nevertheless, Odaenathus remained loyal to Gallienus, never challenging his authority to appoint his own officials to provincial commands. The fruitful symbiotic relationship that developed in Palmyra between local initiative and centralized control demonstrates the continuing effectiveness of the traditional Roman policy of allowing regional rulers a large measure of self-determination in their dealings with the central Roman administration.

In fact, Gallienus faced a far worse situation in the west than in the east. Although he was able to deploy an army to regain control of the Balkans that had much greater battlefield mobility than traditional legionary forces, Gallienus could not reverse the effects of the revolt on the Rhine that had begun in AD 260. The leader of that uprising, Postumus, proclaimed the 'Empire of the Gauls' from his headquarters in Trier (Augusta Treverorum) and ruled the western provinces, including Spain and Britain, until his death in a military coup in the summer of AD 269. In AD 268, Gallienus, whose major effort to unseat Postumus had failed when he was wounded in battle during AD 265, fell victim to a plot by his own senior officers while trying to suppress yet another rebellion, staged this time by a senior commander in northern Italy.

A new model of governance

The eight years of Gallienus' sole reign presented a new model for governing the Roman empire that would, with refinements, re-emerge time and again over the next two centuries, before the western empire ceased to function altogether. This model conceived the empire not as a monolithic whole but as a series of self-contained units. The eastern provinces from Egypt through what is now Turkey formed a natural unit, as did the Central European provinces along with Italy and – for the present, at least – North Africa, whose surplus grain was crucial for Rome's survival. The provinces north and west of the Alps could look after themselves. In the long run, the main issue would be whether Central Europe should be joined to the eastern provinces or remain as a unit of empire in conjunction with Italy. While North Africa remained secure, Italy's importance remained unquestioned; the key question yet to be posed was what would happen to the empire if North Africa should ever be lost?

The death of Gallienus coincided with yet another crisis. The Central European tribes launched a major attack in AD 268 by both land and sea. The emperor who succeeded Gallienus, a Balkan general named Marcus Aurelius Claudius (AD 213–270), comprehensively defeated his barbarian foes in two key battles later that summer, crushing the Goths at Naissus and the Alamanni at Lake Benacus. Emperor Claudius II's accession came as the regimes in both Gaul and Palmyra were undergoing radical changes; Odaenathus was killed by an assassin from within his own entourage at the spring festival of Elagabal at Emesa in AD 268, while the government of Gaul descended into temporary chaos after Postumus' murder. Yet Claudius completely mismanaged the opportunity that these changes presented. He was unable to turn the situation in Gaul to his advantage and wrecked good relations between Rome and Palmyra by insisting that Odaenathus' position as general had died with him. After the defeat of a Roman expeditionary force in western Turkey, Palmyrene armies took over direct control of Arabia and Egypt. The driving force behind the operation was Odaenathus' young widow, Zenobia.

Claudius did not survive long enough to deal with the situation in the east. He died of disease while on campaign in the Balkans in the early part of AD 270, and was remembered ever afterwards as a great hero for his victories in AD 268. After a brief period of conflict, power passed to another of Gallienus' former marshals, again a man from the Balkans. This man would become the emperor Aurelian.

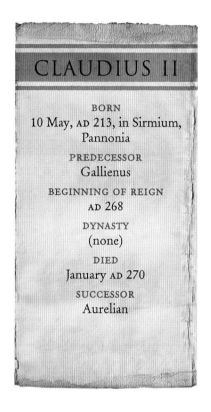

CLAUDIUS II

BORN
10 May, AD 213, in Sirmium, Pannonia

PREDECESSOR
Gallienus

BEGINNING OF REIGN
AD 268

DYNASTY
(none)

DIED
January AD 270

SUCCESSOR
Aurelian

Claudius II is credited with averting the crisis of the third century through his defeat of the barbarian tribes. Yet his short reign was also characterized by missed opportunities to forge useful alliances.

Steadying the Ship of State: Restoration of the Imperial Office (AD 270–305)

Aurelian faced daunting challenges when he came to power. The events of AD 268–269 had upset the equilibrium between the three parts of the empire, and the northern tribes were once more on the move. Between AD 270 and 271, Aurelian was forced into a desperate defence of Italy. Despite losing at least one major battle and having to put down a revolt in Rome, he finally swept the enemy from his part of the empire. Aurelian then went on to cement good relations with the Roman people, constructing a massive new ring of defensive ramparts around the capital. At the same time, he took the bold step of renouncing Roman control over Trajan's Dacian provinces.

Aurelian's achievements as emperor ranged from mundane but popular reforms such as adding pork to the subsidized food supply in Rome to vital consolidation of the empire's frontiers in the north and east. In recognition, the senate bestowed the honorific title 'restitutor orbis' ('restorer of the world') on him in AD 74.

After achieving stability at home and commencing the withdrawal from Dacia, Aurelian's next step was to launch a two-pronged invasion of Syria through Egypt and Asia Minor with the aim of crushing the armies of Zenobia and capturing Palmyra. He rapidly achieved his objective, but sought reconciliation over revenge; Zenobia was taken to Rome, where she remarried. Her descendants were serving in the senate more than a century later. Back in Syria, many Palmyrene officials were allowed to remain in their posts, possibly as a reward for abandoning their erstwhile masters when Aurelian invaded. It appears that Aurelian tried to make the transition back to direct Roman control as painless as possible. Yet however well-intentioned his policies, they did not work; no sooner had he embarked on his homeward journey

The Porta Asinara in the Aurelian Walls in Rome. Built between AD 271 and 273, this 12.5-mile (20-kilometre) long fortification gave the capital much-needed new protection against attacks by barbarian tribes.

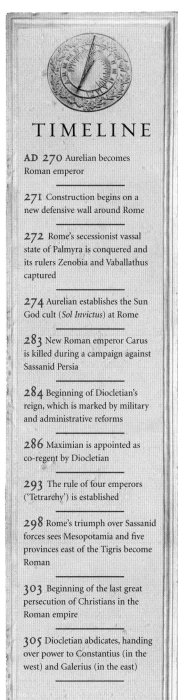

TIMELINE

AD 270 Aurelian becomes Roman emperor

271 Construction begins on a new defensive wall around Rome

272 Rome's secessionist vassal state of Palmyra is conquered and its rulers Zenobia and Vaballathus captured

274 Aurelian establishes the Sun God cult (*Sol Invictus*) at Rome

283 New Roman emperor Carus is killed during a campaign against Sassanid Persia

284 Beginning of Diocletian's reign, which is marked by military and administrative reforms

286 Maximian is appointed as co-regent by Diocletian

293 The rule of four emperors ('Tetrarchy') is established

298 Rome's triumph over Sassanid forces sees Mesopotamia and five provinces east of the Tigris become Roman

303 Beginning of the last great persecution of Christians in the Roman empire

305 Diocletian abdicates, handing over power to Constantius (in the west) and Galerius (in the east)

than an anti-Roman faction in Palmyra seized control of the city and defended it to the death. This time Aurelian showed no mercy. Palmyra's long history as one of the great trading posts of antiquity came to an abrupt end when his forces sacked the city in AD 273. The remainder of the trade that it had once controlled now shifted northwards to the cities of Mesopotamia.

The rehabilitation of Elagabal

Victory in the east had one other momentous outcome. One of the decisive battles against the Palmyrenes took place near Emesa (Homs), and when victory was assured, Aurelian suddenly announced that he had received aid from none other than the local sun god, Elagabal, who had been restored to his home under Alexander Severus some 50 years before. In homage, Aurelian ordered that the god's cult be reintroduced to Rome. In contrast to Elagabalus' theatrical observances, the deity was now worshipped in more sober fashion as the 'invincible sun,' with none of the exotic trappings of the earlier cult. No one in Rome seems to have objected to the revamped cult, and Aurelian's action set an important precedent for the close identification

ZENOBIA

A rare example of a powerful female ruler in the ancient world, Septimia Zenobia was born in around AD 240 into the family of a Palmyrene noble named Antiochus. She married the ruler of her home town of Palmyra, Odaenathus, and bore him a son, Vaballathus.

When her husband was murdered in the spring of AD 269 Zenobia took over as regent for Vaballathus. When Claudius refused to recognize her son's succession to the position of his father (something expected by the Palmyrenes, but out of line with Roman practice), she ordered her armies to overrun Egypt,

By all accounts, Zenobia was extremely attractive and gifted, and could speak several languages, including Greek, Arabic and Latin.

where she apparently presented herself as the descendant of Queen Cleopatra VII. Yet her armies were unable to resist the forces of Aurelian when they invaded Palmyra in AD 272.

After putting up a brave defence, Zenobia and her son were captured and taken as hostages to Rome. There is no record of what became of Vaballathus, but we are told that, after parading Zenobia in golden chains at his triumph in AD 274, Aurelian, struck by her dignity, installed her in a sumptuous villa at Tibur (Tivoli), and permitted her to marry a Roman senator. It is not recorded when she died.

of an emperor with a non-Roman divinity. The rationale for this new cult – a divine vision experienced by an emperor – would be invoked several decades later when Constantine introduced a heavily Romanized form of Christianity to the capital.

In reintroducing the cult of Elagabal, the new emperor dramatically reversed the avowedly chauvinistic, Romanocentric attitude to religion taken by Decius and Valerian. Aurelian's approach was far more in tune with the spirit of the age; he and his successors all came from the provinces, and as a result had a better feel for what would play well to an empire-wide audience. In tune with this trend, the concept of *virtus* that had for so long been the lynchpin of the personality cult of the emperor also began subtly to change. *Virtus* ceased to be identified with the moral code of ancient Rome, and instead became part of a more homogenized form of imperial propaganda with wider appeal.

Aurelian next turned his attention to the breakaway Gallic empire. Tetricus I (AD 271–273), the most recent incumbent of the Gallic throne, realized that his days as ruler were numbered. Accordingly, he signalled his willingness though diplomatic channels to relinquish his throne and, in a face-saving exercise, arranged with Aurelian to desert to the Roman camp when the two armies met in battle at Chalôns-en-Champagne. As a reward for his compliance, Tetricus was allowed to go into retirement with a sinecure administrative post in southern Italy. Within four years, then, Aurelian had achieved the seemingly impossible task of restoring the unity of the Roman empire.

Success was, however, fleeting. There were many parts of the empire
that had become freshly militarized in the years of chaos and that
were still not fully reintegrated within the imperial system, including
parts of Gaul, Syria, Egypt and southern Turkey. Aurelian did not
command the loyalty of all of his military commanders, and he
further compounded the problems of the empire by issuing a
'reformed' coinage that destroyed the existing tariff relationship
between gold and silver, causing rampant inflation that was not cured
for generations.

Confusion reigns supreme

In the late summer of AD 275, as he prepared for another campaign,
Aurelian was murdered in Thrace (European Turkey) by members of
his staff. Although his record as an administrator would forever be
marred by his monetary reform, his other achievements had endeared
him to the rank and file. The army buried him with great ceremony
near Perinthus, where he was killed, and lamented him as the saviour
of Rome.

Aurelian's assassins quickly realized that whatever plans they may have
had for the future were fated to founder on the opposition of the army.
They withdrew temporarily to the deserts of Jordan, where pockets of
resistance against the peace Aurelian had imposed on Palmyra still held

L. DOMITIUS AURELIAN	M. CLAUDIUS TACITUS	PROBUS	CARUS	CARINUS
BORN AD 214, in Dacia	BORN c. AD 200, in Terni, Umbria	BORN AD 232, in Sirmium, Pannonia	BORN (unknown date) in Narbo (Narbonne), France	BORN (unknown date)
MARRIED Ulpia Severina	MARRIED Cornelia Supra	PREDECESSOR Marcus Claudius Tacitus	CHILDREN Marcus Aurelius Carinus, Marcus Aurelius Numerian	FATHER Marcus Aurelius Carus
PREDECESSOR Claudius II	PREDECESSOR Aurelian	BEGINNING OF REIGN June, AD 276	PREDECESSOR Probus	MARRIED Magnia Urbica
BEGINNING OF REIGN 9 September, AD 270	BEGINNING OF REIGN 25 September, AD 275	DIED October, AD 282	BEGINNING OF REIGN October, AD 282	PREDECESSOR Carus
DIED September, AD 275, at Caenophrurium, Thrace	DIED June, AD 276, in Tyana, Anatolia	SUCCESSOR Carus	DIED August, AD 283, in Mesopotamia	BEGINNING OF (SOLE) REIGN August, AD 283
SUCCESSOR Marcus Claudius Tacitus	SUCCESSOR Probus		SUCCESSOR Carus and Numerian	DIED AD 285, Velika Morava, Serbia
				SUCCESSOR Diocletian

During his reign, Probus seems to have been generally unpopular with the army. One legend surrounding his death claimed that he was killed by overworked soldiers in the Balkans.

out. Loyalist officers now fell to considering the question of who should succeed as emperor. Their candidate was a general by the name of Marcus Claudius Tacitus (*c.* AD 200–276; no relation to the famous historian), who proved incapable of resolving the tensions that still seethed within the high command. While the army was engaged on operations in central Turkey, Aurelian's assassins infiltrated its main camp and slew Tacitus too.

The period of turmoil did not end with the murder of Tacitus. It had been his intention that the throne would pass to his brother Florian; yet that too was unacceptable to the army in the east, which promptly proclaimed its own general Probus (AD 232–282) as emperor. Florian failed to suppress the revolt, and Probus assumed leadership of the whole empire. He duly summoned a 'reconciliation' meeting with Aurelian's assassins. The meeting ended with a dinner party at which Probus resolved the dispute that had divided the governing class for more than a year by murdering his guests. Having seized power in such a violent manner, Probus spent most of his reign trying to suppress uprisings in areas as diverse as southern Turkey, Egypt and Gaul. In each case, these revolts arose as a result of particular local tensions, but they all combined to undermine his authority in Rome. In AD 281, the praetorian prefect, Marcus Aurelius Carus, realized that he had sufficient support to overthrow Probus, and promptly did so.

Nefarious machinations

Carus decided that the best method of consolidating his rule was to embark upon a punitive military expedition against Rome's old enemy, the Persians. In the aftermath of the deaths of Shapur I of Persia in AD 272 and his successor Hormizd I the following year, the Sassanian empire found itself weakened and fraught with discord. Claiming that he was avenging Valerian's disgrace, Carus was able to invade Iraq with relative ease. Then something went terribly wrong. Tradition has it that Carus' tent was struck by lightning. This may indeed have been the case, or perhaps the historical sources used the phrase as a euphemism for mutiny. Whatever the truth, it is clear that Carus' younger son, who had accompanied him east with the title of Caesar, now became Numerian Augustus, while his elder brother, who had remained at home, became Carinus Augustus.

Carinus' and Numerian's succession incurred the displeasure of powerful elements in the eastern army. Numerian was murdered after the army left Antioch in the summer of AD 284. However, it appears that the only thing that his assassins could agree upon was that it was time for him to go; unable to decide on a successor, they concealed Numerian's dead body in a litter, claiming that an eye infection prevented him from appearing in public. Eventually, the stench of the decomposing body became intolerable, leaving everyone in no doubt that the emperor was dead. Forced to act, the general staff halted just outside Nicomedia in western Turkey and on 20 November, AD 284 selected a mid-grade officer named Gaius Aurelius Valerius Diocles as a compromise candidate. Standing on a high platform that had been erected some miles from the city, Diocles accepted the acclamation of the troops, drew his sword, and cleft the praetorian prefect Flavius Aper, whom he accused of having murdered Numerian, in two. Shortly afterwards, Diocles took the Latinized name Gaius Aurelius Valerius Diocletianus; he is known to history simply as Diocletian.

Carus' successes against the Persians in AD 283, avenging the many Roman defeats during the previous decades, earned him the honorific 'Persicus maximus'. Many commentators are sceptical that his death really was caused by a bolt of lightning.

DIOCLETIAN

BORN
c. AD 245, in Dalmatia, Croatia

PREDECESSOR
Carinus

BEGINNING OF REIGN
20 November, AD 284

END OF REIGN
1 May, AD 305

DIED
AD 311 or 313, in Split, Croatia

SUCCESSOR
Constantius Augustus and Galerius

Stability at last

As Diocletian set out to contest the throne with Carinus in the spring of AD 285, few could have predicted that any great change would result. The contenders were typical third-century emperors who based their claims to power on the ability of their army to defeat those of their rivals. Whichever man won would be expected to spend the rest of his reign fighting on the frontiers until some northern barbarian, Persian or other Roman ended his life.

Alongside structural modifications to the army from the mid-third century onwards, the nature of imperial power had undergone a change over the 15 years prior to Diocletian taking office. Gallienus had been the last emperor to reside regularly at Rome. Aurelian, to be sure, had given the city new walls and a new god, but had spent most of his time on the march. So too had his successors, and that had

The New Roman Army

The armies that Carinus and Diocletian led against one another in AD 285 were radically different from the legionary forces that had been the mainstay of Rome's army until the mid-third century. The old Roman army had experienced its demise in the military catastrophes that occurred under Decius, Gallus and Valerian. Although there were still many units called legions, these were no longer the large bodies comprising some 5500 heavily armed and armoured infantrymen that could trace their lineage back to the armies of the republic. Legions now tended to number no more than 2000 men, were more lightly armoured and trained in new tactics. The main strike force of the army, which was gradually being separated from units that were primarily assigned to frontier protection, contained higher proportions of cavalry than was the norm before AD 250. In many ways it was a better army, capable of a wider range of tactical manoeuvres, and capable of adapting to a variety of enemies. Unlike the army of the Severan era, the new Roman army was designed to fight Rome's enemies on their own terms. The new-look army enjoyed notable success from the opening year of Aurelian's reign (AD 275) onwards.

Horsemen of the Roman cavalry. Mounted units, with their ability to launch swift attacks, formed a key element in the revitalized army of the later third century.

important consequences for the composition of the governing class. The most obvious of these was that senators now only rarely enjoyed access to the emperor's charmed inner circle of advisors. As emperors spent increasingly less time at Rome, senators no longer had the ready social access that had been an important feature of the Antonine age. In consequence, while there were a few who still managed to achieve prominence under the new emperors, only one of the new emperors (Tacitus) had been a senator before taking office. Rather, the people who had chosen Claudius, Aurelian and Tacitus were all army generals, while Probus and Carus were both victors in civil wars. As the role of the senate declined, so too did that of the imperial court. With the emperor on the march, most courtiers were removed from regular contact with their master, which had the effect of concentrating power in the hands of those staff members whom the emperor chose to take with him.

One negative result of the extreme centralization of power in the emperor's camp became evident in the rebellions that dogged the reign of Probus: if people could not get access to the emperor, they took matters into their own hands. The new system of authority was in fact not worthy of the name, and it did not take Diocletian long to decide that, if he managed to defeat Carinus, major changes would need to be made. Diocletian did indeed win his victory, largely through treachery and desertions, and began to emerge from the shadow of more powerful men who had thought to install him as their placeman.

The new era began in the immediate aftermath of the victory over Carinus, when Diocletian married one of his daughters to a relatively junior officer named Maximian (c. AD 250–310), raised him to the position of deputy emperor, or Caesar, and dispatched him to show the eagle of the new regime to the western provinces. After initial success in quelling rebellions in Gaul, Maximian was made Augustus, with the proviso that important decisions would only be made in consultation with Diocletian. The relationship between the two men was presented to the empire through their symbolic association with the gods Jupiter and Hercules. As the chief emperor, Diocletian gave directions, while Maximian played the role of Hercules by wandering the earth to smash the foes of civilization. The association with these gods clearly expressed the nature of the *virtus* of the two emperors. Since the new relationship was also intrinsically familial – Hercules was the son of Jupiter – the *domus* was now intertwined once more with the concept of *virtus* in a way that had not been seen since the early days of the empire.

A Roman signet ring portraying the figures of Jupiter and his son Hercules. Diocletian and Maximian consciously modelled their relationship on that between the two deities. Maximian even went so far as to style himself 'Herculius'; however, his identification with Hercules had none of the pantomimic quality of Commodus' self-aggrandizement.

Devolving power

Diocletian was not content merely to reshape the outward image of government. Over the course of the next decade he replaced the ramshackle administrative system he had inherited into a bureaucracy unlike anything the Roman empire had seen before. Out went the notion that the emperor was a friend rather than a boss, and out too went the obsolete conceit that the empire had a single capital. Diocletian plainly did not find the city of Rome agreeable: in 21 years as emperor he only visited the capital twice, spending in total less than six months there. The centre of power would henceforth be wherever the emperor chose to reside. A quasi-imperial residence already existed at Sirmium in the Balkans, where Marcus had died; it was soon joined by similar sites at Aquileia and Milan in northern Italy and Trier in Germany. Other significant administrative complexes were established at Antioch (perhaps too close to the Persian frontier to be a primary residence), Carnuntum on the Danube, and Thessalonica in northern Greece. Most significantly, Diocletian decided that his main residence would be at Nicomedia in northwestern Turkey. Nicomedia, formerly the capital of the kingdom of Bithynia, controlled all the key routes running from east to west through Asia Minor. The establishment of the imperial seat here indicates that Diocletian deemed this area – from where he had easy access to either of the two main frontier armies – the optimal site for the new capital.

Diocletian's military and administrative reforms were necessary steps in bringing the empire back under firm control. However, his subdivision of local government into even more units than before saw the imperial bureaucracy grow to sprawling proportions. This would have a debilitating effect on the later history of the empire.

Diocletian's decision to govern away from Rome was accompanied by a gradual, but thorough, reshuffling of the way in which government was organized. The tradition of dividing offices according to social class had largely ended in the middle of the third century. Most offices were now in the hands of men who, though technically equestrians, had little in common with the officials of the Antonine age. The hyperinflation that resulted from Aurelian's currency reform meant that the traditionally high salaries of these officers were now relatively modest. Although the annual pay of a legionary had been set at 1250 denarii in the period after Caracalla's reign, a lower-level equestrian, whose salary had not been increased, now made just 20 times the salary of a humble infantryman, as opposed to 60 times in the second century. The property valuations that had defined the equestrian and senatorial order in the Augustan age were likewise now meaningless. These changes had a levelling effect, placing the imperial office within the reach of men who would, in the past, have remained local dignitaries or have had little prospect of advancing beyond the level of a unit commander. People who disliked Diocletian would claim that he was little better than a barbarian of peasant background. This accusation, though false, reflects the fact that government was no longer the preserve of multi-millionaires who would now have felt distinctly uncomfortable taking orders from people who were so unlike themselves.

The new civil administration had four main elements. Provincial governors reported through the praetorian prefects, and were henceforth to be responsible only for the administration of justice and the delivery of taxes in produce. The office of the *res privata*, the descendant of the old *patrimonium*, took over responsibility for the collection of all taxes paid in coin, the output from mines and the minting of coins. The equestrian secretariats of the old empire were now subsumed, along with the legal staff, under the authority of the *magister*

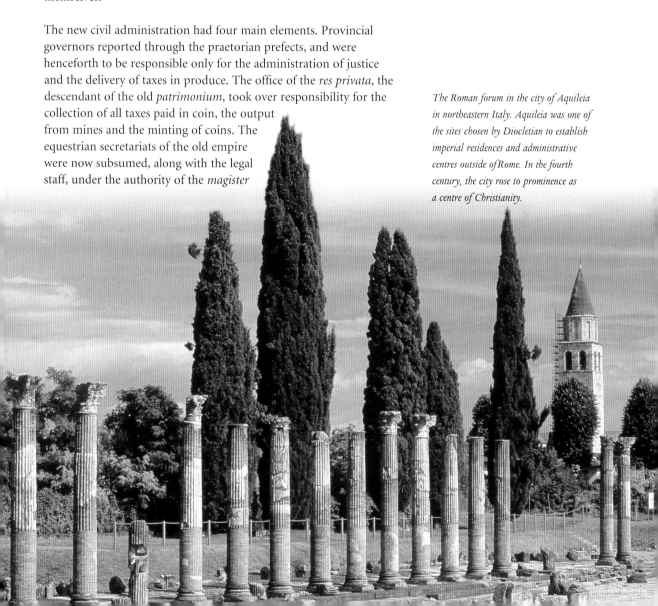

The Roman forum in the city of Aquileia in northeastern Italy. Aquileia was one of the sites chosen by Diocletian to establish imperial residences and administrative centres outside of Rome. In the fourth century, the city rose to prominence as a centre of Christianity.

officiorum, master of offices, while the operations of the various palaces continued to be under the control of *cubicularii*, now more numerous than ever before and more likely to be eunuchs.

Birth of the tetrarchy

For the present, the army was under the direct command of each Augustus, with *comites* or *duces* commanding larger formations. The most momentous change in the system, however, came about as a result of a series of major setbacks suffered by Maximian in attempting to suppress a revolt that broke out along the Rhine and in Britain under Carausius, formerly the senior commander in the area. Carausius' rebellion began in AD 288, but within three years Maximian had driven his forces out of most of northern Gaul. However, when he attempted to capitalize on this success by invading Britain, his fleet was destroyed in a storm. Carausius took advantage of this disaster to reoccupy parts of the Gaulish mainland. In AD 293 Maximian, whose authority was threatened by the difficulties he was experiencing, appointed a deputy emperor to take charge of the campaign. Diocletian followed suit, with the understanding that the two deputies, or Caesars, would one day succeed the current Augusti. This refined system of rule was known as the Tetrarchy ('rule of four'). The new Caesars were Flavius Constantius (*c.* AD 250–306) and Gaius Galerius Valerius Maximianus (known simply in English as Galerius; *c.* AD 250–311). Both Constantius and Galerius were experienced soldiers, and their appointments relieved the Augusti of the need to take personal control of potentially risky military operations. To celebrate their new offices, the two men married into the families of their patrons; Constantius married Theodora, daughter of Maximian while Galerius took Valeria, daughter of Diocletian, as his wife.

At the time of his promotion to the rank of Caesar, Constantius had one son by a woman named Helena – allegedly a barmaid from the Balkans – whom he continued to support. This son, whose name was Constantine, was around 18 years old in AD 293 and was shortly dispatched to Nicomedia to be educated at Diocletian's court alongside Maximian's slightly younger son, Maxentius (*c.* AD 278–312). In time, both would become emperors.

Constantius soon proved his worth, driving Carausius' forces out of Gaul, invading Britain and bringing the breakaway state back under central government control. Galerius' record was initially more chequered. After years of internal turmoil, the Sassanian regime had recovered its sense of purpose under the leadership of Shapur I's son

A porphyry carving of the four tetrarchs. This sculpture, which is thought to have been made in Alexandria in the fourth century, was looted from Constantinople by the Fourth Crusade in 1204 and built into the fabric of St Mark's Basilica in Venice.

Narseh (r. AD 293–302), who had seized the throne in a coup d'état in AD 293. Narseh took great exception to Roman support for the restoration of an Arsacid ruler in part of Armenia. In AD 297 he invaded Armenia and, pushing south, inflicted a serious defeat on Galerius who had been lured into giving battle around Carrhae, which now had the unique distinction of being the only city to witness three major Roman defeats.

Diocletian was less than impressed with Galerius' performance. He came in person to Antioch, where he made Galerius march before his chariot for more than a mile before the assembled army, a powerful statement that emperors were responsible for military failure. Of more practical value was a new plan of campaign that drew Narseh into the Armenian mountains where Galerius was able to win a decisive victory in AD 298, forcing the Persians to surrender five provinces east of the Tigris, and, with them, direct access to the Armenian highlands. It was perhaps the greatest victory won by a Roman army since the time of Marcus Aurelius.

The strength of the new collegial system of government was further demonstrated, even as Galerius advanced against Narseh, by the fact that Diocletian and Maximian were able to direct their energies towards quelling local disturbances in Egypt and Spain, while Constantius set up his headquarters at Trier to launch repeated assaults against the Franks, a loose federation of Germanic tribes along the lower Rhine, and the Alamanni in southern Germany. It was with some justice that the propagandists of the regime trumpeted the restoration of the Roman world. It was also at this time that Diocletian turned his attention to domestic policy.

Domestic reforms

Throughout the AD 280s and 290s a pair of jurists named Gregorius and Hermogenianus had tried to systematize the huge corpus of Roman law. In AD 291 Gregorius produced a collection of the legal opinions of previous emperors that were still regarded as valid sources of law, while Hermogenianus updated the collection in AD 298 to include the rulings of Diocletian. The urge to set the legal record straight was just one part of a concerted effort to change the way in which the reformed imperial administration governed its subjects. In AD 296 Diocletian introduced a new tax system that aimed to create a coherent definition of the taxable units for the basic taxes across all the provinces (this reform is thought to have caused the revolts that engaged the two Augusti while Galerius was defeating the Persians).

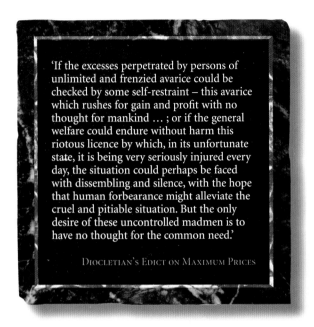

'If the excesses perpetrated by persons of unlimited and frenzied avarice could be checked by some self-restraint – this avarice which rushes for gain and profit with no thought for mankind … ; or if the general welfare could endure without harm this riotous licence by which, in its unfortunate state, it is being very seriously injured every day, the situation could perhaps be faced with dissembling and silence, with the hope that human forbearance might alleviate the cruel and pitiable situation. But the only desire of these uncontrolled madmen is to have no thought for the common need.'

DIOCLETIAN'S EDICT ON MAXIMUM PRICES

A settler in one of the Roman-occupied provinces of Germany paying his taxes to the local magistrate (curialis) responsible for collecting imperial revenues. This third-century relief comes from Neumagen near the major Roman city of Trier.

Prompted chiefly by complaints from the army about the dwindling purchasing power of their salaries, in AD 301 the emperor introduced a new system of coinage, followed by an edict fixing maximum prices for goods and services throughout the empire. The effort was a failure, but, like Diocletian's other fiscal measures, demonstrated his conviction that the government could reform the conduct of the empire's subjects to make them more efficient servants of the regime. Crucial to all of this was the view that the emperor no longer existed to serve the state but rather that the state, having been saved from its enemies, should serve the emperor.

By the end of AD 301, Diocletian had survived longer than any emperor since Septimius Severus, but he was also in his sixties. What would happen next? Diocletian was giving very clear indications that he did not intend to die in office; he had constructed a grand palace at Spalatum (Split), near his homeland of Salonae in modern Croatia, to which he intended to retire. But what of Maximian, and what of the Caesars? Constantius, who had been appointed a few weeks before Galerius, would naturally succeed to the position of Augustus that Diocletian intended to vacate, while Galerius might be expected to wait until Maximian, who had been in power for one year less than Diocletian, decided that it was time for him to leave as well. Constantine and Maxentius were being groomed as the Caesars of the

DIOCLETIAN'S MONETARY REFORMS

In the last year of his life, Aurelian altered the traditional system of Roman coinage based upon the notional tariff of 25 silver denarii to one golden aureus, throwing the economic system of the empire into chaos, and causing massive inflation. Diocletian's currency decrees were intended to stabilize the coinage. From AD 294 onwards, a new silver coin (*argenteus*) and gold coin, the *solidus* (worth 1000 denarii) were issued; the *argenteus* was the first new silver coin in decades, while the *solidus* replaced the since-devalued *aureus* and had a higher standard of purity. The word 'soldier' ultimately derives from this coin, since troops came to be paid in *solidi*. However, although these coins held their value during the emperor's reign, the extensive minting of them only stoked inflation. To make matters worse, the wide-circulation, lower-denomination copper coinage failed to hold its value relative to gold.

Accordingly, Diocletian issued his *Edictum de Pretiis Rerum Venalium* ('Edict on Maximum Prices') in AD 301. The preamble to the edict displayed a rather naïve understanding of inflationary forces, ascribing them solely to unscrupulous traders' 'avarice'; to remedy this situation, the emperor then went on to impose maximum legal prices on a wide range of goods and services, including wheat, millet, lentils, different varieties of wine and beer, sewer cleaning and the teaching of arithmetic.

Those who failed to comply were threatened with severe penalties. Even so, the measure was a failure; goods simply vanished from the market, while the limits that it imposed on wages hit those on fixed incomes (soldiers, for example) especially hard. By the end of Diocletian's reign, the edict had largely fallen into disuse.

next generation. Yet Diocletian appears suddenly to have changed his mind over the succession, as relations between the eastern and western courts grew strained. He had not seen Maximian in more than a decade, and there is no evidence that he had ever met Constantius as Caesar. Moreover, neither of the western emperors enforced the edict on maximum prices, which they may rightly have regarded as wholly unworkable. To complicate matters further, Galerius' wife gave birth to a son: where would Diocletian's new grandson now fit into the scheme of things if the grown-up children of the western emperors were allowed to succeed?

A late spasm of persecution

On 24 February, AD 303 Diocletian introduced a further strain into the relationship between east and west. It was on this day that he posted an edict at Nicomedia ordering all Christians to sacrifice to the traditional gods. Their communal property was seized, and those who refused to recant their faith faced the loss of their civil rights and even capital punishment. It was now more than forty years since Gallienus had brought the persecution instituted by his father to an end, and some 30 years since Aurelian had referred the decision of a dispute among the Christians of Antioch to the bishops of Italy – and the question of the relationship between Christians and non-Christians in the empire had ceased to be a burning issue. By this stage, Christians were well represented in the army and the court. Most significantly, many were also employed in the higher education establishment at Nicomedia, where the seminal early Christian teacher, Lactantius (*c.* AD 240–320) may first have met Constantine.

LACTANTIUS – A KEY EARLY CHRISTIAN

Born in around AD 240 in North Africa, Lucius Caelius Firmianus Lactantius was a scholar who taught rhetoric throughout the eastern Roman empire. He was a committed Christian, and was notable for presenting its tenets in such a way that it became more appealing to educated non-Christians. His treatise *Institutiones Divinae* ('Divine Institutions'), written between AD 303 and 311 pointed out the futility of pagan beliefs and attempted to establish the reasonableness and truth of Christianity as a response to pagan critics. Lactantius was unorthodox in his approach to the Christian faith, teaching that the truth of Christian revelation was proved through works of traditional literature rather than through

An early Christian mosaic in the basilica at Aquileia. At the top of the inscription is 'chi rho,' the Greek symbol for Christ.

the Old Testament. Yet he was a seminal figure in fostering discourse between Christians and non-Christians as the new religion expanded in the course of the third century and lost much of its earlier anti-establishment polemical edge.

As the effects of Diocletian's 'Edict Against the Christians' took hold, Lactantius' tone became more embittered. His grisly work *De Mortibus Persecutorum* ('On the Deaths of the Persecutors') sought to demonstrate that emperors who persecuted his faith had all met hideous deaths, illustrating his thesis with the fates of Diocletian and his colleagues. Yet in this treatise he largely exonerates Diocletian of blame, claiming instead that he was driven to his persecution of Christians by Galerius.

The result of Diocletian's edict was to fuel the fire of Christian fundamentalism in some areas and alienate men like Lactantius. The rationale behind the edict, which upset long-established relationships, is hard to fathom. The fact that the edict ceased to be enforced within 18 months of its promulgation – only to be renewed with especial vigour by Galerius when he stepped into the role of Augustus – suggests indeed that Lactantius was right to explain it as a matter of politics more than of faith, and to suggest that the bigotry which was the driving force behind the measure was a particular hallmark of Galerius. Certainly, the responses of the Tetrarchs varied greatly; Constantius largely ignored the edict, while Maximian's enforcement of it was less than enthusiastic. The measure served to highlight sharply differences between the eastern and western rulers on the very eve of an important journey that Diocletian planned to make to Rome in AD 304 to celebrate his and Maximian's 20 years of shared power.

In ordering this joint celebration, Diocletian unilaterally took it upon himself to add a year to the period that Maximian had actually spent in office. At their meeting in Rome, Diocletian spelt out the intention behind his deliberate miscounting to his fellow senior member of the

Tetrarchy; now that he and Maximian had the 'same' number of years in power, he expected them both to abdicate on the same day. Concurrently, he announced that he had already chosen the new Caesars, one of whom was a general named Flavius Valerius Severus (d. AD 307), and the other the nephew of Galerius, Maximinus Daia (c. AD 270–313). The principle enshrined in this pronouncement was that emperors made emperors; inheritance was not to be considered a decisive factor in the succession.

Renouncing the purple

Maximian and Constantius must have been infuriated by Diocletian's decision, but there was little they could do about it. As was only fitting after a 20-year reign in which he had effectively restored Rome to a position of dominance not seen since the time of Septimius Severus, Diocletian's personal authority was unbounded. Although not all of his actions could be regarded as prudent – the edicts on maximum prices and Christian persecution being cases in point – he possessed genuine wisdom. He was modest enough to realize that he could not govern on his own, and willing to entrust great power to a man (Constantius) who was plainly not part of his inner circle, and also consistent enough in his belief that the nature of the imperial office needed to be changed that he did what no other emperor had ever dared do – he voluntarily renounced the most powerful position in the world.

On 1 May, AD 305, Diocletian removed the purple cloak that symbolized his authority and draped it around the shoulders of Maximinus Daia. Galerius ascended to the rank of Augustus at Sirmium. Maximian handed over power to Severus outside Milan, while Constantius became Augustus at Trier.

Withdrawing to his retirement palace, Diocletian spent his time growing cabbages. When asked later to resume office, he allegedly replied, 'If only you could see the vegetables planted by my own hand ... you'd never think of asking such a thing'.

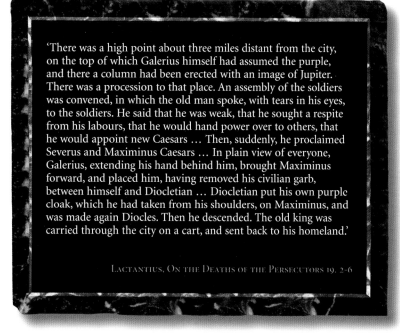

'There was a high point about three miles distant from the city, on the top of which Galerius himself had assumed the purple, and there a column had been erected with an image of Jupiter. There was a procession to that place. An assembly of the soldiers was convened, in which the old man spoke, with tears in his eyes, to the soldiers. He said that he was weak, that he sought a respite from his labours, that he would hand power over to others, that he would appoint new Caesars ... Then, suddenly, he proclaimed Severus and Maximinus Caesars ... In plain view of everyone, Galerius, extending his hand behind him, brought Maximinus forward, and placed him, having removed his civilian garb, between himself and Diocletian ... Diocletian put his own purple cloak, which he had taken from his shoulders, on Maximinus, and was made again Diocles. Then he descended. The old king was carried through the city on a cart, and sent back to his homeland.'

LACTANTIUS, ON THE DEATHS OF THE PERSECUTORS 19. 2-6

Beginnings of the Christian Empire: The Reign of Constantine (AD 305–337)

Even as Diocletian set off on the long journey that would end at his retirement palace, and Maximian retired to a villa outside Rome, the succession plan began to fall apart. The reason was simple; although Constantius was now senior Augustus, he was far from content in his new role. He also saw a way to take advantage of new administrative structures that came into force just as he acceded to the highest office.

Constantine I came to power in AD 306, but only gained absolute control over the empire 18 years later, with the defeat of his last rival Licinius. He is often referred to as the 'first Christian emperor', but at the same time as espousing Christianity retained the title of 'pontifex maximus' and as late as AD 320 issued coins bearing the image of Roman gods.

Although the Tetrarchic system established four separate imperial courts, under Diocletian the empire was not formally divided into administrative districts. The likely reason for this was that an informal arrangement was deemed perfectly adequate in a situation where no-one challenged Diocletian's authority over the empire as a whole. Now, as a result of the tensions surrounding the succession, the empire was split into four praetorian prefectures, with each prefect controlling three dioceses. Each of these was under the control of a *vicarius* – so-called because the office-holder acted 'in lieu of' (*vice*) the praetorian prefect for the purposes of day-to-day administration.

Sowing the seeds of destruction

Under this new administrative system, Galerius and his prefect administered the three dioceses comprising the Balkan provinces, Maximinus ruled the three from the Dardanelles to Egypt, Severus controlled Italy, Africa and Spain, while Constantius held sway in Gaul and Britain. All of them, theoretically at least, were subordinate to Constantius. The four prefectures roughly mirrored the natural tax distribution zones of the second-century empire, with one major exception: the inclusion of Egypt with the east rather than with Italy marked a significant redistribution of resources towards Syria and the new capital district in northern Turkey. This is not to say that Rome did not still get grain from Egypt, and was not still a major market for the trade in luxury goods from the Far East via Egypt, but it did signify that other areas had grown in importance. The administrative joining of Egypt to the east reflects the fact that the natural economic and cultural divisions of the empire were beginning to shape the formal administrative structure in ways that would, in the long run, contribute to the downfall of the empire in the west.

However, any idea of the collapse of the western empire – or any inkling that the empire was now less than a century away from permanent division and partial occupation of its territories by barbarians – would have been far from the minds of Diocletian's successors. There was no shortage of more immediate concerns to occupy them. No sooner had he come to power as the western Augustus than Constantius demanded the return of his son Constantine, who was effectively a hostage at the court of Galerius. He had other children, several of them boys, but they were all young, and it seems that the offspring of his early romance with Helena held a special place in his affections. Constantius now had firm designs on his oldest son becoming emperor. Even if Galerius had guessed his colleague's intentions, he was in no position to refuse him.

> 'So great that although your father left you imperial power, nevertheless you were content with the title of Caesar and preferred to wait for the same man to declare you Augustus who so declared him. Thus indeed you judged that this imperial power would be finer not if you had acquired it as an inheritance by right of succession, but if you earned it from the supreme emperor as due reward for your merits.'
>
> LATIN PANEGYRIC 7.5.3 (TR. NIXON)

Since Maxentius had been handed back to Maximian, there was no justification for keeping Constantine from his father. And so, having secured the return of his son by the end of AD 305, Constantius left to campaign in northern England. On 25 July, AD 306 he died at York, and, evidently at his behest, the army declared Constantine emperor.

Galerius was furious, but was powerless to act, especially since Maxentius, inspired by developments in Britain, claimed the throne in Rome. His father Maximian came out of retirement to support him,

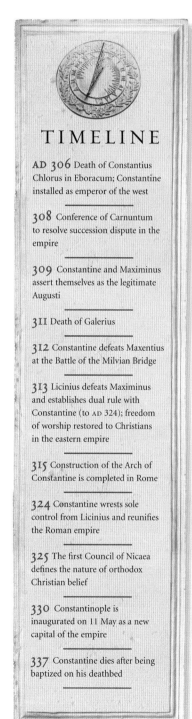

TIMELINE

AD 306 Death of Constantius Chlorus in Eboracum; Constantine installed as emperor of the west

308 Conference of Carnuntum to resolve succession dispute in the empire

309 Constantine and Maximinus assert themselves as the legitimate Augusti

311 Death of Galerius

312 Constantine defeats Maxentius at the Battle of the Milvian Bridge

313 Licinius defeats Maximinus and establishes dual rule with Constantine (to AD 324); freedom of worship restored to Christians in the eastern empire

315 Construction of the Arch of Constantine is completed in Rome

324 Constantine wrests sole control from Licinius and reunifies the Roman empire

325 The first Council of Nicaea defines the nature of orthodox Christian belief

330 Constantinople is inaugurated on 11 May as a new capital of the empire

337 Constantine dies after being baptized on his deathbed

CONSTANTIUS

BORN
31 March, *c.* AD 250

MARRIED
(1) Helena; (2) Theodora

CHILDREN
(by 1) Constantine; (by 2)
Flavius Dalmatius, Julius
Constantius, Flavia Julia
Constantia, Eutropia,
Anastasia

PREDECESSOR
Diocletian

BEGINNING OF REIGN
1 May, AD 305

DIED
25 July, AD 306, in Eboracum
(York), Britannia

SUCCESSOR
Constantine

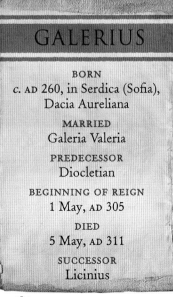

GALERIUS

BORN
c. AD 260, in Serdica (Sofia),
Dacia Aureliana

MARRIED
Galeria Valeria

PREDECESSOR
Diocletian

BEGINNING OF REIGN
1 May, AD 305

DIED
5 May, AD 311

SUCCESSOR
Licinius

and when Severus tried to quell the revolt he found that the loyalty of the army, which had served for years under Maximian, was suspect. Before the end of the year, he was imprisoned in a villa near Rome, and subsequently killed. Both factions now courted Constantine, who was recognized as Caesar by Galerius even as he contracted a formal marriage with Maximian's prepubescent daughter, Fausta (as she was still a child, marital relations were postponed for the better part of a decade).

The empire fragments

In the summer of AD 307 Galerius invaded Italy. Constantine remained formally neutral, which probably guaranteed the failure of the expedition. With the limited forces at his disposal, and Constantine the only potential source of reinforcements, Galerius simply did not have enough manpower to lay siege to the capital (now surrounded by Aurelian's massive defensive wall). Maximian, who plainly anticipated this turn of events, refused to engage in open battle. Faced with an impossible siege and a shortage of supplies, Galerius was forced to withdraw. The fact that he got out of Italy alive is testimony both to his own force of character and to the loyalty of the troops he had led for many years in the Balkans. It also testified to the fact that Diocletian's reforms had only reinforced the tendency for the Roman army to divide along regional lines. This had occurred once before, in AD 193 – in the power struggle following the death of Commodus – and now it was patently obvious that the four main armies were essentially separate entities. The paradox of Diocletian's reforms was that, while he sought to concentrate all power in the college of emperors, he actually succeeded in creating a number of separate governments that could operate independently of one another. Diocletian's dominant personality had held the system together, and it is significant that, in the wake of his failure to defeat Maxentius, Galerius turned again to his mentor for help.

Diocletian came out of retirement in AD 308, but made it clear that he was only doing so to aid Galerius. Given the great support he still commanded and the potential for enormous bloodshed, it is fortunate for all involved that Diocletian had a real abhorrence of civil war. After a confusing spring in which Constantine and Galerius squared up to one another, while Maximian tried to remove Maxentius from power, failed and fled to Gaul, a meeting was summoned at Carnuntum in lower Austria, from which Maxentius was excluded. The outcome of the conference was that Galerius agreed that Constantine could call himself Augustus in the regions he controlled already, and Caesar elsewhere. This made it possible for Galerius to appoint a new Augustus, an experienced general named Licinius (c. AD 250–325) to replace the fallen Severus. With the principle of collegiate government re-established, and with Galerius clearly recognized as the senior member of the college, Diocletian retired once more to his palace, where he lived in peace for the final three years of his life, tending his vegetable garden.

It is one of the ironies of this period that Galerius, who tried so hard to uphold Diocletian's system, even constructing a massive retirement palace of his own at Roumaliana (Gamzigrad) in the Balkans, was fated to succumb to a malignant disease, possibly bowel cancer, a few months before his former mentor. His principal achievement had been to keep the peace between his fractious colleagues. During this uneasy peace, Constantine took advantage of the lull to hone his skills as a general, while Maximinus did nothing more constructive than work up a profound loathing for Licinius, who had effectively been promoted over his head. Maximian lived with Constantine until AD 310, when he suddenly tried to seize power for himself in southern France while Constantine was away campaigning on the Rhine. The attempt failed, and Maximian committed suicide (it is unclear whether he did so with or without the active collusion of his son-in-law).

Immediately after the death of Galerius, the surviving Augusti and Caesars split into two factions; Maximinus allied himself with Maxentius, and Constantine with Licinius. The war that loomed in

A Roman army using state-of-the-art military technology to storm a city. In the foreground, soldiers prepare a siege crossbow (right) and a type of catapult known as an onager (meaning 'ass', from the fierce recoil kick it gave when fired). In the middle distance, troops approach the walls under a gallery, while in the background, an assault is being made from a siege tower. Galerius' bid to suppress Maxentius faltered on his lack of heavy equipment to mount a serious siege of Rome in AD 307.

185

'In Hoc Signo Vinces'

The story of Constantine's conversion has been modified down the ages. In AD 313, the author of a eulogy to the emperor claimed that when sacrifices to the traditional gods were not propitious, he remained confident because he had faith in *mens divina*. Lactantius, writing a few years after Maxentius' defeat, said that Constantine had a dream in which a young man told him to put the symbol of Christ on the shields of his men before the battle of the Milvian Bridge. Years later, in his *Life of Constantine*, the Christian historian and theologian Eusebius (c. AD 275–339) wrote:

'If someone else reported it, it would perhaps not be easy to accept; but since the victorious Emperor himself told the story to the present writer a long while after ... and confirmed it with oaths, who could hesitate to believe the account, especially when the time that followed provided evidence for the truth of what he said? About the time of the midday sun, when day was just turning, he said he saw

'The Emblem of Christ Appearing to Constantine,' by the Flemish painter Peter Paul Rubens (1577–1640), depicting the emperor's conversion.

with his own eyes, up in the sky and resting over the sun, a cross-shaped trophy formed from light, and a text attached to it which said, "By this sign conquer". [In hoc signo vinces].

He was, he said, wondering to himself what the manifestation might mean; then, while he meditated, and thought long and hard, night overtook him. Thereupon, as he slept, the Christ of God appeared to him with the sign which had appeared to him in the sky, and urged him to make himself a copy of the sign ... and to use this as protection against enemy attacks.'

There has been intense debate about what exactly it was that Constantine saw, but most sources agree that his conversion took place in the months leading up to the invasion of Italy.

AD 312 looked ominous indeed; the two sides had roughly equivalent armies, and neither had a clear strategic advantage. The threat of Maximinus constrained Licinius from lending significant aid to Constantine, while Constantine could not help Licinius until he had dealt with Maxentius.

Showdown with Maxentius

The invasion of Italy was a daunting task. Maxentius' army was supplemented by a series of fortified cities in the north, while Rome itself had so far proved unassailable. Constantine was plainly worried, and now set out upon a spiritual odyssey that would transform the history of Europe. While in Gaul, he had followed what was by now the traditional practice of letting it be known that he had a guardian divinity – in his case *Sol Invictus*. This may have been more than just self-aggrandizement on Constantine's part, since he was evidently a deeply pious person. But what if his faith in the gods was misplaced? It would not have escaped his attention that Galerius had been a devoted follower of the traditional gods yet had still failed utterly.

In the spring of AD 312, Constantine suddenly announced that he placed all his confidence in *mens divina*, the 'Divine Mind'. It is not clear what he meant to signify by this term, and contemporary polytheistic propagandists writing immediately before and after the invasion supply no clue. It is altogether likely that, with an army that consisted of traditional believers behind him, Constantine did not wish to be more specific. He may well have speculated that the one deity that Galerius despised, the Christian God, now held the key to his fate. Later commentators are in no doubt that this was the point when Constantine became convinced he had been given signs that the God of the Christians would be on his side.

The uncertainty over the precise nature of his conversion is fully in accordance with Constantine's generally enigmatic character: he could be rash yet patient; he had the ability to listen and to change course when he realized he had made an error, yet placed enormous confidence in his own judgement; although no intellectual, he was extremely bright. He could be both compassionate and utterly ruthless. But what was beyond all dispute was Constantine's genius as a military commander, possibly the greatest general Rome had seen since the time of Julius Caesar.

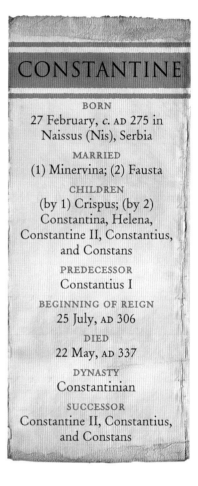

CONSTANTINE

BORN
27 February, *c.* AD 275 in Naissus (Nis), Serbia

MARRIED
(1) Minervina; (2) Fausta

CHILDREN
(by 1) Crispus; (by 2) Constantina, Helena, Constantine II, Constantius, and Constans

PREDECESSOR
Constantius I

BEGINNING OF REIGN
25 July, AD 306

DIED
22 May, AD 337

DYNASTY
Constantinian

SUCCESSOR
Constantine II, Constantius, and Constans

The relationship between Constantine and the eastern emperor Licinius had always been uneasy. The truce they concluded after their first clash in AD 317 was broken seven years later when Constantine declared war against his rival and defeated him.

Constantine's invasion of Italy was one of the most brilliant military operations in ancient history. Sweeping aside Maxentius' northern armies, and drawing them into battle before they could take refuge behind their fortifications, by the early autumn he was already advancing on Rome. The effect of the defeats in the north was that Maxentius could not retire behind the walls of Rome and wait for Constantine to exhaust his supplies. His reputation in tatters, he had to risk all in one final encounter. So it was that Maxentius led his army out of Rome on 28 October to a place near the Milvian Bridge called Saxa Rubra north of the Tiber to challenge Constantine. The final battle was swift and decisive. Maxentius was killed in the rout, and Constantine entered Rome in triumph.

The alliance with Licinius

Within weeks of the victory over Maxentius, Constantine was on his way back north. Meeting Licinius at Milan, he spoke to him of the power of his new god, and cemented their alliance by giving him his half-sister, Constantia, in marriage. It was now up to Licinius to deal with Maxentius' ally Maximinus.

Maximinus proved an obliging enemy; his crossing of the Dardanelles at the head of his field army in April AD 313 saved Licinius the trouble of waging war in hostile territory. So thorough was the victory that Licinius won near the city of Adrianople, some 150 miles (220 km) west of modern Istanbul, that Maximinus could mount no serious resistance when Licinius pursued him back into his own territory. As Licinius closed in on his stronghold at Tarsus in Anatolia (southern Turkey), Maximinus realized that the game was up and committed suicide. During his retreat, one of Maximinus' last acts had been to issue

In an attempt to stop Constantine's army from entering Rome along the Via Flaminia, Maxentius' troops made a stand near where the road crossed the River Tiber at the Milvian Bridge. The day of the battle was the sixth anniversary of Maxentius' accession as western emperor, supposedly a good omen, but Constantine's superior generalship won the day. Heavy losses were inflicted on Maxentius' forces as they retreated in confusion across the narrow bridge.

THE ARCH OF CONSTANTINE

The Arch of Constantine, standing between the Colosseum and the Palatine Hill and erected with staggering speed between AD 312 and 315, was designed as a monumental expression of the emperor's role within the state. The frieze along the lower register illustrates the main inscription on the arch, which proclaims that Constantine liberated Rome by force of arms from a tyrant (Maxentius), and restored proper civil government. Although Constantine is not shown taking part in the battles, his presence with the army is made clear by the inclusion of the wagon that served as his conveyance on the campaign. This is very much in the tradition of imperial ideology and

The frieze on the Arch of Constantine shows scenes of the emperor's campaign against Maxentius, but carefully avoids any triumphal depiction of the capture of Rome.

iconography since Diocletian, which present the emperor not as a man of action but rather as the director of operations. Other panels show Constantine personally meeting with the senate and people of Rome. In addition to the narrative panels, other sculptures, taken from the monuments of Antonine emperors, have been re-carved to show Constantine and Licinius participating in other traditional activities such as hunting, offering sacrifices to the gods and addressing the soldiers. Unlike Trajan's Column, no attempt was made to portray other members of the imperial houshold in any detail.

---

an edict declaring that the Christians in his part of the empire, against whom he had staged a series of persecutions, were free to practise their religion in peace. Licinius, whose wife was a Christian, followed this with an edict of his own restoring property confiscated in the persecutions. The combination of these edicts with the earlier edicts of Constantine restored Christianity to the position of equality with other religions that it had enjoyed in the years after Gallienus.

Although Licinius and Constantine both believed that Christians should have the freedom to worship, there was little else upon which they agreed. While it was possible for decrees of one emperor to be recognized as legally binding in the territory of the other, in practice the tendency was increasingly for the two to go their separate ways. Key documents have survived showing that Licinius' army was granted slightly different benefits from that of Constantine, and the bureaucracies of the eastern and western empires had little interchange with one another. Although there were now effectively two Roman empires, each one consisting of six of the 12 dioceses, neither man yet dared to take a step that would signal a decisive break. Nor would either yet conceive a succession plan. Licinius' position was straightforward, since he, as yet, had no son. For

'The senate and people of Rome dedicated this arch, decorated with images of his triumph, to the imperator Caesar Constantine Augustus, pious and fortunate, because, by the extraordinary impulse of the mind of the divinity, he, with his army, avenged the Res Publica upon the tyrant and his whole faction at the same instant.'

INSCRIPTION ON THE ARCH OF CONSTANTINE IN ROME

The state that Diocletian bequeathed to his successors consisted of 12 dioceses, equally divided between the western and eastern parts of the empire. The immediate aim of Diocletian's administrative reforms had been to devolve power away from Rome, but their unforeseen long-term consequence was to weaken the cohesion of the empire.

Constantine, the situation was somewhat more complex. He had a son, Crispus, the offspring of a relationship with a woman named Minervina, who had died before his marriage to Fausta. Initially, Constantine was equivocal in promoting the claims of this boy, whose circumstances were reminiscent of his own. However, the situation changed radically between AD 315 and 316, when first Constantia and then Fausta produced sons. Between the birth of the two boys, Constantine and Licinius concluded an agreement that their sons should not be placed in the line of succession, and arrived at a compromise whereby Bassianus the husband of Constantine's half-sister, Anastasia, would be declared Caesar. Yet shortly after the birth of Fausta's first son – which meant that, if he stuck to the compromise, Constantine would now be sacrificing two of his children's hopes for one of Licinius' – Constantine executed Bassianus on a charge of treason. Anticipating conflict, both emperors had already prepared for war.

Constantine attacked in the autumn of AD 316 and succeeded in driving Licinius out of most of his territory in the Balkans, but then overreached himself. Manoeuvring with great skill, Licinius cut his adversary's supply lines, forcing Constantine to make peace on far less advantageous terms than might otherwise have been the case. The result was that Constantine gained just one of the three Balkan dioceses on a permanent basis and was obliged to recognize three Caesars: Constantine's eldest son, Crispus, the infant Constantine and the infant Licinius. The treaty was concluded on 1 March, AD 317, and remained in force for seven years.

Although Constantine spent much of his time after signing the treaty with Licinius commanding his army in the Balkans, he still found time to sire three more children with Fausta, two daughters and a son. By AD 324, with a household full of potential heirs, Constantine decided to be rid of Licinius for good. Declaring war in the summer, he drove his enemy out of the Balkans by the early autumn and forced him to surrender at Nicomedia in November. The defeated Licinius was granted clemency and sent into exile in Thessalonica. But shortly thereafter, Constantine 'discovered' that he was at the centre of a conspiracy and ordered his death.

Nova Roma

No sooner had he defeated Licinius than a new problem arose for Constantine regarding the Christians of the eastern empire. Adherents of the faith were engaged in a bitter dispute over the true nature of God, arising from ideas developed by Arius (c. AD 250–336), a theologian from Alexandria. The Arian controversy, as it became known, had caused a deep rift in Christian communities, which were split between rival leaders. Constantine had some experience of such disputes, having already tried to resolve an extremely unpleasant schism that developed in the Christian community of North Africa soon after he defeated Maxentius. On that occasion, the schism had resulted not from doctrinal differences but from practical disagreements over whether it was better to appease persecutors of the faith or to resist and run the risk of greater violence. When Constantine's officials arrived in North Africa to restore property seized in the persecution, they found themselves confronted by two diametrically opposed factions that had adopted entrenched positions. To determine which had the better claim, Constantine referred the matter to a series of church councils, all of which ruled against the party which claimed that resistance to the authorities was in accord with God's will.

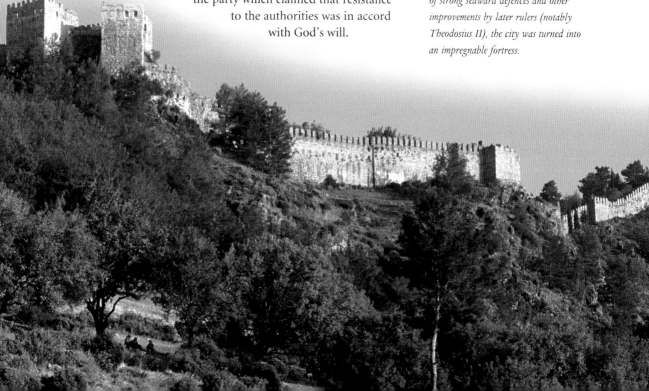

A section of the landward defensive walls of Istanbul (Constantinople). The fortification of Constantinople was begun in AD 324 and over time, with the addition of strong seaward defences and other improvements by later rulers (notably Theodosius II), the city was turned into an impregnable fortress.

THE COUNCIL OF NICAEA

The Council of Nicaea was the first 'universal' council of the Christian Church, including bishops from the west as well as the east. The issue that divided the Christian community of the east prior to AD 325 arose out of a dispute between an Alexandrian priest, Arius, and his bishop, Alexander. Arius actually represented mainstream Christian thought at the time, which held that Jesus, as the Son of God, was subordinate to his father, and of a similar, rather than identical essence. Alexander maintained that the Father and the Son were of the same substance. At the council of Nicaea, which also tried to reach an agreement on the date of Easter, Constantine offered a creed that would, as a result of its adoption by the universal council, be the essential statement of belief for all Christians in the empire. It contained the compromise formulation that God the Father and God the Son were 'consubstantial'. The Nicene Creed was the first such universal creed, and is still the basic statement of the faith for many Christian denominations, making it the most widely read document ever composed by a Roman emperor.

ARRIVS BISCHOP.

Arius of Alexandria, portrayed in a mediaeval print. His depiction here is somewhat fanciful – Arius was never actually made a bishop.

The defeated faction refused to abide by the decisions of the councils, and after a brief bout of persecution, Constantine washed his hands of the whole affair. Yet although his intervention in this dispute was unsuccessful, Constantine had learned a valuable lesson: third-party arbitration would not stop Christians from fighting with each other. He would need to intervene personally to get the warring parties around the negotiating table.

Thus it was that in AD 325, Constantine summoned the bishops of the east to a grand council at Nicaea, a town on the coast of Anatolia. After a show of listening to both sides in the dispute, the emperor offered a compromise formula that delivered a new creed expounding the nature of God. This was a seminal event in the history of the Christian Church. Since not only eastern but also a few western bishops were present, the council of Nicaea was the first conference that claimed jurisdiction over the Christian community as a whole. It was also an important moment in relations between the secular and religious leaderships. Constantine's action showed that the emperor could exert authority in spiritual matters, thus setting a precedent for later emperors who would regard such intervention as part of their remit.

Around the same time, Constantine conceived the idea of building a new capital in the east. Perhaps because of its association with earlier regimes, Nicomedia was deemed unsuitable, and so his choice finally came to rest on the ancient city of Byzantium on the Bosphorus. This settlement, which was ideally placed to give the emperor easy access to Rome's northern frontier on the Danube and its eastern frontier on the Euphrates, was now to be refounded as Constantinople. The design of the new capital was intended to mirror Constantine's attitudes towards both government and religion.

The new city arose with remarkable speed. The centrepiece of the building programme was the imperial palace, with a massive Hippodrome attached, seating 80,000 people, as a venue where the emperor could meet his subjects. In addition, he ordered construction of a vast new church, while retaining the city's older temples. Christianity was to be presented as a faith that could supplement and enhance the regime without requiring that the old ways be repudiated. The same principle was applied to the way in which the new city was populated. Constantine did not force people to come to the city, but instead rewarded those who chose to move. Likewise, rather than create a new senate, an act that would have offended senators in Rome, he simply accorded privileges to senior officials who chose to relocate to his capital. To beautify the new capital, cities throughout the east were invited to send famous monuments of antiquity to adorn its public spaces.

Crispus was proclaimed Casesar by Constantine in AD 317, and shortly afterwards made commander in Gaul. He seemed certain to succeed his father until a disastrous and mysterious turn of events led to his sudden downfall and execution in AD 326.

Turmoil and divisions

Although Constantinople was never meant to replace Rome, but rather to augment it, its founding did nevertheless raise the question of how the western empire would now be run. Constantine was personally committed to the east, but his son Crispus, who had distinguished himself during the war with Licinius, had long been based at Trier. However, before the end of AD 326, the peace of the imperial household was shattered, with Crispus arrested, tried for treason and executed, and Fausta banished into internal exile, where she died within a couple of years. The reason for this dramatic turn of events is shrouded in mystery. A later pagan writer concocted a lurid tale of how Fausta had lusted after her stepson, and when he refused her advances, claimed that he had attempted to rape her, which led to his execution. According to this same author, Fausta's plot had been exposed by the emperor's mother, causing an enraged Constantine to lock his wife in an overheated bath house until she died. Nothing in this story is borne out by the facts as we know them. A more likely explanation was that a major rift had occurred between father and son regarding the future direction of government, and that Fausta had objected to the treatment of her stepson. Constantine seems to have interpreted Crispus' disagreement as potentially treasonous and acted precipitately. Perhaps a sign that he came to regret what happened was the fact that Fausta's sons remained in line for the succession, and that he never remarried.

Now lacking an empress, Constantine was forced to turn to his mother for help. The aged Helena was sent on a grand tour of the east, where she visited Palestine and was present as a massive new programme of church building was inaugurated in the Holy Land. The sacred sites of the Christian religion were honoured with their own churches, such as the Church of the Holy Sepulchre in Jerusalem, built over the supposed tomb of Christ, as well as churches at the site of the Ascension and the Nativity. Her participation in these events later gave rise to the legend that she found the fragments of the True Cross – on which Christ was crucified at Golgotha – in Jerusalem.

While Constantine's guiding principle was that religion should act as a unifying force in the empire, the exercise of secular authority during his reign caused ever-deepening divisions. As the central government asserted more control over local affairs – an inevitable consequence of Diocletian's policy of smaller, more numerous provinces – each region found that it had increasingly less freedom to define its own relationship to the centre. Conversely, the more extensive governing structures generated regional bureaucracies that were perfectly capable of functioning on their own. Constantine's empire was still split into four prefectures, while his army was now firmly divided between frontier units, the *limitanei*, and units attached to mobile reserve formations, the *comitatenses*, a system begun by Diocletian. In addition to this functional compartmentalization, the army was also divided into three main commands – the West, the Balkans and the East – with each front under its own *magister peditum* (master of infantry) and *magister equitum* (master of cavalry). The different parts of the army, like the different bureaucracies, were increasingly regional in character, with the western sector being heavily recruited from Franks and Alamanni as well as people from within the frontier zone, while the Balkan army increasingly included large numbers of Goths, who had

On an eighth-century fresco painting, Emperor Constantine and his mother Helena (St Helen) are seen holding the True Cross. Legend claims that Helena had nails from the cross placed in her son's helmet and his horse's bridle to give him divine protection in battle.

replaced the earlier tribes north of the Danube over the course of the third century. It was only in the east, where the central Anatolian plateau offered a seemingly endless supply of hardy recruits to serve alongside Syrian and Armenian troops, that the imperial army could still broadly be described as 'Roman', (though many of these soldiers were only acclimatized to Roman ways after they had enlisted).

In the late 330s, as Constantinople expanded into a major city, Constantine confronted the need for a firm plan of succession. He still had three sons and two daughters by Fausta, and a number of nephews, the children of his half-brothers and sisters. Although much of his adult life had been spent eliminating rivals, Constantine felt that there was no intrinsic reason why the empire should have only one emperor. Indeed, the fact that a man who had ruled the entire empire on his own for 13 years should feel that collegial government would work best when he passed on speaks volumes about how deeply divided along regional lines the empire now was. Considering his succession, Constantine even looked beyond his immediate family, elevating his nephew Dalmatius (d. AD 337) to a position equal to that of his own sons as Caesar and making another nephew, Hannibalianus (d. AD 337) king of Armenia, with the evident intent that he should rule a fifth prefecture as soon as it could be acquired. This prefecture would be in Iraq, and in AD 337 Constantine began to plan a massive invasion to bring this region finally under Roman control.

The legacy of Constantine

Yet Constantine, whose first spell of military service is thought to have been as a junior officer in Galerius' successful campaign against Narseh some 40 years earlier, was fated never to return to Iraq. In the spring of AD 337 he fell dangerously ill and died on 22 May after having himself baptized. His body was taken to Constantinople, where it was interred in the great mausoleum he had built for himself in his new city. Although he died a Christian, he intended to be buried as a Roman emperor in the tradition of Diocletian or Galerius. It was only later that his son, Constantius, transformed the mausoleum into the Church of the Twelve Apostles. This was just one of many indications that Constantius failed to appreciate the importance of Constantine's conviction that a person could be both a Roman emperor and a Christian concurrently, rather than simply a Christian emperor.

Constantine was a very dangerous person to be related to: his execution of a son, a wife, a father-in-law and two brothers-in-law is a record of domestic carnage unequalled in the annals of Roman history.

Yet he reigned for nearly 31 years after his seizure of power in Britain. His longevity as emperor may in part be attributed to his great personal ability, yet it also highlights radical changes in the way that the imperial office was now perceived at Rome. While the emperor might now have colleagues in the imperial office, the position was inherently less collegial than it had been when Commodus succeeded Marcus. Commodus had been surrounded by men whose personal status was independent of their position at court. By contrast, in the empire of Diocletian and Constantine status at court defined status beyond the walls of the palaces. Although the post of senator was still highly attractive – ensuring a person great wealth (while also rendering him liable to new taxes) – the mere fact of sitting in the senate no longer guaranteed access to power at the imperial level.

The imperial role changes

In the course of his 20-year reign, Diocletian had fundamentally changed the landscape of power, driving home the point, time and again, that emperors could be created only by other emperors. When the army assembled to watch him retire it was not being invited to the ceremony in order to choose a successor, as it had done in the murky hours after the death of Pertinax or in the Danubian camp of Severus. It had gathered to pay homage to the man whom Diocletian had already marked out as the new Caesar. The emperor would still be presented, and, indeed, present himself through his edicts to the public as a creature of *virtus*, but as the community of Romans had extended far beyond Rome, the *virtus* of the emperor was an increasingly artificial construct, detached from the *domus*, which was now on a grander scale, and definitely off limits to the average person. If, as Diocletian realized, the emperor could only rule effectively if he was distanced from his subjects, then he could no longer be the ideal dinner companion. The Severans had fatally compromised the old system by courting only one element of the empire – the army – and offering no viable alternative.

As the successors of Septimius Severus failed in

A modern sculpture outside the imposing English cathedral of York Minster commemorates Constantine's proclamation as emperor in the town in AD 306. The Christian connection is made clear by the familiar inscription on the plinth – 'By this sign conquer'.

CONSTANTINE BY THIS SIGN CONQUER

the collective exercise of *virtus*, their conduct within the *domus*, ranging from the ghastly to the bizarre, undermined their authority.

However, internal factors alone cannot explain the transformation of the imperial office from one that depended upon the collective action of members of the aristocracy in Rome to one of mastery over an imperial bureaucracy. For much of the trouble that followed the reign of Alexander Severus, due measure of blame must be apportioned to failures by the military. While the inability of the army to defeat either the Sassanians under Ardashir and Shapur or the northern tribes was partly due to the sheer skill of these adversaries, the major role played by the inflexibility of Roman generals cannot be ignored. It was only after the disasters of the AD 250s that new, more professional, fighting soldiers came to the fore and built a new, more flexible army.

One key question remained: now that the emperor controlled an imperial rather than a Roman bureaucracy, could the empire survive with just one emperor? The bureaucracy naturally divided along the major economic lines of the empire, suggesting that multiple emperors would provide a better focus for regional administrations. Diocletian had believed as much, and at the end of his life it appears that Constantine thought so too.

This intricately carved marble sarcophagus (second century, from Acilia) is adorned with sculptures of prominent members of the Roman ruling élite. Between the reigns of Diocletian and Constantine, power steadily devolved away from Rome and the traditional senatorial class.

LOSING
CAESAR

*Relief sculpture of a battle scene. After the relative
stability of Constantine's reign, the Roman empire,
especially in the west, found itself increasingly beset
by wars and invasions.*

Carving up the Empire:
From Constantine's Sons to Valens
(AD 337–375)

In the century and a half after the death
of Constantine, the western empire
ceased altogether to be governed by
Rome, while the east continued to
assert its essential Roman ancestry
for almost a millennium. These
momentous developments occurred
under a system of governance that
had first seen the light of day in the
late second century. Yet key differences
distinguish earlier attempts to find a more
practical way of administering the empire from the
modus operandi of Constantine and his successors.

The eldest son of Constantine, Constantine II, was given command over Gaul, Britannia and Hispania on his father's death. He was made regent for his younger brother Constans, and it was his refusal to hand over guardianship of the latter's realm when Constans came of age that sparked a fatal clash between the brothers. Constantine II was killed as he invaded Italy in AD 340 to assert his authority.

Towards the end of a life spent unifying the empire, Constantine clearly concluded that it should be carved up into four prefectures and run by a college of emperors. The division of the monolithic empire into more manageable administrative units had already been foreshadowed in the reign of Marcus Aurelius. Marcus authorized the creation of large military commands encompassing several provinces in both the east and the Balkans. The tripartite division of the empire that began under Gallienus in AD 260 was a later variation on this same theme. Yet Constantine's scheme, while preserving the naturally self-contained units of the Balkans and the east, further split the western Mediterranean away from Europe north of the Pyrenees and the Alps. Geopolitically, this represented a natural division; the two regions had been separate entities before the advent of the Augustan empire and continue to be thought of as essentially distinct from one another to the present day.

A sprawling bureaucracy
The prefectural model also harked back to Diocletian's dispersal of power in the AD 290s. The only difference was that in Constantine's system the college was made up of blood relatives, whereas Diocletian's

The Roman empire at the death of Constantine in AD 337.
The prefectures that he brought into being are indicated by
the four different coloured zones on this map.

had ultimately placed more of a premium on experience, supported by marriage into the imperial family. Hand-in-hand with their conviction that the empire needed collegiate government went the firm belief that it was in the empire's best interests not to be governed from Rome. This particular aspect is what distinguishes the shared governance schemes of the fourth century from those of earlier periods.

With the benefit of hindsight, it is tempting to regard the empire that Augustus created as an anomaly that was inevitably doomed to failure. Yet hindsight, as we know, is always twenty-twenty. The more remarkable fact is how long the Roman empire in this guise managed to sustain its precarious balancing act – 290 years all told, from Augustus' seizure of Alexandria to Shapur's capture of Valerian, the final death knell of unitary rule.

The empire had always been defined by its systems of taxation and provincial administration; as the style of government changed, then so too did the empire. The system of governance that Augustus put in place was surprisingly decentralized, as were the modes of provincial government that operated in the centuries that followed his reign. One consequence of this decentralization was that the emperor was obliged to negotiate with different groups and balance the interests of one against another. Under the Augustan and Antonine system, personal status determined the broad outlines of a career, as emperors were constrained to recruit their senior officials from people who were usually important in their own right. By contrast, after the death of Diocletian, all power flowed outwards from the palace; personal status

TIMELINE

AD 337 Constantius II orders the massacre of all male offspring of the marriage of his grandfather Constantius I and Theodora

340 Emperor Constantine II is killed at Aquileia in a civil war against his brother Constans

350 Constans is killed, as the usurper Magnentius takes control of the western empire

353 Constantius II defeats Magnentius and becomes sole ruler of the Roman empire to 361

357 Julian wins a major victory over the Alemanni at Strasbourg

359 The Synod of Rimini, Constantius II's final attempt to impose a variant of the Nicene Creed as the statement of faith for the eastern and western churches

361 Death of Constantius II; Julian the Apostate takes the purple

363 Julian is killed invading Persia

364 Valentinian I becomes western emperor, with his brother Valens emperor in the east

368 Picts and the Franks launch sustained attacks on Britain (to 372)

375 Valentinian I dies and is succeeded by his young sons Gratian and Valentinian II was determined by the offices that a person held rather than the other way round. As central government expanded, the pressure to obtain these offices became ever greater, and official power was increasingly defined by a person's ability to secure jobs within the government for his clients. It is one of the great paradoxes of imperial history that as the struggle for status became ever more focused on the palace, the emperor actually lost power rather than gained it. Before a century had elapsed after the death of Constantine the bitterest partisan battles would be fought not over who should be emperor, but rather over who should control the offices that gave access to him. In other words, Caesar was by now little more than a figurehead.

The fractious sons of Constantine

Constantine had hoped that his sons and nephews would manage to govern the empire among themselves. These hopes foundered on the ambitions of Constantius II (AD 317–361), the second of his sons by Fausta. The cause of the discord between Constantine's heirs is lost in the mists of time, but in the late summer of AD 337, Constantius suddenly ordered the arrest and execution of Dalmatius and Hannibalianus, as well as that of every other male descendant of Constantius I and Theodora, with the exception of the sons of his wife's brother, Julius Constantius. These boys, Gallus and Julian, were taken away to Nicomedia, where they were confined in Diocletian's former palace. The three sons of Fausta now assumed the title of Augustus, though it appears that the eldest, Constantine II (AD 316–340), was made regent for the youngest, Constans (AD ?323–350), who was still a minor.

Relations between the brothers soon proved to be as little imbued with Christian charity as their actions towards their cousins had been. Animosity between Constantine II and Constans – or perhaps more accurately the staff of Constans – reached boiling point by the spring of AD 340.

CONSTANTINE II

BORN
AD 316, in Arles, southern France

FATHER
Constantine I

MOTHER
Fausta

PREDECESSOR
Constantine I

BEGINNING OF JOINT REIGN
22 May, AD 337

DIED
AD 340, near Aquileia, northern Italy

SUCCESSOR
Constans

CONSTANS

BORN
c. AD 323 (?)

FATHER
Constantine I

MOTHER
Fausta

PREDECESSOR
Constantine I

BEGINNING OF JOINT REIGN
22 May, AD 337

DYNASTY
Constantinian

DIED
AD 350 in southeastern Gaul

SUCCESSOR
Constantius II

Constantine II led an army from his domain (the western empire) into his younger brother's territory (Italy and Illyricum), claiming that he was on the way to help Constantius II, who was then engaged in a tough struggle against the Persian King Shapur II (r. AD 309–379). As he did so, Constantine was ambushed and killed. And so, no military help ever arrived for Constantius from the west; the court of Constans, which annexed all Constantine II's lands after his death, apparently harboured a deep suspicion of the eastern establishment.

The hostility of the western court was a genuine problem for Constantius, since his resources for the war against the Persians – a conflict his father had been planning just before his death – were limited. Unlike earlier rulers, he could not draw troops from the entire empire. Even so, his forces and those of the Sassanid empire were fairly evenly matched. Despite Shapur II's best efforts over the next decade, he failed to gain any significant advantage, while Constantius was content to remain on the defensive.

A would-be theologian

Constantius was far less quiescent on the matter of his subjects' faith. The point at issue was not that he had been raised as a Christian; the same was true of Constans, yet he turned out to be far less dogmatic in his attitudes than his elder brother. Constantius' unyielding stance was the source of many quarrels with powerful opposing forces in the Eastern Church, notably those in Alexandria led by Bishop Athanasius. Constantius convened council after council in an attempt to arrive at a modified version of the Nicene Creed that would restore church unity.

After Constantine's death, it became apparent that Constantius II, who received the eastern empire as his inheritance, was the most ambitious and ruthless of his three sons. He ordered that his father's funeral be postponed until he could come from Antioch to Constantinople to preside, and then purged the imperial dynasty of any potential rival claimants to the throne. He also fancied himself an intellectual, taking an active and unhelpfully dogmatic part in the affairs of the Christian Church.

CONSTANTIUS II

BORN
7 August, AD 317, in Sirmium, Pannonia

FATHER
Constantine I

MOTHER
Fausta

MARRIED
(1) daughter of Julius Constantius, (2) Eusebia, (3) Faustina

CHILDREN
(by 3) Faustina Constantia

PREDECESSOR
Constantine I

BEGINNING OF JOINT REIGN
22 May, AD 337

DYNASTY
Constantinian

DIED
3 November, AD 361 at Tarsus, Cilicia (southern Turkey)

SUCCESSOR
Julian

ATHANASIUS OF ALEXANDRIA

Although Bishop Athanasius (c. AD 293–373) spent much of his career in exile from his see in his home town of Alexandria, his thinking had an enormous impact on the development of the Christian interpretation of Roman history. He divided emperors between 'true believers' – that is to say, Trinitarians who followed the Nicene Creed – and Arians. He also promoted an ascetic lifestyle, which he popularized through his biography of St Anthony (AD 251–356), the Egyptian founder of the monastic movement. Although Arianism did not long survive the death of its originator Arius in AD 337, accusations of Arianism continued to be raised for many decades. For example, Romans frequently accused Germanic peoples of following this ideology after AD 381, when the emperor Theodosius reasserted the primacy of the Nicene Creed at the Council of Constantinople.

Athanasius was a vigorous opponent of Arianism throughout his life. His fierce opposition to this doctrine brought him into conflict with the ruler of the eastern empire, Constantius II.

However, all such efforts failed, since disputes about the nature of God masked deeper concerns about the nature of imperial authority. Doctrinal matters were presently to be the cause of a serious rift between Constans and Constantius. As early as AD 341, differences between the brothers emerged in their attitude to polytheism. Constantius made moves to abolish public sacrifice, which Constans initially went along with. However, he then chose to reinterpret the proscription as applying only to secret sacrifices that involved casting spells to distress one's neighbours or seeking information about the health of the emperor (practices that had always been illegal).

The following year, when yet another council of eastern and western bishops was summoned, this time at Serdica (modern Sofia, Bulgaria), to discuss proposed 'improvements' to the Nicene Creed, matters came to a head. The western churchmen, sensing that they enjoyed strong support at the court of Constans, rejected the eastern document and demanded that Athanasius be permitted to attend. In AD 344, and for most of AD 345, the storm clouds of civil war appeared to be gathering, as different consuls were recognized in the two parts of the empire. Then, quite suddenly, Constantius, who was hard pressed by the Sassanians, gave in and allowed Athanasius to return to Alexandria.

The challenge of Magnentius

Though Constans had emerged victorious from this clash, major problems were looming for him elsewhere. He had been forced to spend the bulk of the AD 340s in the Danubian lands. The bureaucracy that had once served his brother Constantine in Gaul began to resent the lack of attention it was receiving, with results that would ultimately prove fatal to Constans when he decided to visit there in AD 349. On 18 January, AD 350 Flavius Magnentius (AD 303–353), the commander of the Gallic armies, declared himself emperor and hired assassins to murder Constans. Meanwhile, Constantius' rule teetered on a knife-edge, as Shapur II once again attacked his eastern frontier.

Constantius recognized that the problem he faced in the former realm of Constans would take years to sort out, and that nothing could be done about it until the Persian threat had abated. Thus it was that Constantius delayed his response until Shapur withdrew after a failed siege of the key stronghold of Nisibis in Mesopotamia in the summer of AD 350. Even then, before venturing west to take on Magnentius, Constantius saw that he would need to appoint a reliable deputy – someone who could show the dynastic flag during his absence but not do anything rash to put his realm at risk. Having no son, he called his oldest cousin, Gallus, out of the enforced seclusion in which he and his half-brother Julian (AD 331–363) had been living for the past decade and appointed him Caesar. At the same time, he released Julian from house arrest, allowing this keen scholar to resume his education at Constantinople and other cities along the Aegean seaboard.

Advancing into the Balkans during the winter of AD 350, Constantius first received the submission of the army under Vetranio and then prepared to deal with Magnentius. Diplomatic negotiations brought some significant desertions from Magnentius' camp before the two emperors met in battle at Mursa, a city near Sirmium on the Danube (modern Osijek in Croatia) in AD 351. The outcome was a bloody disaster for both sides, with Magnentius losing some two-thirds of his force while Constantius allegedly sacrificed nearly 40 per cent of his own army. This horrific casualty rate was a sign of just how great the

The usurper Magnentius posed a serious threat to the rule of Constantius in AD 350–353. Constantius was only saved from having to confront an invincible alliance under Magnentius in the west when his sister Constantia persuaded the commander of the Balkan armies, Vetranio, to declare himself emperor. This desperate and temporary expedient succeeded in preventing the Balkan army from joining forces with Magnentius.

'Not long afterwards, Magnentius was overthrown at the battle of Mursa, and nearly taken prisoner. Thus perished large forces that could have conquered any enemy and assured lasting peace throughout the empire.'

EUTROPIUS (4TH CENTURY HISTORIAN), BREVIARIUM HISTORIAE ROMANAE, 10. 12

antipathy between the different sections of the army had become, and of the difficulties any emperor would face if he tried to insist upon unified government. But insist Constantius must, for he could not possibly share power with a rival as determined as Magnentius. Constantius completed the destruction of the western regime at the battle of Mons Seleucus in Gaul in the spring of AD 353.

The victory over Magnentius gave Constantius only temporary respite from governmental crisis. Gallus forgot that his appointed role was merely to act as a figurehead for the regime, and began to quarrel with senior officials in the east, who refused to report to him. In the west, an effort to reward an officer named Silvanus for betraying Magnentius backfired when members of the court conspired against him, whereupon he declared himself emperor. Constantius ordered Gallus to leave Antioch and executed him for treason at the end of AD 354 and arranged Silvanus' assassination in AD 355. Yet these crises convinced him that he needed more help. For this he turned to Julian, who was appointed Caesar in Gaul, with express instructions to prevent a recurrence of the troubles that had doomed Gallus.

'Frequent messages concerning the desperate state of Gaul, where everything was laid waste by the barbarians and there was none to resist them were distressing Constantius. Worrying for a time about how he might prevent these disasters by force while remaining in Italy, as he desired – he thought it was dangerous to take himself off to a distant part of the empire – he hit upon the correct plan, and decided to associate his cousin Julian, who had recently been summoned from Greece and still wore the student's cloak, in the imperial power.'

AMMIANUS MARCELLINUS, HISTORY 15.8.1

In the course of his extensive education, Julian had secretly converted from Christianity to paganism under the tutelage of Maximus of Ephesus, a Neoplatonic philosopher who showed him a flaming – and talking – statue of the goddess Hecate that he kept at his house. Maximus believed that philosophers who were party to secret knowledge of the gods could induce revelations, and he used the statue to convince impressionable individuals like the young Julian of the truth of his claims.

Julian the schemer

Julian may have been eccentric, but he was by no means stupid. He recognized that Constantius governed by sowing fear and suspicion among senior officials, who looked to him as the ultimate arbiter of all their affairs. One of the most telling anecdotes from Constantius' reign concerns the general Ursicinus, who was sent to murder Silvanus. When he arrived at Silvanus' headquarters, Silvanus greeted him as an old friend, assuming that Ursicinus was as disillusioned with

THEURGY

The central tenet of theurgy was the belief that humans could control the action of the gods through intense study of the divine world. The doctrine was based on the Chaldaean Oracles, texts allegedly written by a man named Julianus in the time of Marcus Aurelius (historians now believe that they were composed much later). These writings disclosed 'secret' knowledge about the gods, imparted to mortals by the gods themselves.

The actual practice of theurgy among a small group of philosophers in the eastern empire was introduced at the end of the third century by Iamblichus (c. AD 245–325), a native of Syria, and promoted by certain philosophers who traced their ideas to those of Plotinus, the third-century AD founder of Neoplatonism. A great deal of magical ritual, sacrifice and invocation was involved in the theurgical litany.

Constantius' reign as he was. Indeed, this was a fair appraisal of Ursicinus' state of mind – Ammianus Marcellinus (c. AD 330–395), one of his staff officers, meticulously documented his incessant moaning about how badly treated he felt. Even so, he still feared Constantius enough that he thought it better to assassinate his friend than defy his emperor. In such circumstances, then, if Julian were to survive, he would need to find a way to exploit Constantius' tyrannical style of rule to his own advantage.

In the wake of Silvanus' murder, Ursicinus and an officer named Marcellus were put in command of military forces in Gaul. In AD 356 they were ordered to conduct manoeuvres to intimidate the Alamanni, an operation that went off tolerably well, while Julian played his role as imperial figurehead in the campaign. In the winter, however, Julian was cut off, well within Roman territory, by a band of Frankish raiders. He escaped, but thereafter histrionically dramatized the incident, suggesting that his near-death experience was the result of a desertion of duty by his senior military commanders. Ursicinus and Marcellus were duly replaced by an officer named Barbatio, who was ordered to coordinate an operation with Julian in AD 357 similar to that of the previous year. Julian did as little as he could to help, perhaps hoping that Barbatio would run into trouble and retreat, which is indeed what happened. Julian, however, had reckoned without the consequences of his own subterfuge, and suddenly found himself confronted by an army of Alamanni near Strasbourg.

Even allowing for the fact that most of what we know comes from Ammianus, whose critical faculties were occasionally impaired by his partiality for Julian, the result of this encounter exceeded Julian's wildest hopes. His victory was total, including the capture of the king of the Alamanni, and established his reputation as a commander to be reckoned with. Even Constantius, who was in the Balkans at the time, seemed genuinely impressed, and began to entrust Julian with real authority.

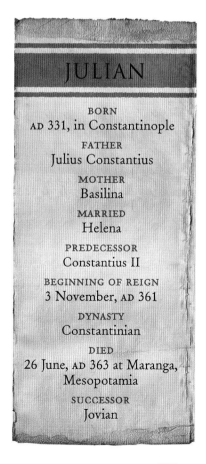

JULIAN

BORN
AD 331, in Constantinople

FATHER
Julius Constantius

MOTHER
Basilina

MARRIED
Helena

PREDECESSOR
Constantius II

BEGINNING OF REIGN
3 November, AD 361

DYNASTY
Constantinian

DIED
26 June, AD 363 at Maranga, Mesopotamia

SUCCESSOR
Jovian

Watch, learn and strike

Over the course of the winter, Julian won further credit, this time at the expense of the praetorian prefect in Gaul in a dispute over tax collection. This matter was dealt with by correspondence. In his dealings in Gaul, Julian emulated his cousin in avoiding personal entanglements with senior officials. Constantius had come to realize that maintaining a certain aloofness bred exactly the kind of constructive fear that was needed to keep officials in line. Julian did likewise, surrounding himself with a few close friends and staying clear of day-to-day administration.

All the while, as he built his own group of supporters and won the loyalty of select units of the army, Julian knew that he only had a limited amount of time to play with. Dreams revealed to him that he was destined to overthrow his cousin, and he entered into treasonous correspondence with his spiritual gurus. Constantius grew suspicious and so, in AD 358, he replaced a number of Julian's closest advisers with his own placemen. But then larger problems obtruded and demanded his attention, as Shapur II once again threatened war in the east. At the same time, he became embroiled again in doctrinal debate. In these circumstances, it would have been counterproductive to remove Julian, who was at least efficient and, as far as Constantius knew, not openly disloyal.

The Persian invasion ground to a halt before the city of Amida in the summer of AD 359. Ammianus, who was present, recorded the scene as the enemy carefully prepared his siege lines around the fortress for over two months. Meanwhile, Constantius was idle, awaiting the outcome of discussions on the Holy Trinity at Sirmium. Even when Amida fell, Constantius did not act. Yet the garrison's courageous stand had so seriously delayed the Persians' timetable for a summer offensive that they now withdrew. This would only be a temporary reprieve, however. If Constantius was to defeat Shapur, he would need more men, and the only person who was in a position to supply troops, having successfully pacified the Rhine frontier, was Julian.

Constantius had few options open to him when he elevated Julian, and likely had more than an inkling of his cousin's oddness. Yet he could not have known quite how eccentric Julian would turn out to be. Later Christian writers dubbed him 'Julian the Apostate' for his rejection of Christianity and revival of the worship of the old gods.

Julian saw his chance. Antipathy to Constantius ran high both in the western army and among influential opinion-makers in Gallic society. Mainstream Christians in particular – now rejoined once more by Athanasius, who had been exiled from Alexandria for a third time in AD 355 – had come to regard the emperor as the Antichrist. Western troops were all too aware that units transferred east as a penalty for supporting Magnentius never came home – five were wiped out at Amida alone – and so refused point-blank to leave Gaul. These were disciplined soldiers, but they saw their loyalty as being primarily to the areas from which they came. Julian exploited their discontent, and in March AD 360 allowed himself to be proclaimed Augustus by troops who were in transit to the eastern front. Constantius' authority in Gaul collapsed and the new Augustus wrote saying that he would be content to split the empire with his cousin, who had no choice but to concede while Shapur threatened his borders.

'We waited there [Amida] for two full days, and when the sun rose on the third, we saw the whole circuit of the lands, which we call the horizon, filled with innumerable columns of soldiers, and the king himself, gleaming in magnificent attire.'

AMMIANUS MARCELLINUS, HISTORY 17.6.22.

Julian did not wait for Constantius to regroup. In the summer of AD 361 he invaded the Balkans and reached Naissus, where he stopped to gather his strength and bombard the cities of the east with propaganda leaflets justifying his rebellion. He now began to worship the old gods openly, and after 3 November had even more reason to put his faith in them. It was on that day that Constantius suddenly died of a fever in southern Turkey.

Desperate ploys

The brief reign of Julian is most noteworthy for his abortive attempts to revive traditional cult. If he had not combined this effort with a spectacularly ill-advised invasion of Iraq, it is conceivable that he might even have reversed the steady trend towards Christianization begun by Constantine. On the other hand, Julian's brand of religious fundamentalism was as distasteful to thinking pagans as it was to Christians. In dealing with the Christians, he held back from conducting persecutions, and tried instead to foment discord within their communities. He did this by recalling various bishops to the sees from which Constantius had exiled them for doctrinal nonconformity. Thus it was that Athanasius returned as archbishop of Alexandria after a pagan mob there had murdered the former incumbent (and Julian's former guardian) George of Cappadocia. Julian did not punish the Alexandrians for their act, but in various other places, when violence broke out between Christian communities, his response was to impose heavy sanctions upon them.

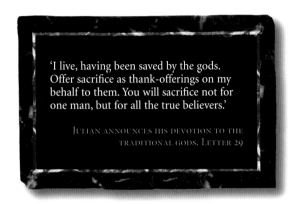

Julian also created new provincial priesthoods to raise the profile of traditional pagan worship by engaging in lavish public sacrifices. The intention was that his new priests should mount a challenge to the Christian establishment, which, for all its internal divisions, had won genuine credit for dispensing charity to widows and the sick. This initiative failed; not only were aristocratic pagan priests totally unused to doing charitable works, but they also simply lacked the infrastructure to compete.

Equally problematic was Julian's attempt to encourage the Jews to restore the Temple at Jerusalem, destroyed in the revolt of AD 70. His sole motivation was to disprove Jesus' prophecy, as reported in the gospels, that the Temple would remain a ruin. All of Julian's plans ultimately turned to dust; in AD 362 work in Jerusalem was halted by an earthquake. That same year, Athanasius was again evicted from Alexandria when he dared to convert several prominent pagans to Christianity. Worse still, the people of Antioch, where Julian overwintered, displayed open contempt for him after he controversially removed the bones of a Christian martyr from the site of an oracular shrine he planned to reopen. He also tried to blame the Christians of Antioch when a famous local temple was consumed by an accidental fire. Ultimately, he concluded that the only way out of the impasse he had got himself into was to undertake a massive assault against Persia.

Outflanked in Iraq

Julian launched his invasion of Iraq in the spring of AD 363. His strategy was to force the Persian king to negotiate by threatening his capital at Ctesiphon. The ultimate plan was to install Shapur's relative Hormizd (son of the former ruler Hormizd II), who was accompanying Julian, as a puppet ruler of some part of the realm. This was a foolish plan bedevilled by slapdash preparation. Julian brought with him no siege train, and was totally wrong-footed when Shapur refused to engage in a risky set-piece battle. Shapur had the luxury of being able to play a waiting game and win the war by exploiting Julian's woeful logistics. And so, as Julian advanced down the Euphrates, the Persians flooded the irrigation canals behind him, making it impossible for him to withdraw the same way that he had come.

Things went from bad to worse. Ctesiphon refused to surrender to a general who lacked the proper equipment to lay siege to it. Julian was forced to beat an ignominious retreat up the Tigris, harassed all the while by Persian delaying tactics designed to slow his withdrawal as he ran desperately short of food and other supplies. On 26 June, Julian was mortally wounded during a Persian attack on his rearguard. A relatively junior officer, Jovian (*c.* AD 332–364), was chosen by the general staff to serve as emperor and continue the retreat. On 1 July, he reached an agreement with Shapur, whereby the starving remnant of his army would be granted safe conduct to Roman territory in return for certain concessions. These included restoring to Persia the provinces seized by Diocletian and surrender of the fortress of Nisibis, which Shapur had failed to capture three times in the reign of Constantius.

Brothers in power

Jovian might not have been a bad emperor. The surrender to Shapur was hardly his fault, and in his short reign he tried to bring confessional peace to the empire. Athanasius, the symbol of ecclesiastical resistance to imperial control, was permitted to return to Alexandria. At the same time, Jovian took only limited action against former supporters of Julian, and recognized that he could only secure power though negotiation with various entrenched interests in the bureaucracy.

St George of Cappadocia, pictured on a Byzantine bas-relief sculpture. He was venerated as a Christian martyr after his murder by a pagan mob in Alexandria. Edward Gibbon identified him with the St George who became the patron saint of England, Ethiopia, Georgia, Greece, Serbia and many other countries, but there is much doubt about this attribution.

Before he had a chance to get a firm grasp on the reins of power, however, he died on 17 February, AD 364. The official line was that a coal fire asphyxiated him in his bedroom. The fact that there was no investigation of his death hinted at murder. But if this were the case, those responsible had no clear plan for the future. It was not until 26 February that another comparatively junior officer, Valentinian (AD 321–375), was presented to the army as the general staff's candidate. The soldiers duly proclaimed him emperor, and, a few weeks later, as Valentinian realized that he would be spending a great deal of time in the west, he requested that they proclaim his brother, Valens (AD 328–378), as his co-emperor.

Julian the Apostate falling in battle near Ctesiphon in Persia. His ill-prepared invasion of Mesopotamia, motivated by a heady combination of military adventurism and religious fanaticism, resulted in an unmitigated disaster for the Roman army.

Constantius and Julian were strong personalities who had constantly reasssigned senior officials to prevent the formation of powerful patronage networks. Yet, like the rank-and-file soldiers, senior bureaucrats tended to come from the regions where they served. Imperial authority simply set the seal on the power they had already acquired by cultivating connections within each bureau of government. All power was now centralized within the palace and was no longer based on the principle of collegiality. This meant that emperors were now obliged to negotiate with various diverse local power structures masquerading as representatives of a central government. The men who surrounded the throne had a vested interest in preventing effective imperial interference in their fiefdoms. They got exactly the emperors they wanted in Valentinian and Valens.

The nature of the new regime became apparent in September AD 365 when Procopius, a distant relative of Julian, whom Julian had allegedly designated as his successor before invading Iraq, staged a coup in Constantinople. In line with his lenient treatment of Julian's former confederates, Jovian had allowed Procopius, who did not press his claim, to retire to his estates in central Turkey. Valens now stirred things up by ordering Procopius' arrest. Procopius evaded capture and reappeared in the capital to win control of two legions. For several months, it looked as though he would unseat Valens. When Valentinian learned of the revolt, his advisors dissuaded him from intervening, emphasizing that it was vital he should remain in Gaul to repel any barbarian invasion. If Procopius prevailed, they would work out a way to deal with him later.

In the end, though, Valens was saved by the intervention of Arbitio, a member of Constantius' inner circle whom Julian had cashiered. Arbitio, whose personal authority was plainly far greater than that of Valens, convinced many of Procopius' men to switch sides prior to the battle that would decide who became emperor. In the course of the battle even more of Procopius' men deserted his ranks, and he was captured and executed.

'A wonder! By chance the corpse of the accursed one,
Crossing over towards the rampart met me near the city!
And the Magus took and fastened on a tower
The standard sent from the east,
So that this standard-bearer would declare to the onlookers
That the city was slave to the lords of that standard.'

EPHRAIM OF NISIBIS, HYMN AGAINST JULIAN 3

The message of Procopius' coup was loud and clear. Valens and Valentinian were welcome to rule, but if they wanted to stay in power, it was essential that they respect the interests of their top civil servants. Valens' success was largely due to the fact that, once the western armies had returned home, most eastern officials were still Constantius' appointees, who hated Procopius for his links with Julian.

Corrupt sinecures

Valentinian remained on the throne for 11 years, and Valens for 14. In the west, Valentinian ruled through a small circle of associates who had supported his rise to power. Many abused their privileged position for years. In North Africa, for instance, a major scandal erupted at the start of Valentinian's reign, when the region's long-serving military commander, Romanus, arrived in the city of Leptis Magna to deal with the problem of ongoing attacks by desert raiders. After remaining there for 40 days, he suddenly demanded 4000 camels from the city's long-suffering inhabitants and, when these were not forthcoming, simply abandoned them to their fate. The people of Leptis Magna protested, but Romanus exploited his connections at court to ensure that no action was taken against him, even as the nomads resumed their raids. The issue dragged on for years, and Romanus continued all the while to feather his own nest. Indeed, Romanus' corruption only became the subject of scrutiny in a massive shake-up of government after Valentinian's death.

Similar corrupt practices flourished in Rome, where members of the senatorial aristocracy were charged with a range of offences of a largely personal nature (e.g. consulting magicians and adultery). Senators lodged vigorous protests, but were delivered a rude snub, as the official they most detested was promoted to the praetorian prefecture. The most significant feature of this incident is not that the representations of the senate failed to achieve their desired effect, but that this body now clearly saw itself as quite separate from the imperial court. The Roman senate had once been the pool from which future emperors were drawn, and a partner in the governance of the realm. Now, with only limited access to key posts, and the emperor living far away in Constantinople, it was reduced to acting as just another civic petitioner.

The senatorial prosecutions and the tribulations of the people of Leptis Magna, which were symptomatic of a court that exercised arbitrary power, help explain an event that was not only the most extraordinary of the reign of Valentinian, but also one of the most remarkable in the entire history of Rome. Valentinian fell seriously ill in AD 367, and the

JOVIAN

BORN
c. AD 331, in Singidunum (Belgrade)

FATHER
Varronianus (commander of Constantius II's personal guard)

PREDECESSOR
Julian

BEGINNING OF REIGN
26 June, AD 363

DIED
17 February, AD 364 in Dadastana

SUCCESSOR
Valentinian I

two principal factions at the court, described simply by Ammianus Marcellinus as the 'Gauls' and 'those with better aims' met to decide whom they should choose as his successor in the event of the emperor's death. There was evidently no question of consulting Valens, or even Valentinian himself. When Valentinian recovered, he punished none of those responsible but instead had his son, Gratian, declared Augustus. The bureaucracy allowed him to have his way, but it was clear from what had gone before that the government of the west felt no responsibility to the emperor in the east, nor to the dynastic principle. The situation in the east was no different.

Casting the runes

In AD 371 a group of officials consulted a bizarre prophetic device (an ancient form of ouija board) to determine who the next emperor should be. The answer it gave was understood to indicate Theodorus, a Gaulish official. Even more curiously, when Theodorus was informed of his selection, Ammianus claims that he planned to tell Valens. Yet he was pre-empted by the praetorian prefect Modestus, who wanted to secure the succession for an easterner, and launched an investigation into treasonous magical practices. Many senior officials were executed. Since Valens had no son yet, the matter of the succession was left open for the time being.

Valentinian, who had a ferocious temper, died of an apoplectic seizure in AD 375. Gratian stepped in as Augustus in Gaul, and his supporters immediately set about purging all of Valentinian's former confederates. The Balkan commander Merobaudes, who was one such ally, saw the writing on the wall if he failed to interpose some new titular authority between himself and the new ruler. Indeed, he seems to have planned for just this eventuality with the collusion of Valentinian's second

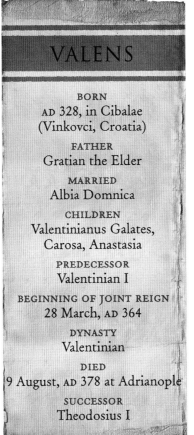

VALENTINIAN I

BORN
AD 321, in Cibalae
(Vinkovci, Croatia)

FATHER
Gratian the Elder

MARRIED
(1) Marina Severa, (2) Justina

CHILDREN
(by 1) Gratian, (by 2)
Valentinian II

PREDECESSOR
Jovian

BEGINNING OF JOINT REIGN
26 February, AD 364

DYNASTY
Valentinian

DIED
17 November, AD 375 at
Brigetio on the Danube

SUCCESSOR
Gratian and Valentinian II

VALENS

BORN
AD 328, in Cibalae
(Vinkovci, Croatia)

FATHER
Gratian the Elder

MARRIED
Albia Domnica

CHILDREN
Valentinianus Galates,
Carosa, Anastasia

PREDECESSOR
Valentinian I

BEGINNING OF JOINT REIGN
28 March, AD 364

DYNASTY
Valentinian

DIED
9 August, AD 378 at Adrianople

SUCCESSOR
Theodosius I

AN ANCIENT SÉANCE

During excavations at Pergamum (modern Bergama in western Turkey), German archaeologists found a private divination kit similar to the one that Ammianus Marcellinus describes in his account of Theodorus' 'conspiracy' against Valens in AD 371, in his *History of the Later Roman Empire*. In that instance, the diviners used a tripod from which a ring was suspended. Placed above the tripod was a dish engraved with all the letters of the Greek alphabet. When the question was posed who the next emperor would be, the oscillations of the ring pointed successively to the letters theta, eta, omicron and delta. The interpreters took this to denote an official named Theodorus. Ammianus recounts the testimony given at their subsequent trial by the two main officials responsible for organizing the séance, Patricius and Hilarius:

On this fragment of a frieze, the gods Apollo and Hercules are shown arguing over the Delphic tripod. Divination continued to be widely practised in the late Roman empire.

'My lords, in an unlucky moment we put together out of laurel twigs in the shape of the Delphic tripod the hapless little table before you. We consecrated it with cryptic spells and a long series of magical rites, and at last made it work. The way in which it did so ... was this. It was placed in the middle of a room thoroughly fumigated with spices from Arabia, and was covered with a round dish made from the alloys of various metals. The outer rim of the dish was cunningly engraved with the twenty-four letters of the alphabet separated by accurate intervals. A man dressed in linen garments and wearing linen sandals ... officiated as priest. After uttering a set prayer to invoke the divine power which presides over prophecy, he took his place above the tripod as his knowledge of the proper ritual had taught him, and set swinging a ring suspended by a very fine cotton thread which had been consecrated by a mystic formula. The ring, moving in a series of jumps over the marked spaces, came to rest on particular letters.'

Their full confession failed to save the hapless Patricius and Hilarius. Ammianus records that 'both the accused were fearfully mangled by the torturer's hooks and taken away unconscious'.

wife, Justina. She had a son, also named Valentinian, and within five days of the announcement of the elder Valentinian's death, the younger Valentinian was proclaimed Augustus, with authority over Illyricum. Gratian and Valens accepted the proclamation as a *fait accompli*.

Whatever Valens thought of the proclamation of Valentinian, he soon found himself beset by far more urgent problems. As Valentinian II came to power, he was engaged in a fierce struggle with the Persians over control of Armenia. As if this were not serious enough, news reached him the following year in Antioch of a massive movement of peoples north of the Balkan frontier. The Goths were coming.

Enemies at the Gate: The Barbarian Invasions (AD 376–411)

The Goths were not exactly an unknown quantity to the Romans. Having first arrived in the region to the north of Rome's border along the Danube around the end of the second century AD, they took part in the extensive raids that kept much of the Roman army tied down in the 250s and 260s. During the course of the next century, they divided into two main groups, the Tervingi, who inhabited the region around the Dneister River, and the Greuthingi, who occupied the lands bordering the Danube.

A Roman cavalryman battling a Gothic invader. Although, over time, the Roman empire began to assimiliate its Gothic neighbours, the sudden huge influx of Goth refugees fleeing from the Hunnish invasions created insuperable tensions, making conflict inevitable.

Over time, many Goths were recruited into the Roman army, while Constantine sponsored an effort to spread Christianity among them. The main agent of conversion was a Goth priest named Ulfilas (*c.* AD 311–383), who was ordained a bishop by Athanasius' great enemy, Eusebius of Nicomedia. The effects of his missionary work were deeply ambivalent, both at the time and later. From the Roman point of view, when Athanasius' brand of Christianity finally triumphed at the end of the century, Goths were regarded as heretics. In Ulfilas' own time, Gothic leaders who did not convert regarded him as an agent of the imperial government and persecuted his flock. As a result, Constantius II was forced to grant Ulfilas and some of his followers permission to move into Moesia Inferior (northern Bulgaria). Otherwise, contacts between the Roman and the Goths were regulated through Roman border posts. This was an uneasy coexistence, with occasional upsurges of violence, the most recent of which had been sparked by the Goths' alleged support for Procopius. A truce was concluded in AD 369, in which both parties agreed to maintain the status quo.

Invaders from the north

The ensuing peace, however, was shattered by the Huns – a semi-nomadic people from the Eurasian steppes. Although Roman sources describe in great detail the sudden irruption of these fearsome barbarians into northeastern Europe in the years immediately before AD 376, the truth about their appearance is probably somewhat more prosaic. As semi-nomads, the Huns would have long depended to some degree on neighbouring settled communities of Goths for their subsistence. It is not known what soured this relationship, but it is apparent that the Huns began to carry out massive raids against the Tervingi from the mid-370s onwards.

The Huns' success was due in large part to their adoption of a devastatingly effective piece of military hardware: a powerful form of recurved bow that enabled them to take down their opponents at long range. This weapon instantly rendered useless traditional Gothic tactics that relied on spear-armed cavalry engaging in close combat. A series of defeats threw the Tervingi into political turmoil, causing many to leave their lands and seek refuge among the Greuthingi, who also now began to suffer raids from the Huns. A large number of Greuthingi now decided to abandon their traditional territory and, like the Tervingi, seek refuge within the empire. As Ulfilas' flight shows, the empire was seen as a safe haven for Goths who could no longer live as they wished north of the border. This time, however, the sheer numbers involved made old models of accommodation unworkable.

Valens saw the displaced Goths as a potential source of recruits, and hoped to regulate the flow of refugees by allowing only the Greuthingi to enter Roman territory. Although this was a perfectly measured response, it would have required a great deal more advance planning than Valens had given it to make it work. The total number of Greuthingi is thought to have been in the region of 30,000–40,000 people, some 10,000 of whom were men of fighting age. With most of Valens' field army deployed in the east, there were not enough troops to control the situation. Moreover, even if it had been properly managed, the supply network was wholly inadequate for catering to such a huge influx of hungry people. Relations with the immigrants

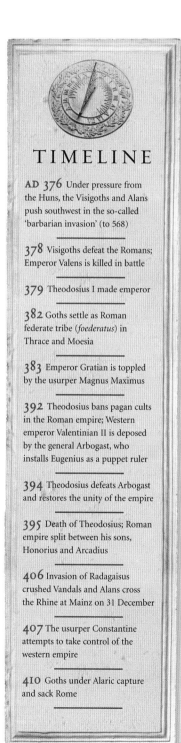

TIMELINE

AD 376 Under pressure from the Huns, the Visigoths and Alans push southwest in the so-called 'barbarian invasion' (to 568)

378 Visigoths defeat the Romans; Emperor Valens is killed in battle

379 Theodosius I made emperor

382 Goths settle as Roman federate tribe (*foederatus*) in Thrace and Moesia

383 Emperor Gratian is toppled by the usurper Magnus Maximus

392 Theodosius bans pagan cults in the Roman empire; Western emperor Valentinian II is deposed by the general Arbogast, who installs Eugenius as a puppet ruler

394 Theodosius defeats Arbogast and restores the unity of the empire

395 Death of Theodosius; Roman empire split between his sons, Honorius and Arcadius

406 Invasion of Radagaisus crushed Vandals and Alans cross the Rhine at Mainz on 31 December

407 The usurper Constantine attempts to take control of the western empire

410 Goths under Alaric capture and sack Rome

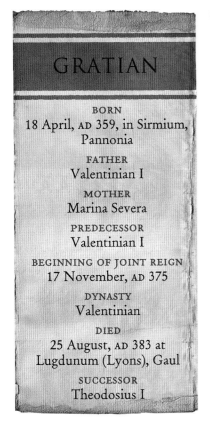

GRATIAN

BORN
18 April, AD 359, in Sirmium,
Pannonia

FATHER
Valentinian I

MOTHER
Marina Severa

PREDECESSOR
Valentinian I

BEGINNING OF JOINT REIGN
17 November, AD 375

DYNASTY
Valentinian

DIED
25 August, AD 383 at
Lugdunum (Lyons), Gaul

SUCCESSOR
Theodosius I

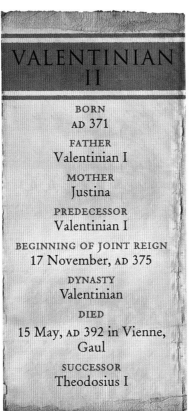

VALENTINIAN II

BORN
AD 371

FATHER
Valentinian I

MOTHER
Justina

PREDECESSOR
Valentinian I

BEGINNING OF JOINT REIGN
17 November, AD 375

DYNASTY
Valentinian

DIED
15 May, AD 392 in Vienne,
Gaul

SUCCESSOR
Theodosius I

swiftly deteriorated and, after a botched Roman effort to seize the leaders of the Greuthingi at a banquet in AD 377, they broke down completely.

The outbreak of war with the Greuthingi opened the frontier to other tribes, and by the summer of AD 377 the number of new arrivals swelled to around 80,000. When set against the overall population of the empire – still probably in the range of 60 million – this figure might appear negligible. Yet it represented a huge number of people concentrated in one area, and it would have required close coordination on the part of the three governments of the empire to bring the situation under control. As Valens made peace with Persia, neither the government of Valentinian II nor that of Gratian sent reinforcements to help the eastern emperor. Gratian, who was at least willing to help, was held up by insurrection among his forces on the lower Rhine. The Balkan commander Merobaudes, who was closer, did nothing except secure his own territory against Goth incursion. In AD 378, Gratian finally advanced east. Meanwhile Valens marshalled his forces, but still hoped that a diplomatic solution might be found.

In August, AD 378 the main Goth force encamped near Adrianople (the Turkish city of Edirne, in Thrace). Valens could delay no longer, and on 9 August made his move. His defeat was so complete that two-thirds of his army perished with him on the battlefield. The Goths, after realizing that they could not take Constantinople, and heeding the famous words of one of their leaders that they should try to attack walled cities, moved on to the hitherto unravaged lands of central Bulgaria and Serbia.

Gratian was in something of a quandary. As senior surviving emperor, he could simply claim

> 'We are at peace with walls.'
>
> VISIGOTH CHIEFTAIN FRITIGERN (D. C. AD 380)

The Battle of Adrianople

The battle of Adrianople, fought on 9 August, AD 378 near the present-day Turkish village of Muratcali, pitted Valens' Roman field army of the east, numbering between 30,000 and 40,000 men, against the Goths and other tribes that had crossed the Danube after 376. The strength of the Gothic army was probably around 30,000 men. After marching eight miles (11 km) from their camp, the Romans deployed in line against the Goths, who had taken up defensive positions in front of their wagon laager. Following a parley between Valens and the Goth commanders, some units on the Roman left launched an attack on the Goths (quite possibly without orders). The Gothic cavalry, which had been away from the camp, then attacked and routed the Roman left, and subsequently encircled and destroyed the centre of the Roman force. Two-thirds of the Roman army is said to have perished. The emperor Valens was among the casualties, but his body was never found (perhaps because the Goths set fire to a farmhouse where he was taken after being wounded). Adrianople was the most crushing defeat suffered by Rome since a Republican army was annihilated by Hannibal at the Battle of Cannae six centuries earlier.

Stele carving of a Gothic warrior on horseback. The intervention of cavalry forces in the Battle of Adrianople was decisive in the rout of the Roman army.

sovereignty over the east, but could not be sure that the eastern bureaucracy would accept him. Instead of doing battle with the Goths, he appointed two senior military commanders, one for the eastern frontier, the other for Illyricum, a rather ill-defined title that probably comprehended authority over the idle armies of Valentinian II as well as the remnants of Valens' forces in the Balkans. As commander in the east he selected a man with the portentous name of Shapur (evidently a Persian who had entered Roman service), while the man he chose to take military control of Illyricum was Theodosius.

Striking a deal

Theodosius was the son of the man who had been Valentinian I's *magister militum* (literally 'master of the soldiers'). This post was created in the early AD 370s, establishing a new level of command above those held by the master of infantry (*magister peditum*) and master of cavalry (*magister equitum*). Over time, it would become the most prestigious post within the military bureaucracy.

Yet when Theodosius the Elder took on the role in AD 373, his position was precarious to say the least. Dispatched to North Africa to suppress a minor revolt, he uncovered the corrupt conduct of Romanus and sent him for trial in Italy. The trial was conducted by Merobaudes, who promptly found Romanus innocent, and in addition ensured that his cronies at the court of Valentinian I charged Theodosius himself with treason. He was executed in AD 376.

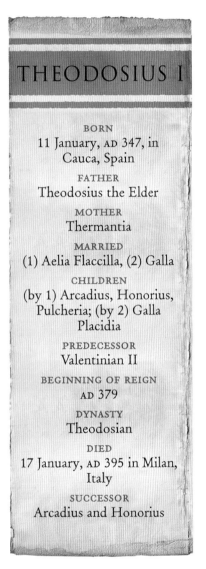

THEODOSIUS I

BORN
11 January, AD 347, in
Cauca, Spain

FATHER
Theodosius the Elder

MOTHER
Thermantia

MARRIED
(1) Aelia Flaccilla, (2) Galla

CHILDREN
(by 1) Arcadius, Honorius,
Pulcheria; (by 2) Galla
Placidia

PREDECESSOR
Valentinian II

BEGINNING OF REIGN
AD 379

DYNASTY
Theodosian

DIED
17 January, AD 395 in Milan,
Italy

SUCCESSOR
Arcadius and Honorius

It is probable that the scandalous death of the elder Theodosius sparked the violent reaction against Valentinian's inner circle, whose members now fell from power. This event would doubtless also have had repercussions at the court of Valentinian II. Certainly, Gratian's choice of the younger Theodosius – now in his thirties and with no experience of such a senior command – was more a message to the regime of Merobaudes than it was a threat to the Goths. Even at moments of extreme crisis, it seemed, internal bureaucratic politics were of prime importance.

Perhaps Theodosius' chief quality was that he was a fast learner. After defeating Sarmatian raiders, he promptly allowed himself to be proclaimed emperor in January AD 379. This may all have been part of Gratian's plan; certainly the outcome was not unwelcome to Gratian's retinue of officials, who lent Theodosius vital support over the next couple of years, and the young Gratian recognized Theodosius' claim to the throne without demur. Perhaps he and his advisors felt that anyone who wanted to be Augustus in the east under the circumstances that obtained in AD 379 was welcome to the job. Theodosius knew that he needed to tread carefully, for he could not really claim the throne, or indeed show himself in Constantinople, until the problem of the Goths had been resolved. He therefore set up court at Thessalonica.

The shared experience of victory and pillage was gradually shaping the Goths who had ventured south from their original homeland into a cohesive new community. More than anything they now wanted a place that they could call home, and sought it within the bounds of the Roman empire. Theodosius was initially hostile, but after suffering a defeat at their hands in AD 380, made peace with the Goths. They were granted autonomous lands in the Balkans under the control of their own chiefs in return for service, when required, with the army of the east. Such subsidized barbarian tribes were known as *foederati* ('federates').

Blueprint for break-up

Although the treaty of AD 382 might appear to hark back to a happier age when the emperor controlled a multi-ethnic state through careful diplomacy and overt displays of personal *virtus*, it was in fact a blueprint for the break-up of the Roman empire. The idea of client states and independent allies was nothing new; in the past Rome had allowed Palmyra to raise a powerful army, and fostered a variety of relationships with its subjects as a way of strengthening the empire. But this treaty was fundamentally different, inasmuch as there was now no

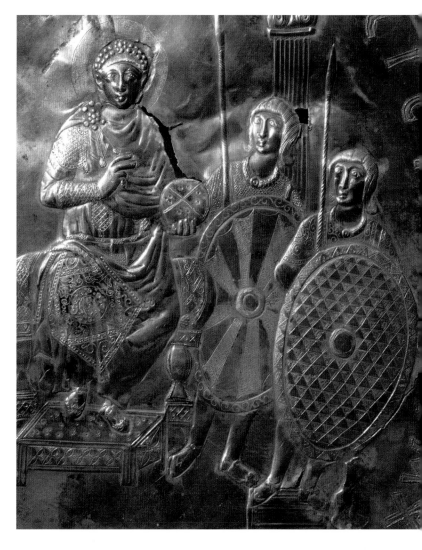

apparatus for interaction between Rome's federates and the central government that was not dictated (and tainted) by the vested interests of the bureaucratic elite. In other words, instead of becoming staunch and valued allies of the Roman people or the Roman empire, the Goths were to be mere pawns in the endless internal power struggle between different parts of the Roman bureaucracy.

Another reason for the incipient dissolution of the empire was the growing gap in prosperity that opened up between the east on the one hand and the centre and west on the other. Not only did the treaty with the Goths mean that no more tax revenues would flow to the western empire from the regions they occupied, but the foregoing years of war had also done terrible damage to the empire's infrastructure in the Balkans. Large swathes of countryside took years to recover from such depredations. By contrast, improving relations with Persia after the death of Shapur II in AD 379 meant that no such devastation was visited on the eastern empire. In consequence, there developed a substantial difference between the logistical capacity of the empire to the east of the Bosphorus and that of the empire to the west. To further exacerbate the problem, the inability of the eastern, western and central bureaucracies to unite behind a common set of objectives meant that deterioration in one area was now unlikely to be repaired through the altruistic cooperation of the others.

The Missorium of Theodosius is a votive platter that was made to commemorate the tenth anniversary of this emperor's reign. This detail shows Theodosius' son Arcadius with two soldiers. Despite bellicose anti-German statements by Theodosius at the beginning of his reign, many soldiers, including the men depicted here, were of German origin.

The interventions by Gratian, whose generals continued to help Theodosius up until the treaty of AD 382, stand as an honourable exception to the general rule that each region was left to fend for itself. Certainly, Theodosius did not reciprocate Gratian's loyalty. In AD 383, Magnus Maximus, the commander of the British garrison, took advantage of serious discontent with Gratian's management of affairs

ST AMBROSE

Born in the city of Trier in around AD 340, Ambrose rose to become one of the leading figures of early Christianity; together with SS Augustine of Hippo, Gregory, and Jerome, he is considered one of the four 'doctors of the Church', scholars whose teachings had a seminal influence on the development of Roman Catholicism.

Ambrose was appointed bishop of Milan in AD 374, and in this role used his formidable learning and skill at preaching to exert enormous influence well beyond the pulpit. So great was his influence that Ambrose repeatedly succeeded in challenging the secular ruler; perhaps the most notable instance was in AD 390, when he made

'The Four Doctors of the Church' by the Flemish artist Jacob Jordaens (Ambrose is shown far right). Despite his sometimes fraught relationship with Theodosius, Ambrose delivered a eulogy at the emperor's funeral.

Theodosius perform penance for a massacre that his soldiers had conducted in Thessalonica.

Ambrose died on 4 April, AD 397. According to legend, his great eloquence derived from the fact that, when he was a child, a swarm of bees landed on his face and did not sting him, but left behind a drop of honey on his lips: bees and beehives therefore often appear in the iconography associated with this saint.

in Gaul by invading the province. Encouraged by Merobaudes, the Gaulish army deserted Gratian, and Theodosius responded by recognizing Maximus as a member of the imperial college. It was only when Maximus launched a sudden invasion of Italy in AD 386, driving Valentinian II into exile in Theodosius' part of the empire, that the relationship between the two men broke down. In AD 388, Theodosius invaded Maximus' realm. Caught off guard by the speed of the invasion, Maximus was captured outside Aquileia and summarily put to death. Valentinian was restored to power, but in name only. In fact, Theodosius' marshals began to exert an iron grip over the region. Prominent among them was his *magister militum*, the Frankish general Arbogast (d. AD 394), who ruthlessly mopped up any remaining sympathizers of Maximus and placed Valentinian under virtual house arrest in Vienne after Theodosius returned to Constantinople. In AD 392, Valentinian tried to depose Arbogast and paid with his life.

Showdown with the pagan

The fact that Arbogast was not a pure-blooded Roman effectively disqualified him from taking the throne himself; no such official sanction existed, but there was enough residual anti-German sentiment in the empire to make it impossible. Instead, he selected a senator named Eugenius to play the role, thereby assuring himself of the loyal backing of the senate. In all of this, there were also unmistakable signs of religious antagonism. Arbogast was a pagan, and there was also growing resentment among pagan members of the aristocracy at the power that certain bishops, notably Ambrose of Milan, had acquired under Gratian and Theodosius.

The civil war that broke out between Arbogast and Theodosius in AD 394 thus had many of the hallmarks of a religious conflict. Historical sources reveal that Arbogast openly placed his faith in the power of the old gods. Meanwhile, Theodosius, a devout Christian, had issued a law banning all forms of sacrifice in AD 392. On campaign against Arbogast, he made much of his devotion to his God. When the two sides met at the Battle of the Frigidus on 6 September, Theodosius attributed his eventual victory to the intervention of a violent storm, which he proclaimed a divine miracle. Arbogast and Eugenius were executed and Theodosius moved into Italy to re-establish his authority.

A Roman bust of the god Serapis. This Hellenistic-Egyptian deity was widely worshipped in Roman Egypt. A sign of growing intolerance against paganism came when a Christian mob destroyed a major Serapeum (the temple dedicated to the god) in Alexandria in AD 392 and subsequently lynched pagan philosophers in the city. Emperor Theodosius turned a blind eye to these outrages.

Before leaving on campaign, Theodosius had elevated his teenaged son, Arcadius (AD 377–408), to the rank of Augustus in the east, a sign perhaps that he intended to remain in the west for some time. That was not to be; in January AD 395, he died at the age of 49 in Milan.

Theodosius was the last emperor who could claim to rule the bureaucracies of both east and west. Following his death, these were divided into two equal parts, with the Balkan dioceses of Illyricum and Macedonia going to the west, and Moesia and Thrace going to the east. With Illyricum went the land settled by the Goths after AD 382. The

Stilicho with his wife Serena and their son Eucherius, portrayed on an ivory diptych from around AD 400. Despite his undoubted skill as a general, Stilicho's non-Roman ancestry prejudiced imperial courtiers against him, and he eventually fell victim to their intrigues in AD 408.

specifics of this division determined the future course of Roman history, for the Goths now became an exclusively western rather than an eastern problem.

Stilicho and Alaric

Theodosius' *magister militum* during the campaign against Arbogast was a man called Stilicho (*c.* AD 359–408), the son of a German officer and a Roman mother. At Theodosius' deathbed, Stilicho announced that he had been appointed as guardian for the emperor's successors Arcadius and his brother Honorius (AD 384–423). Also serving in the army that invaded Italy was Alaric, a leader of the Gothic community that Theodosius had settled in the Balkans after the treaty of AD 382. On the first day of the Battle of Frigidus, Theodosius is said to have ordered these Gothic commanders to launch a series of attacks on their compatriot's defensive works that cost the lives of 10,000 Goths all told. Theodosius allegedly boasted that he had simultaneously destroyed two enemies of Rome – the Goths and Arbogast. However, this story was greatly exaggerated – the number cited was in fact the entire number of warriors deployed by the Goths. Even so, the result seems to have displeased Alaric, even as Arcadius' government recognized him as leader of the Goths who returned to Lower Moesia.

Meanwhile, following the death of Theodosius the next year, Stilicho travelled with the eastern army as far as Thessalonica, where messengers from the eastern government, then dominated by the praetorian prefect Rufinus, sent word that if he personally came any closer to Constantinople, his force would be regarded as a threat and attacked. Stilicho handed control of the eastern army over to Gainas, a Goth who had risen to high command under Theodosius. When the army reached Constantinople, Gainas promptly arranged for Rufinus to be assassinated at a military review. With a loyal supporter now in charge of the eastern army, Stilicho might well have imagined that he had succeeded, at minimal cost, in making himself effective master of the empire. However, this would not turn out to be the case; Gainas allied himself with Eutropius, the eunuch who dominated the court of Arcadius. At their prompting, Arcadius refused to acknowledge Stilicho's claim to be his guardian.

ENEMIES AT THE GATE

The complete lack of cooperation between the two governments in the face of a series of crises over the next seven years demonstrated that the empire was more firmly divided than ever. In AD 397–398, Stilicho received no assistance from the east in quelling a major uprising in North Africa, nor when Alaric burst forth from his enclave to raid the Greek peninsula. Stilicho caught Alaric's forces in a potentially fatal trap in the northern Peloponnese in AD 399, but in allowing him to slip away, Stilicho may have had at the back of his mind the idea that Alaric might one day prove useful in the event of a war with the east.

In Constantinople, Gainas now gave further evidence of his treachery, though this time he went too far. Sent to suppress a serious revolt against the eastern empire by a group of Goths in Phrygia under the chieftain Tribigild, Gainas apparently cut a secret deal with his Gothic counterpart. His aim was to deflect blame for the failure of his campaign onto his erstwhile ally Eutropius; this tactic succeeded and Eutropius was dismissed and executed. A year later, Gainas again blackmailed the imperial government, forcing the resignation of Eutropius' successor, Aurelian. But then he immediately overplayed his hand by demanding a special church for his men to practise their Ulfilan brand of Christianity in the capital and higher office for himself. The people of Constantinople rose up, slaughtering thousands of his men and driving the rest from the city. When Gainas tried to lead his surviving men back across the Hellespont, naval forces destroyed their transports, and Gainas fled into Thrace where he, and his surviving followers, were caught and slaughtered by Uldin, king of the Huns, who had recently joined forces with Arcadius. Uldin sent Gainas' head to the emperor as a gift.

In AD 401 Alaric launched an invasion of Italy; with no Roman army in his way, he advanced easily

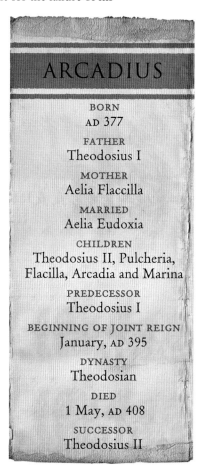

ARCADIUS

BORN
AD 377

FATHER
Theodosius I

MOTHER
Aelia Flaccilla

MARRIED
Aelia Eudoxia

CHILDREN
Theodosius II, Pulcheria, Flacilla, Arcadia and Marina

PREDECESSOR
Theodosius I

BEGINNING OF JOINT REIGN
January, AD 395

DYNASTY
Theodosian

DIED
1 May, AD 408

SUCCESSOR
Theodosius II

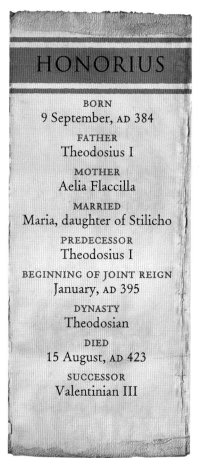

HONORIUS

BORN
9 September, AD 384

FATHER
Theodosius I

MOTHER
Aelia Flaccilla

MARRIED
Maria, daughter of Stilicho

PREDECESSOR
Theodosius I

BEGINNING OF JOINT REIGN
January, AD 395

DYNASTY
Theodosian

DIED
15 August, AD 423

SUCCESSOR
Valentinian III

The Notitia Dignitatum is a list of all the offices and military units in both the eastern and western Roman empires from the imperial court down to provincial level. The keeper of the list was the *primicerius notariorum*, one of whose jobs was writing letters of appointment for officials. The Notitia, which was preserved through the Middle Ages in a single manuscript, appears to have been composed around the time of the division of the empire between Honorius and Arcadius. The listing of eastern officials reflects the situation in AD 395. For the west, it was updated twice, once in around AD 408, and again in

c. AD 420. One critical issue that emerges from the western section is that nearly 50 percent of the army had to be replaced during Honorius' reign, and that casualties were extraordinarily heavy in the Gallic army, where 21 of 37 units were created while Honorius was emperor. These losses resulted both from barbarian invasions across the Rhine and Constantine's revolt.

Aside from the information that it provides about the state of the army, the Notitia is notable for the remarkable illustrations it contains for each office, and the shield designs for each unit in the army.

into northern Italy, drove Honorius from his palace at Milan to the city of Asta, and besieged the emperor for several months until Stilicho arrived with part of the field army from Gaul. On Easter Sunday, AD 402, Stilicho attacked the now largely Christian Goths as they prepared for their religious observances near Pollentia. Despite being caught by surprise, Alaric managed to withdraw with the bulk of his army intact and fought a running war with Stilicho until the following summer, when Stilicho cornered and defeated him near Verona. Yet although Alaric had staged two uprisings in under a decade, Stilicho regarded him as more useful alive than dead, signing a pact with him and allowing him to return to the Balkans. He evidently still took the view that Alaric could play a part in furthering his own ambitions.

Stilicho's lenient treatment of Alaric contrasts sharply with his handling of the next group of invaders to cross his path. In the summer of AD 406, Radagaisus led an armed migration of the Alamanni from the upper Rhine into Italy. So huge was this displacement of people that Stilicho judged the western field army unequal to the task of defeating his new foe. Accordingly, he turned to the accomplished mercenary leader, King Uldin of the Huns. Uldin's appearance at the head of a large cavalry force enabled Stilicho to force the surrender of his enemies. Around 10,000 of Radagaisus' men were taken into imperial service for use in the defence of Italy, while many thousands of others were sold into slavery.

The eastern emperor Arcadius was dominated throughout his 13-year reign by his advisors, notably the praetorian prefect Rufinus and his successors, the eunuch Eutropius and Flavius Anthemius.

Invaders cross the Rhine

Disaster followed hard on the heels of victory. On 31 December, AD 407, the Rhine froze over, allowing a second massive invasion wave to crash down upon Gaul. This time the invaders were relatively new arrivals – the Vandals, Alans, and Sueves, all of whom came from central Europe. The bulk of Stilicho's field army was still caught up further south and there was nothing he could do to prevent the destruction of the Rhine frontier. The tribes that crossed the frontier on this occasion would never leave Roman territory; the integrity of the frontier first established by Augustus, and stabilized by Tiberius, would never be fully restored. Around the same time, the commander of the Roman army in Britain, Constantine, declared himself emperor and moved into Gaul. Driving the recent invaders south and west he rapidly took control of the Gallic dioceses.

Stilicho was in a genuine quandary. Uldin had gone home, and he was unwilling to commit his own army to open battle against Constantine. Instead, he contented himself with garrisoning the passes over the Alps. Stilicho also faced a number of other difficulties. The western emperor Honorius, now in his early 20s, had taken Stilicho's daughter as his wife but had come to detest her. He was also surrounded with courtiers who wanted to be rid of Stilicho. Moreover, there remained among the Romans a deep-seated dislike of Germans. While it was the case that most of the army was now German, the same was not true of the civil administration. Tensions between civil servants and German soldiers had played a large part in the upheaval in Constantinople that led to the downfall of Gainas. There had also been occasional violent attacks on Germanic units in other imperial cities. In the wake of Adrianople the *magister militum* of the east ordered the massacre of Goths serving in the Roman army there. Now, with what could not have been worse timing, Arcadius died. The eastern regime replaced him with his seven-year-old son, Theodosius II, on 8 May, AD 408.

Stilicho's first instinct was to lead an army east, but at the same time he had to watch Constantine and find some way of dealing with the renegade Alaric. Breaking his parole, Alaric had in the meantime advanced on northern Italy and was demanding a huge tribute in return for a promise of good behaviour. Stilicho's response was to pay the tribute to Alaric and suggest that it would be better for him go to Gaul to fight Constantine.

Map of the city of Constantinople, showing its formidable seaward defences and (far right) the Column of Arcadius. Erected between AD 402 and 421, this grand monument stood for many centuries as the centrepiece of the Forum of Arcadius on Xerolophos Hill. Its elaborate relief sculptures depicted the defeat of Gainas' Goths in AD 400. The Column of Arcadius was demolished as a threat to public safety in the 18th century, and only its base now remains.

This stratagem proved to be Stilicho's downfall; the anti-German prejudice in the western imperial establishment now reached fever pitch. On 13 August, soldiers mutinied as Honorius reviewed them in Pavia and murdered a number of Stilicho's generals; eight days later, Stilicho himself was killed in Ravenna. The new leader of the government, Olympius, then ordered a massacre of the 'Germans' in the army – in this case former followers of Radagaisus – who were thought to be loyal to Stilicho. The survivors fled to join Alaric. Realizing that there was now no Roman army of any strength between himself and Rome, Alaric bypassed the emperor and made straight for the city. The senate voted to pay him a massive bribe and to negotiate a fresh deal with Honorius that would give Alaric new status within

The feckless emperor Honorius shown feeding birds inside the imperial palace. Honorius was as foolish as he was bigoted, and was further hampered by being surrounded by inept and unimaginative advisors. Pragmatic considerations eventually dictated his removal from power.

the Roman hierarchy. When Honorius refused to go along with this, Alaric returned to Rome with an even longer list of demands. These included a homeland for his people in Switzerland and southern Austria, and the rank of *magister militum* for himself. Though Honorius' officials were willing to accede to this demand – to do so would give them a decisive edge against Constantine in Gaul – Honorius refused outright.

New thinking was needed to find ways of assimilating immigrants into imperial society. With many Germans serving in the army, even after the massacre of AD 408, and many still in the officer corps, a pragmatic solution should have been possible. With this in mind, in AD 409, after another siege of Rome, the senate proclaimed a new emperor, Priscus Attalus, who with its blessing made common cause with Alaric.

The fall of Rome

Alaric seems genuinely to have believed that the empire would last forever and that the imperial government alone could grant security to his people. The problem was that he still lacked the wherewithal to realize these goals. Attalus had little influence with the bureaucracy, and Alaric's army had no siege equipment. These two shortcomings meant that Alaric would still have to treat with Honorius; however, having recently gained reinforcements from the east, Honorius refused to deal with him. Betrayed at every turn, Alaric deposed his puppet emperor and appeared once more before the walls of Rome. On 24 August, AD 410 the Goths found that a sympathizer had left the Salarian Gate open. For the first time in 800 years, a man who was not part of the Roman hierarchy took control of the capital.

The fall of Rome revealed many things. In terms of political power, it demonstrated just how little the city now mattered: Honorius and his government were still secure in Ravenna, as was Theodosius II in Constantinople, while the field army remained encamped on the border with Gaul. In terms of Roman culture, the sack of Rome was more momentous. While Jerome in Palestine lamented the event as an unsurpassed catastrophe, Augustine, the bishop of Hippo in North Africa, responded to pagan claims that the sack of the city was the result of the conversion of the state to Christianity by writing his massive treatise *City of God*, in which he argued that political history was of little consequence when compared with the history of God's relationship with humanity. After all, he contested, far worse things had happened in the past, before the rise of Christianity.

In support of Augustine's argument, a Christian from Spain named Orosius wrote a seven-volume work entitled *History against the Pagans*, the bulk of which recounts disasters before the birth of Christ. The city of Rome was a symbol of a world that was past, rather than of the world that was to come. It was eminently possible for there to be a civilized world that was both Christian and Roman and that did not depend on any specific political order. For the Goths, the situation was even more problematic. Alaric had played his last card, and still not gained the office that he wanted or a homeland for his people. He died a year later in southern Italy.

Alaric's entry into Rome in AD 410. The Gothic leader and his men left the capital after three days of highly organized, but relatively non-violent, looting. Some contemporary and later commentators saw the sack of Rome as a signal disaster and a portent of much worse to come. Yet given the prevarication and shifting allegiances of Rome's leaders, this event can be seen as a deserved come-uppance.

'But when the bright light of all the world was put out, or, rather, when the Roman empire was decapitated, and, to speak more correctly, the whole world perished in one city, "I became dumb and humbled myself"…'

SAINT JEROME, COMMENTARY ON EZEKIEL, PREFACE TO BOOK 1

Final Decline and Fall:
The Collapse of the Western Empire
(AD 411–476)

At the start of the fourth century AD the governments of the eastern and western Roman empires faced essentially the same problem – the movement of peoples from central Europe towards the central tax-generating zones around the Mediterranean. One of the most intriguing questions of European history is why the western regime failed within 70 years of Alaric's sack of Rome, while the eastern continued, in varying forms, until the Ottoman capture of Constantinople in 1453.

In his 19-year reign as king of the Huns, Attila conducted campaigns of such ferocity against the western and eastern Roman empires that his name became a byword for terror and destruction.

Certainly, Asia Minor had the geographical advantage of being protected from attack by the Bosphorus, yet this fact alone is not as decisive as it might at first appear. This narrow body of water was no real barrier to a determined enemy, and the walls of Constantinople still needed to be manned by large and well-led defensive forces. The main reason that the eastern empire survived the movement of peoples and the western empire did not is that in the crucial decades of the early fifth century the government of the east was far more efficient than its western counterpart.

Wasted opportunities

The western empire lacked coherent direction between the death of Stilicho and the advent of a new regime led by Theodosius' daughter Galla Placidia in the AD 430s. By then, there was no salvaging anything that resembled the western empire of the past. Too much territory had already fallen under the political control of immigrants who could have been peacefully assimilated into the power structure of the empire if Honorius' court had not been staffed by bigoted incompetents. The primary interest of these officials was self-advancement, and their ways of securing it conspiracy and murder. In addition, the emperor himself was hamstrung by his pathological prejudice against 'Germans'. In the end, German communities that could not be assimilated were set

The emperor Theodosius II ordered the walls of his capital
Constantinople to be strengthened as soon as he took office in AD 408.
Work proceeded under the direction of the praetorian prefect Anthemius
and was completed within five years.

upon each other in a destructive cycle of violence that saw ever more territory prised from the direct control of the emperor, and ever more land in the provinces laid waste. Tribes that had already decamped once to move into the empire were not so attached to the districts where they settled that they were unwilling to move on to some other area they had not yet ravaged. Ultimately, this led to the catastrophic passage of the Vandals from Spain to North Africa in AD 429, and the loss of North Africa to the Vandal king Geiseric in AD 439. Thereafter, the western government simply lacked the resources to govern alone, while its bureaucrats were unwilling to surrender their authority to the only government with the power to help, the regime in Constantinople.

The government of the east, by contrast, functioned relatively smoothly in the 30 years after the revolt of Gainas, largely due to the immensely able stewardship of the empresses Pulcheria (AD 399–453) and Eudoxia (AD 401–460), who were able to construct a coherent regime with reasonably orderly patterns of advancement despite their personal antipathy to one another. When the violent incursion of the Huns under Attila occurred in the AD 440s and 450s, the eastern government was strong enough to survive. It did so by adopting the policy of diverting potential enemies to the west, whose failed regimes it had only limited interest in supporting.

TIMELINE

AD 412 Visigoths under Athaulf migrate from Italy to Gaul

423 The death of Emperor Honorius sparks power struggles in the western empire

425 Valentinian III comes to power as western emperor

429 Geiseric becomes king of the Vandals (to 477) and under pressure from the Visigoths migrates to found a state in North Africa

434 Attila takes over leadership of the kingdom of the Huns, centred on Pannonia

450 Theodosius II dies in Constantinople

451 Aetius defeats Attila at the battle of the Catalaunian Plains

453 Death of Attila sees Hunnish influence in Europe wane

454 Valentinian murders Aetius

455 Supporters of Aetius murder Valentinian; end of the Theodosian dynasty; Vandals under Geiseric sack Rome

456 Ricimer becomes kingmaker in the western empire

476 Romulus Augustulus is deposed by Odoacer, spelling the end of the western Roman empire

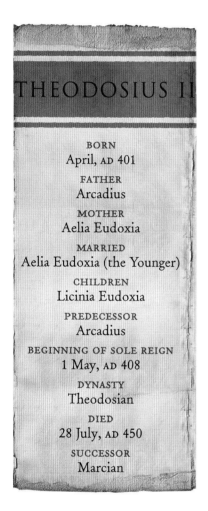

THEODOSIUS II

BORN
April, AD 401

FATHER
Arcadius

MOTHER
Aelia Eudoxia

MARRIED
Aelia Eudoxia (the Younger)

CHILDREN
Licinia Eudoxia

PREDECESSOR
Arcadius

BEGINNING OF SOLE REIGN
1 May, AD 408

DYNASTY
Theodosian

DIED
28 July, AD 450

SUCCESSOR
Marcian

Around this time, an important change occurs in the language that Roman writers use to refer to the empire. As late as the AD 430s, the historian Olympiodorus, the principal source for later accounts of the period, was still writing in terms of the eastern and western parts of the empire. Yet the younger Priscus of Panium – an immensely gifted historian who also played a minor role in the government of the period, serving on an embassy to Attila – wrote instead of the 'western' and 'eastern Romans'. Ostensibly a quibbling linguistic difference, Priscus' terminology in fact indicates that the two states were now distinct entities, pursuing quite different policies when it suited them. Shortly after Priscus brought his history to an end in the early AD 470s, the western empire collapsed completely, leading to the abolition of the imperial office after AD 476, and, within a decade, to the creation of a new Gothic state in Italy. This polity joined the other successor states that had already developed in Rome's western provinces.

Ensuring the dynastic succession

The story of the decline of the western empire is initially that of two empresses: Galla Placidia (c. AD 388–450), the long-suffering daughter of Theodosius I, and Pulcheria, the sister of the emperor Theodosius II. Galla Placidia was one of the prizes abducted from Rome by Alaric in AD 410. In the years after the sack of Rome she accompanied the Goths, now led by Athaulf, the half-brother of Alaric, as they moved to Gaul. There then ensued a complex series of events culminating in the collapse of the regime of the usurper Constantine III. At the same time, the Vandals and Sueves, the invaders of AD 407, occupied Spain, wreaking havoc on its inhabitants, and Athaulf's Goths, now called the Visigoths, took over territory along the southern coast of Gaul.

In AD 414, Athaulf married Galla and proclaimed Priscus Attalus – the emperor installed and deposed by Alaric who had remained with the Goths – as his own emperor. Athaulf's ultimate ambition is revealed by the fact that when Galla bore him a son at the end of AD 414, the child was named Theodosius. Since Honorius was childless, the boy would have been an obvious candidate for the succession if he had lived, but he did not survive infancy. A year later, Athaulf was murdered, and his successor returned Galla to Constantius, the *magister militum* of Honorius' regime, and acceded to the Roman request to attack the tribes in Spain. In AD 418, after years of slaughter in Spain, the Visigoths were rewarded with land of their own around Toulouse.

The empire in the west was by now a shambles. Britain, which had expelled the representatives of Constantine III in AD 410, was barely part of the empire any longer. Its tiny garrison was fully occupied defending the country against raids by the tribes north of Hadrian's Wall (the Picts and Scots) as well as raiders from across the North Sea (Angles, from Schleswig, and Saxons). The Burgundians, a tribe that had taken advantage of the collapse of the Rhine frontier to establish themselves in Roman territory, occupied a substantial portion of northwestern France. Southwestern France was now the home of the Visigoths; and most of Spain was Roman in name only. The regime in the east was largely untroubled by these reverses. After all, the west yielded no revenue, and was obviously in no position to provide military support should any be needed. As long as Honorius was alive, the government of Theodosius II rested easy in the knowledge that

Map showing the successor states that developed with the break-up of the western Roman empire from the mid-fifth century onwards. A terminal blow was dealt to the western empire in AD 429–439, when the Vandals seized North Africa, Rome's main source of grain, and established an independent kingdom there.

eastern Roman empire

kingdom of Odoacer

kingdom of Syagrius

Burgundian kingdom (Germanic)

Franks (Germanic)

Ostrogoth kingdom (Germanic)

Vandal kingdom (Germanic)

Visigoth kingdom (Germanic)

other Germanic peoples

A fresco painting of St John Chrysostom (AD 349–407). He gained a great following in Constantinople and beyond for his eloquent condemnation of abuses of wealth and power. However, many of his sermons and writings were virulently anti-Semitic and gave ideological succour to the persecution of Jews in the eastern empire.

there was a representative of the dynasty in place. But if that dynasty were to continue, the key figure would be Galla Placidia. Constantius could fairly claim that he had rescued Galla from the hands of the barbarians, and that she should show him due gratitude by accepting his generous offer of marriage. Galla, however, found him abhorrent and the prospect of becoming his wife deeply distasteful. Ever since his defeat of Constantine, the ambitious Constantius had successfully inveigled himself into ever more influential positions within the regime. His self-appointment as a patrician was designed to advance his career still further. Galla was the key to the future of the western empire, for any offspring she bore would guarantee that western officialdom avoided potential takeover by representatives of the dynasty from the east, or another civil war. Although she managed to resist what was essentially a political act of rape for three years, her brother finally forced her to take Constantius' hand on 1 January, AD 418. Their son Valentinian III (AD 418–455) was born before the end of that year, with a second child, Honoria, following shortly thereafter.

In early AD 421, having finally achieved his aim of being named Augustus (a title which the eastern court refused to recognize), Constantius suddenly died. The tensions in government between the 'Germans' and 'Romans', which he had kept in check, resurfaced almost immediately. Even as Constantius, the *de facto* leader of the 'German' group, was rising to power, the court of Honorius had issued a remarkable edict forbidding anyone to wear German dress within the walls of Rome. Galla now became the focus of loyalty for the German soldiers with whom her late husband had surrounded himself. At the same time, Honorius began to hint that he wanted carnal relations with his sister, and Galla fled to the east by the end of AD 423.

Empresses at the helm

The government of the east was far less colourful than that of the west. Although Arcadius was as weak-willed and ineffectual as his brother, he had made a much better marriage. After the revolt of Gainas, his wife Eudoxia (d. AD 404) had forged an alliance with powerful factions at court, and had herself proclaimed Augusta. No woman had held an imperial title since the death of Helena; despite howls of protest from Christian traditionalists, foremost among whom was John Chrysostom, archbishop of Constantinople, Eudoxia made it abundantly clear that she intended to exercise real authority, especially given the shortcomings of her husband in exercising his regnal duties. She died in AD 404, but the precedent she set for strong female rule paved the way for her daughter Pulcheria to become effective regent for her brother, Theodosius II (AD 401–450), who was only eight years old when he ascended the throne in AD 408.

In AD 413, as Pulcheria turned 14 and began to be looked upon as potential marriage material by ambitious politicians, she took a momentous decision that ultimately assured her a unique position in imperial society. Turning down all bids by the praetorian prefect Anthemius – a former key ally of her mother – to arrange a union with one of his relatives, she publicly devoted her virginity to God. Pulcheria was doubtless influenced in her decision by her profound loathing of Anthemius.

Pulcheria subsequently led a reclusive existence in the palace in the company of her younger sisters, who were inspired to follow her example. Together, they created an aura of imperial power that was inextricably linked with the Church. Through her public proclamation of virginity (probably genuine) and her essentially ascetic lifestyle, Pulcheria also helped foster a growing interest in the figure of the Virgin Mary. Thus began the cult of the Virgin and the influential area of ecclesiastical scholarship known as Marian theology. At the same time, however, Pulcheria pandered to more distasteful elements in the early Christian Church. In trying to prevent inter-Christian violence, she consciously acted as a lightning-rod conducting intolerance onto

In this sixth-century mosaic from Hagia Sophia in Istanbul, Emperor Constantine I (right) and the Byzantine emperor Justinian I are shown presenting models of the city of Constantinople to the Virgin Mary. Pulcheria was responsible for promoting the Marian cult in Christianity.

relatively defenceless scapegoats. Jews were persecuted and synagogues destroyed, while pagans were systematically debarred from serving in the administration. In this way, she made her position within Constantinople unassailable; one clear lesson that had emerged from Eudoxia's clash with St John Chrysostom was that whoever managed to harness the passions of fundamentalist Christians would wield enormous power in the capital. On 4 July, AD 414, Pulcheria was made Augusta by Theodosius II.

Even more significantly, the alliance that Pulcheria forged between the imperial office and the Church helped reconcile different groups within the bureaucracy. German generals now stood four-square with traditional aristocrats in the defence of the eastern empire. The institutionalized piety of the regime was clearly demonstrated in AD 415, when the supposed relics of the first Christian martyr, St Stephen were discovered. The relics of Stephen were transported from Jerusalem to Constantinople with enormous pomp and ceremony before being deposited in the household of Pulcheria herself. Although the veneration of relics already had a long history in the early church, the ever more prominent connection between political power and the possession of relics made their collection an important, and lucrative, aspect of Christian devotion and was eventually to become one of the principal bones of contention behind the Protestant Reformation. The dual meaning of the Latin term for the uncovering of relics (*inventio*) – 'discovery' or 'invention' – hints at the focus of later criticism.

On the positive side, the highly Christianized version of the imperial office that took shape in the eastern part of the empire did succeed in bringing the concept of emperorship back in line with contemporary social values. Disputes about doctrine were played out in massive church councils

Part of a mosaic map of Jerusalem and the Holy Land, with the Church of the Holy Sepulchre in the centre. Jerusalem became the focus of ostentatious displays of devotion by the empresses Pulcheria and Eudoxia, especially regarding Christian relics.

Saints Peter and Paul, from a fourth-
century Roman bas-relief sculpture.
As secular and spiritual authority became
ever more closely intertwined in the eastern
empire, imperial rule began to be associated
with the guidance given to the early
Christian Church by the Apostles.

that assembled bishops from all over the empire. These synods were
conducted in Greek rather than Latin, an important concession by an
administration that still issued official proclamations in Latin, even
though few people in the eastern empire used that language in their
daily lives. People from outside the official power structure of the
bureaucracy thus had an opportunity to meet with the emperor, and
hear him declare his attachment to their values, in their own language.
Even if there remained serious disagreements about the nature of God,
and controversial rulings were not universally accepted, there was no
question that the imperial government was now trying to address the
concerns of its subjects. In the time of Augustus, the notion that the
emperor represented the ideal of *virtus* had been essential in defining
the purpose of the office. But as times changed, and the nature of the
office with them, it needed to be imbued with new significance. An
emperor who was the equal of the apostles was far more in tune with
contemporary thought than one whose actions referenced the moral
code of the Roman Republic.

The late western empire

From AD 421 onwards, Pulcheria had to share significant public space
with her brother's new wife Eudoxia, who was just as able as Pulcheria
but also more accepting of doctrinal differences. Although she
converted before her marriage, her background as the daughter of a
pagan family predisposed her to greater tolerance for religious nonconformity. As Theodosius' wife, Eudoxia enthusiastically espoused
Christianity and rivalled Pulcheria in her demonstrations of devotion.
In AD 438–439, for example, she made a pilgrimage to Jerusalem and
brought back precious relics. At least in the short term, personal
rancour between the two women tended to manifest itself exclusively
in the form of religious dispute. While the imperial office was now
conceived of in terms of Christian piety, the contemporary definition
of this virtue did not preclude a ruler from entertaining a lust for
power or meting out vicious treatment to political rivals. As a new
threat emerged on the frontiers of the eastern empire, Eudoxia's
position came under fire. In AD 443 her opponents at court succeeded
in making a charge of adultery against her stick. She was exiled to
Jerusalem, where she lived on until AD 460. Interestingly, she was
allowed to retain her insignia as empress – an admission, perhaps, that
the reason for her exile had had more to do with politics than sex.

Galla Placidia arrived in Constantinople at the very beginning of
Eudoxia's period of ascendancy, and the new empress seems to have
seen in Galla a useful tool to assert her own supremacy. Eudoxia had

been granted the title of Augusta after giving birth to a daughter in AD 421, around the time that Galla fled the west. This infant was now betrothed to Galla's six-year-old son Valentinian III as a symbolic gesture of the eastern court's interest in the succession to Honorius. The issue of succession arose almost immediately, for Honorius died before the end of AD 423, whereupon western officials tried to assert their independence by proclaiming a palace functionary named John as Augustus. He was a poor choice; the Visigoths declared allegiance to the cause of their former queen and began to attack imperial territory in Gaul, and the eastern court made extensive plans for an invasion of the west. The result was a foregone conclusion. John was captured, mutilated and executed in the circus at Aquileia.

Athaulf, king of the Visigoths from AD 410 to 415, led his followers out of Italy in the spring of AD 412. They moved first into Gaul and then to Spain. Before his death in AD 415 Athaulf was briefly married to Galla Placidia, daughter of Emperor Theodosius I; she bore him a son, who died in infancy.

The armies of the east were not sent to occupy the west. Once John was dead, it was Galla's job to govern the west in the name of her son. To do so she had to balance the ambitions of three generals, Flavius, Boniface and Aetius, who had once served her late and unlamented husband, Constantius. These men had played various roles in the recent civil war. Flavius had been recalled from retirement; Boniface, who ruled Africa as a virtual principality, had openly sided with the invaders; while the third, Aetius (*c.* AD 396–454) had appeared at the head of an army of Huns just after John had been killed. Realizing that there was no point in defending a dead man, he paid off the Huns and accepted command of the army in Gaul. Having spent much of his youth as a hostage, first with the Goths of Alaric and Athaulf, and then with the Huns of Uldin, Aetius combined fierce ambition with a genuine knowledge of the people with whom he would have to deal. As an added bonus, he was also a genuinely talented officer. None of these qualities endeared him to the empress, however, who saw in him the image of Constantius, and her antipathy would prove disastrous. Thus it was that when Aetius arrested Flavius on a charge of conspiracy in AD 430, Galla summoned Boniface from Africa to bring him under control. Boniface died in the moment of victory, leaving control of Italy to his son-in-law, Sebastian, while Aetius sought aid from the Huns. With an army of Huns at his back, Aetius returned to Italy. Sebastian fled to Constantinople, and Aetius took control of the western empire, assuming the title of patrician in AD 435, just in time to face the loss of Africa.

Galla's recall of Boniface could not have come at a worse time. After years of warfare both among themselves and against sundry Roman forces, the Vandals, Alans and Sueves had been severely weakened, so much so that one of the two Vandal tribes had virtually ceased to exist, and the Alans had been forced to join with the Vandals to form a new nation. In AD 429, Geiseric (*c.* AD 389–477), the leader of this new confederacy, recognized that there was no future in Spain, where years of conflict had ruined much of the land. He also realized that there was nothing that passed for an effective Roman fleet in the western Mediterranean, and so transported his people across the straits of Gibraltar into Africa. Boniface's effort to organize resistance faltered in the face of his commitment in Italy, with the result that the Vandals gradually established themselves in the western provinces of Africa. Although their advance was halted in AD 435, when Aetius reinforced the African garrison with troops from the eastern empire, this interruption was only temporary. Geiseric captured Carthage in AD 439, and even as Aetius, aided again by forces from the east, assembled a fleet to invade Africa, the Huns appeared, with new leadership and new ambitions, to threaten the Balkan frontier. Eastern help evaporated, and Aetius had no choice but to negotiate a treaty recognizing Vandal control of the only remaining area from which the western empire could draw resources to support a significant army. To ensure the peace, Geiseric continued nominal tax payments from the region under his control in return for the betrothal of Valentinian's infant daughter to his young son, Hunneric. Ever the astute observer, Geiseric wanted security for his people, and had perhaps noted that Athaulf's heir might have been a claimant to the throne. What was good for a Goth would be good for a Vandal, or so he may have thought.

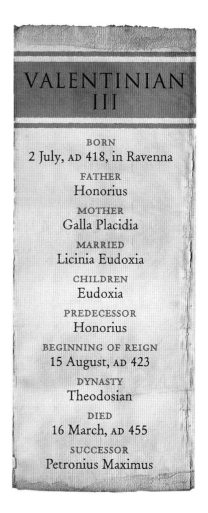

VALENTINIAN III

BORN
2 July, AD 418, in Ravenna

FATHER
Honorius

MOTHER
Galla Placidia

MARRIED
Licinia Eudoxia

CHILDREN
Eudoxia

PREDECESSOR
Honorius

BEGINNING OF REIGN
15 August, AD 423

DYNASTY
Theodosian

DIED
16 March, AD 455

SUCCESSOR
Petronius Maximus

'Geiseric, now most famous for the sack of Rome, was of moderate stature and lame as the result of a fall from a horse, a deep thinker who spoke rarely and despised luxury, was fierce in anger, desirous of gain, skilled in negotiation, and ready to sow dissension to arouse hatred.'

JORDANES, HISTORY OF THE GOTHS 33, 168.

The scourge of God

The new enemies that began to threaten the borders of the eastern empire from AD 443 onwards were the Huns. Ever since their emergence as a major force in the AD 370s the Huns who lived in the Balkans had more often assisted the empire than assailed it. With the exception of a brutal raid by Uldin in AD 407, the leaders of the Huns had chosen to accept large payments from the empire, either to keep the peace on their side of the frontier or to lend significant assistance at

The Huns' annihilation in AD 436 of the first kingdom of the Burgundians (an East Germanic tribe), at Worms in the Rhineland, was so horrific that the event was long preserved in folk memory. It came to form the basis of the famous Middle High German epic poem, the Nibelungenlied. This 19th-century painting portrays the death of the legendary hero Siegfried, who was supposedly staying at the Burgundian court at the time of the slaughter.

moments of crisis. This all changed shortly after the brothers Attila (c. AD 406–453) and Bleda (c. AD 390–445) came to power in AD 434. By far the dominant partner, Attila was a man whose vast ambition was matched by a propensity for ruthless savagery. Initially, Attila followed the traditional Hunnish policy of hiring out large mercenary armies to suppress Germanic enemies of the Roman empire.

Presently, however, Attila realized that his forces were more than a match for the moribund Roman empire. The change in Attila's policy towards Rome is most clearly evident in his demand that the Huns control the frontier. For centuries the Roman empire had regulated trade across the frontier through border crossings, and had maintained a *cordon sanitaire* north of the Danube as a buffer against incursions. Yet when the historian Priscus of Panium accompanied a Roman mission to Attila in AD 449, he reports that he and his fellow legates passed through a deserted zone south, not north, of the Danube that took five days to cross. There could be no more potent demonstration of the reversal of fortunes between the two empires. Well might the Hunnish ambassador Eslas boast that Theodosius was now Attila's subject; by the time he did so, the annual tribute paid by the empire to the Huns had risen sixfold from 350 pounds of gold to 2100 pounds.

This major reversal in status resulted from two massive invasions of eastern Roman territory, the first in AD 441, and the second in AD 447. During these incursions, Roman armies had proved incapable of resisting Attila's armies and Attila had shown that he had the technology to capture fortified Roman cities – battering rams and rolling siege towers. No other northern people had so consummately mastered the techniques of siegecraft, which had hitherto been the preserve of the Romans and Persians. Goths, Vandals and others relied on long blockades or sudden attacks on the rare occasions when they chose to 'make war on walls', and this had given the empire a measure of operational security.

There would be no such security in dealing with Attila, who made extensive use of engineers trained in Roman siege techniques in his army. The effects of Hunnish attacks can still be seen in the massive destruction layers evident at various archaeological sites throughout central Europe.

DATING THE FALL OF THE WESTERN EMPIRE

Given that there had been two extended periods in which there had been no emperor in the west during the decade prior to the deposition of Romulus, the significance of the moment was lost on the historians who wrote closest to the time. The two whose accounts we have are Malchus, who wrote an extensive history of the period from AD 473–474 to AD 491 and Candidus, who covered the period between AD 457 and 491. The work of both historians is known only through later summaries, but both suggest that the deposition of Romulus was still seen as a non-event after AD 491.

It was only in the middle of the sixth century that a western historian, Jordanes, used the deposition of Romulus to mark the end of the western empire. In his *History of the Goths*, he describes the event as follows:

'Not long after Augustulus ['Little Augustus'] was proclaimed emperor by his father Orestes in Ravenna, Odoacer, the king of the Torcilingi, having with him the Sciri, the Heruli and auxiliaries from several other peoples, occupied Italy, and, killing Orestes, drove Augustulus his son from the throne and condemned him to exile in the castle of Lucullus in Campania. Thus did the western empire of the Roman people, which the first of the Augusti, Octavianus Augustus began to rule in the seven hundred and ninth year after the founding of the city [44 BC], perished with this Augustulus in the five hundred and twenty-second year of the rule of his predecessors and those before them, and from that time onwards the Goths held Rome and Italy.'

Defeat at the Catalaunian Fields

Even as Priscus' legation was making its way north to see the great Hun, ambassadors of the 'western Romans' were being browbeaten by Attila. The Hun ruler accused them of 'concealing stolen treasure and protecting the thief' – in other words, harbouring and giving succour to the Huns' enemies. In the past, when levelled at the eastern Romans, such an accusation had always been the prelude to an attack. Attila duly unleashed a massive army from the Balkans on Gaul in AD 451. Things looked bleak for the western empire. Geiseric controlled North Africa, and the only way that Valentinian III's regime could support an army was if it retained the tenuous control of Gaul that Aetius had spent the previous decade building up. But Aetius was a skilled diplomat as well as a good soldier. Recognizing that domination by the Huns was to be avoided at all costs, he forged an alliance with the Visigoths of south-central France and other tribes in the region.

At the height of summer in AD 451, on a vast expanse of flat land outside Orléans variously known as Chalons, or the Catalaunian or Mauriacan Fields, the army of Aetius met that of Attila. It was here that the western Roman army fought its last great set-piece battle, and it was on this day that the independent Visigoths played the decisive role – according to an admittedly pro-Gothic writer – in securing a Roman victory. Attila was driven back to his camp and allegedly planned to commit suicide if the Romans overran it the following day. However, this never came to pass, since Theodoric, the king of the Visigoths, had fallen in battle and Aetius chose not to chance his luck any further. Attila withdrew to the Balkans.

Attila had never before suffered a serious defeat. Aetius seems not to have appreciated the potential harm that such a setback could inflict on a ruler whose unlimited power depended solely upon others' terrified belief in his invincibility. If Attila was to maintain control of his empire, then, staying at home and licking his wounds was not an option. And so, in AD 452, while Aetius was still in Gaul, he returned, this time making straight for Italy. Aquileia was destroyed after a terrible siege, and Milan was taken. But then Attila's attack faltered. Attila did not have the logistical support to advance on Rome, and disease began to take its toll on his army. After receiving an embassy that included the bishop of Rome, now a leading figure in the Roman aristocracy, he agreed to withdraw. Within months he was dead. Legend recounts that, while attending a feast to celebrate his marriage to a woman named Ilico, he overindulged in wine, burst a blood vessel and suffocated. The kingdom of the Huns, dependent as it was upon his personal authority, collapsed in civil war the next year as the many Germanic peoples he had once held in thrall rose up against their masters and defeated them in a huge battle in the central Balkans (the site of which is now lost). The Huns withdrew and resumed their role as occasional mercenaries in Roman service.

The last generation of western Romans

While the great battles had been raging between Attila and the 'western Romans', significant changes had taken place in the political structures of the two empires. Theodosius II died in Constantinople in July, AD 450, followed by Galla Placidia later that same year in Rome. With no eastern heir available from the house of Theodosius, a general named Marcian (c. AD 390–457) emerged as the consensus choice of generals and the palace (Pulcheria even agreed to marry him if he would respect her vow of chastity). Marcian was a different sort of emperor. A career soldier, he made common cause with others who resented the annual tribute payments to Attila. He immediately revoked the tributes and set about reclaiming Roman territory from the Huns while Attila was campaigning in the west.

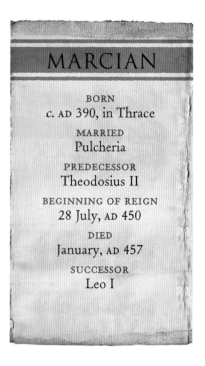

MARCIAN

BORN
c. AD 390, in Thrace

MARRIED
Pulcheria

PREDECESSOR
Theodosius II

BEGINNING OF REIGN
28 July, AD 450

DIED
January, AD 457

SUCCESSOR
Leo I

Valentinian III was furious that he was not consulted about Marcian's actions, but it wasn't his empire. Meanwhile, he had grown increasingly antagonistic towards Aetius, the man who had saved his realm from Attila. His antipathy was encouraged by Petronius Maximus, the most powerful senator of the time, and Heracleius, a eunuch who was the emperor's *cubicularius*. On 21 September, AD 454, Aetius met with Valentinian at Ravenna in the presence of Heracleius. Aetius anticipated that the agenda of the meeting would be the empire's parlous financial state; instead, Valentinian accused him of treason for allowing Marcian to take over the east and attacked him with a sword. Heracleius joined in the brutal assault with a meat cleaver. Valentinian then set about purging Aetius' senior supporters, but failed to reward Maximus sufficiently for his services. Maximus' response was to recruit two soldiers from Aetius' bodyguard as assassins. On 21 March, AD 455 they murdered Valentinian, and Maximus ascended the throne. He forced Valentinian's widow Eudoxia to marry him, and made Eudoxia's daughter (also called Eudoxia) marry his son. This second marriage was a terrible mistake, and was the chief reason why Maximus' reign lasted a mere 11 weeks.

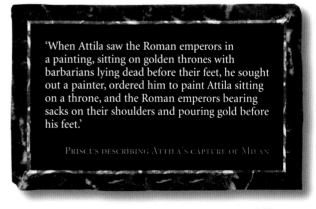

'When Attila saw the Roman emperors in a painting, sitting on golden thrones with barbarians lying dead before their feet, he sought out a painter, ordered him to paint Attila sitting on a throne, and the Roman emperors bearing sacks on their shoulders and pouring gold before his feet.'

PRISCUS DESCRIBING ATTILA'S CAPTURE OF MILAN

The younger Eudoxia had once been betrothed to Geiseric's son. No sooner did Geiseric hear of the marriages in Rome than he claimed that Eudoxia had summoned him to her aid. The Vandal fleet sailed from Carthage and landed near Rome in May, AD 455. When Maximus tried to flee, a mob murdered him. The Vandals then sacked the city for over two weeks, causing terrible devastation.

The vandalizing of Rome opened the final act of the collapse of the western empire, a drama that had begun with Honorius' murder of Stilicho. In the power vacuum that ensued after the deaths of Aetius and Valentinian, a soldier of Germanic origin named Ricimer (c. AD 405–472) who became *magister militum* of the west took upon himself the role of official kingmaker. As *de facto* ruler of the west for the next 14 years, he supported three puppet emperors. Ricimer's success seems to have derived from his ability to deal with the eastern court, which was at that time dominated by another general of Germanic descent called Aspar (c. AD 400–471). Aspar had played a leading role in installing Marcian as emperor, and, after Marcian's death, in promoting an officer from southern Turkey named Leo to be Marcian's successor. Leo, however, had a mind of his own, and wished to be succeeded by a man from his own part of the empire. In AD 469 he overthrew Aspar, and, five years later, put his preferred candidate, Zeno, on the throne.

Cutting the west adrift

The accession of Zeno to the eastern throne effectively sealed the fate of the western empire, for it sparked an immediate revolt by a general named Basiliscus. The revolt lasted for two years and occupied the whole attention of Zeno. As Zeno struggled with Basiliscus, there were growing signs that the office of emperor was losing whatever residual relevance it had in western politics. Thus, when the Burgundian general, Gundobad, ended a five-month interregnum by persuading a man named Glycerius to become emperor, he promptly saw fit to leave Rome, deeming developments in Gaul of greater importance. The effect of Gundobad's departure was to leave Glycerius facing an insurrection by Julius Nepos, commander of the Balkan army. When Nepos learned that Orestes, commander of the army of Italy, was hostile to his bid for power, he returned to his base in Illyricum. Back in Italy, however, Orestes promptly exploited the volatile situation to install his young son, Romulus Augustulus, as emperor. A year later

'... then a certain Roman made himself famous by something he said. When asked by the emperor [Valentinian III] if he had done well or ill in killing Aetius, he replied that he did not know whether he had done well, or perhaps otherwise, but the one thing he did understand well was that he had cut off his right hand with the other.'

PROCOPIUS, HISTORY OF THE WARS, 3.4.28

THE LAST EMPERORS

Petronius Maximus (AD 455)

Avitus (AD 455–456)

Majorian (AD 457–461)

Liberius Maximus (AD 461–465)

Anthemius (AD 467–472)

Olybrius (AD 472)

Glycerius (AD 473–474)

RICIMER'S PUPPET SHOW

Shortly after the Vandals sacked Rome, a senator named Flavius Avitus had himself proclaimed emperor at Arles. Ricimer, *magister militum* in Italy, opposed his accession and when Avitus invaded Italy in AD 456, his army was defeated near Placentia. Avitus surrendered and became bishop of Placentia, dying in office shortly thereafter. Ricimer declined to become emperor and placed an officer named Majorian on the throne. When Majorian failed to defeat the Vandals, whose power had again grown in Spain, Ricimer replaced him with Liberius

Severus (AD 461). The emperor Leo refused to recognize Severus, who died under suspicious circumstances in AD 465. Ricimer did without an emperor until AD 467, when he accepted the eastern general, Anthemius, as his ruler. In AD 472 Ricimer replaced him with Olybrius. Ricimer died on 18 August, AD 472. Olybrius died on 2 November of the same year, leaving the Burgundian general, Gundobad, who had assisted Ricimer in the overthrow of Anthemius, as the chief kingmaker. He appointed his one and only emperor, Glycerius, on 3 March, AD 473.

Orestes died in a mutiny led by a general named Odoacer (AD 435–493), who deposed Romulus and wrote to Zeno announcing that there was no longer any need for an emperor in the west. At the same time, Zeno received representations from Nepos asking the eastern emperor to recognize him. Zeno was sympathetic to Nepos, being related to him through marriage, but was in no position to champion his cause.

The decision to leave the west to its own devices made Zeno the first emperor of a new Roman world, long in formation, that no longer had any need of Rome. The Roman empire had ceased to exist and the classical world was now supplanted by a new era, as the Middle Ages dawned.

Romulus Augustulus surrendering the insignia of empire to Odoacer, an act that effectively brought the western empire to an end. Powerless to intervene, the eastern emperor Zeno had no option but to confirm Odoacer as king of Italy in late AD 476.

Dido's Revenge

At the end of the fourth book of Virgil's *Aeneid*, Dido, the queen of Carthage, curses Aeneas as he sails away to found the city of Rome. Dido is pregnant with his child, but the Trojan hero insists on leaving; the gods have commanded him to establish his own city, a city that will one day rule the world. Dido is not convinced that commitment to an unknown future should be stronger than a sense of duty to the knowable present. The figure whom she dreams will avenge the injustice she has suffered is the great Hannibal, whose invasion of Italy at the end of the third century BC and whose crushing victories over the armies of Rome were to play a formative role in shaping the ancient Roman concept of *virtus*. It was the ability to survive such disasters that defined the greatness of the community of Rome.

This close intertwining of the histories of Rome and Carthage was not Virgil's invention. It was central to the first great original work of Latin literature, Naevius' poem on Rome's First Punic War, a conflict that raged for over 20 years in the mid-third century BC. There was a neat historical symmetry in the fact that, as Rome began its inexorable final decline, an important nail was driven into its coffin by a ruler from the same North African city. Certainly, when the Vandal king Geiseric set sail from Carthage for Aeneas' city in AD 455, the ghost of Dido would have wished him 'God Speed'.

Even so, when Geiseric landed in Italy, the western Roman state still controlled more land than it had when Rome declared war on Carthage in 264 BC. Rome won the earlier war because it was able to mobilize the resources of Italy with enormous efficiency. In the course of that struggle, Italy suffered far heavier casualties than in the war against the Goths in the AD 370s, or even in the bloody civil wars earlier that century. Simple loss of territory cannot therefore explain why Roman Italy in the fifth century AD was no longer able to muster a strong enough army to defend itself. The key difference between AD 455 and 264 BC was not to do with the Italian environment or its population figures, but rather with a fundamental change in the relationship between the state and the people. The armies and navies of the mid-third century BC were comprised of civilians called up from their farms to serve the state, while the civilians of the fifth century AD were bound by the imperial tax structure to their lands. The Romans and Italians who flocked to swell the ranks of the Republic's armies were motivated by a fierce loyalty to their communities, and expected to share in the rewards of victory. The Roman people voted for the Punic wars, and repeated disasters only reinforced their desire for ultimate victory.

Not so the civilians of the fifth century, who had no say in the direction of their state and no reason to love either their emperor or the private armies with which his generals maintained their status at court. Very different too was the attitude of people in the eastern empire. The redefinition of the office of emperor to exploit the religious fervour of the eastern empire's populace meant that the average person there felt a far stronger sense of allegiance to the emperor than did the civilians of the west. Even though religious opinions were often difficult to control, giving rise to innumerable theological controversies that plagued the politics of the eastern empire, meetings summoned with the ostensible purpose of debating matters of faith offered a common forum for people to voice their concerns. Whether by design or accident, the yoking together of imperial and religious ideology lent the eastern government a cohesion that was lacking in the west. The notion that the imperial house existed to protect the faithful was a narrative that proved as potent as the Augustan discourse of *virtus* or Diocletian's discourse of victory. By contrast, the utter failure of governments of the west from Honorius to Valentinian to offer a coherent justification for their existence, together with the bigotry, jealousy and folly that often marked the actions of these rulers, doomed the western empire to decline and fall.

If there is a lesson to be learned from the history of the Caesars from Augustus to Romulus, it is that government must represent the collective moral wisdom of society. It is the duty of an administration not simply to ensure justice and peace for its people, but also to create a viable way for those people to make their voices heard. Government that withdraws from the realities of the world around it, or simply asserts banal 'truths' that have little resonance with the opinions of its people, ultimately only erodes the very foundations of society. The fall of the western Roman empire was not so much the result of barbarian invasion as of a failure of imagination in assimilating the new arrivals. Appeals to prejudice and fantasies about the nature of the world were then, and always will be, a recipe for disaster.

Dido, the legendary queen of Carthage with her lover, the Trojan Aeneas. Heartbroken when he leaves her to found Rome, she commits suicide. Dying, she predicts eternal conflict between Aeneas' people and her own, and invokes the future Carthaginian leader Hannibal with the words 'rise up from my bones, avenging spirit'.

Glossary

aerarium the Roman state treasury, as distinct from the **patrimonium**, which controlled the personal wealth and property portfolio of the emperor.

amphitheatre an elliptical arena surrounded by banked tiers of seating for staging public spectacles such as gladiatorial combats.

Arianism in Christian theology, a doctrine, expounded by Arius of Alexandria in the third–fourth centuries AD, which maintained that the son of God, Jesus Christ, was not of the same 'substance' as god the Father; the Council of Nicaea affirmed that the Father and Son were coequal, coeternal and 'of one substance, thereby declaring Arianism a heresy.

Augustus (lit. 'exalted one') the name conferred by the **senate** on Octavian and adopted as the ruler's title by all subsequent emperors. Under the **Tetrarchy**, the title was used by the two senior imperial colleagues (and 'Caesar' by the two junior colleagues).

auxiliary supplementary troops supporting the **legionaries** of the regular Roman army, auxiliaries were drawn from across the empire. They often deployed specialist fighting skills, as horseman, archers, slingshot-throwers, etc.

Caesar the family name (nomen) of Gaius Julius Caesar and his adoptive son Octavian (Augustus). Caesar came to be used by all Roman emperors as an imperial title. When it was not used in conjunction with the title/name Augustus it signified the heir apparent, a meaning that was strengthened under the **Tetrarchy** when it became the title of the two junior imperial colleagues

Circus Maximus site of a large hippodrome in Ancient Rome, where various equestrian events and festivals were held. Chief among these were the popular chariot races, in which twelve chariots could race abreast around the oval track. The Circus has become a public park in modern Rome.

colonia a free city in a province of the Roman empire, whose inhabitants enjoyed full citizenship and which was exempt from any tribute payments to Rome.

consul the senior magistrate in the Roman administrative system. Prior to the time of Augustus there were ordinarily two consuls elected each year (additional consuls might be elected to replace those who died in office). From Augustus onward, there were usually more than two consuls for each year, though the office still represented the high point of a senatorial career.

cubicularius a **freedman** who held the post of personal attendant to the emperor. Many cubicularii exerted great influence over particular emperors.

Dacia the area, roughly equivalent to modern Romania, north of the River Danube, which became a Roman province after Trajan's victorious campaigns against the tribes there in AD 106. Dacia was abandoned to the Germanic trines after AD 272.

dictator in the Roman Republic, a magistrate granted absolute powers by the **consuls** for a term of six months during times of crisis. Dictators were the only Roman magistrates not to be elected.

diocese in the late Roman Christian empire, a group of provinces under the supervision of a **vicarius**.

domus the Roman household; a key concept in promoting the idea of stability and fidelity in the Roman world. The ability of the head of the household (**paterfamilias**) to maintain order and harmony in his domestic domain was regarded as mirroring the emperor's wise stewardship of the state as a whole.

donativum a 'gift,' usually financial, made by an emperor. Major gifts were expected by members of the military, especially the **Praetorian Guard**, at the beginning of each reign and to mark other significant events.

equestrian: a member of the second aristocratic rank, just below the senate in terms of prestige. From Augustus onwards the equestrian order was defined as being all Roman citizens of free birth who possessed property valued at 400,000 sesterces.

federates (Latin foederati) 'barbarian' peoples, such as the **Goths**, who settled in the Roman empire after being displaced by the **Huns** in the late fourth century AD in return for pledging to serve Rome militarily in time of crisis.

forum a market square or public space in Roman towns. Usually colonnaded and surrounded by temples and public buildings, fora were equivalent to agora in the Greek world.

Franks a confederation of Germanic peoples from the lower Rhine region. Emerging in the third century AD, the Franks settled in northern Gaul in the subsequent centuries.

freedman/freedwoman a slave who had been granted his/her freedom. Freedmen/women remained attached to the households of their former masters, and were often employed in positions of great trust. Employed in the emperor's household, they performed many important functions in those aspects of the government of the empire that were connected with the emperor's household, and could exercise enormous power.

frieze a band of **relief** sculpture decorating the upper levels of stonework on a temple or other monument.

gladiator in public entertainments held at Rome's Colosseum and at other amphitheatres, a slave (or sometimes volunteer) trained in combat. Different types of gladiator specialized in fighting with particular weapons.

Goths a Germanic people of central Europe. The Goths formed a number of different groups in the course of their years of contact with Rome; the most significant were perhaps the Visigoths, who developed out of the people led by Alaric in the early fifth century, and the Ostrogoths, a group that formed in the Balkans at the end of that century.

Huns a semi-nomadic people of Turkic origin, who came to prominence as invaders in eastern Europe from the late fourth century AD onwards. Led by Attila in the mid-fifth century, they wrought havoc in the Balkans and the western empire but their empire broke up shortly after his death in AD 453.

imperator the Roman title from which our word 'emperor' derives. Signifying 'victorious general', it was adopted by Augustus' successors as a standard feature of the imperial nomenclature.

imperium ('power') the authority to rule over the Roman people, once conferred on the kings of the city and after their deposition on magistrates, notably the **consuls**.

imperium maius ('greater power') one of two key powers upon which the legal foundations of the imperial system was based (the other bring **tribunicia potestas**). Imperium maius was power that was 'greater' than that of other magistrates who were therefore supposed to obey orders issued by one who held this power.

legionary a soldier in the regular Roman army; legions, which originally numbered over 5000 men but whose strength was later reduced to 1000–2000, were made up of professionally trained, well-equipped heavy infantry.

lex maiestatis in Roman law, the charge of high treason, a capital offence.

magister equitum ('master of the horse') in the Roman army, the supreme commanding officer of the cavalry units on each war front.

magister militum ('master of the soldiers') a new level of command, created in the late fourth century, above master of infantry and master of cavalry.

magister peditum ('master of the foot soldiers') in the Roman army, the supreme commanding officer of the infantry units on each war front.

Mithraism cult of the sun-god Mithras. Originating in the eastern provinces of the Roman empire, it became increasingly popular during the second and third centuries AD.

municipium an urban centre that had been granted a civic constitution by Rome and whose citizens enjoyed the benefits of Roman citizenship. Compare **colonia**.

Neoplatonism a school of thought combining teachings based upon the writings of the fourth-century BC. Greek philosopher Plato with those of other groups. The founding father of Neoplatonism was Plotinus, whose career spanned the middle of the third century AD.

optimates ('best men') men who tended to support the legacy of Sulla's dictatorship in the generation of Caesar; in other words, inherently conservative members of the **senate**. It was generally used in contrast to the term popularis, or 'supporter of the interests of the people as a whole'.

Pantheon temple built by Marcus Agrippa and repaired by the emperor Hadrian to honour all the gods in the Roman state cult. The building was circular in design and surmounted by a large dome; the term later came to be used figuratively to describe all the gods in any polytheistic belief system.

Parthia name used by the Romans for the territory, primarily in Iran and Iraq, controlled by the Iranian dynasty that preceded the **Sassanid empire** in the early third century AD.

paterfamilias the head of a Roman household (**domus**); Roman law granted the paterfamilias power of life and death (patria potestas) within his home over every member of his family and his servants.

patrician a member of a ruling elite of Rome. The aristocratic families who made up the patrician order claimed descent from the city's original senators, who according to legend were appointed by Romulus.

patrimonium the portfolio of land and other property holdings under personal imperial control (largely acquired through seizures and bequests from citizens) and handed down from one emperor to the next.

plebeian any Roman citizen who was not a **patrician**. Plebeians (or plebs for short) constituted the majority of the Roman populace.

pontifex maximus the high priest of the Roman state cult. Beginning with Julius Caesar, emperors held the post until AD 382.

praetor Roman magistrate, second in rank to the **consul**, responsible for civil jurisdiction.

Praetorian Guard elite imperial bodyguard, first formed under Augustus. Coming to prominence under the influence of their prefect Aelius Sejanus during the reign of Tiberius, the Praetorians

increasingly wielded political power in the appointment of emperors. Their power was curbed by later emperors from Diocletian onwards.

princeps (lit. 'leading man') the most common designation for the emperor from the first century AD onwards.

Punic Roman adjective for the people of Carthage in North Africa and their language. It derives from the Latin Poeni, meaning Phoenician, from the area in the eastern Mediterranean around the ports of Tyre and Sidon, where the Carthaginians originally came from.

quaestor the lowest-ranking Roman magistrate. Quaestors had responsibilities for state finances and public works.

relief a form of sculpture in which the design is raised above a flat background surface.

saeculum a time period theoretically equivalent to the lifespan of the longest-lived person on earth, calculated at either 100 or 110 years. In Rome, the end of a saeculum was marked with extensive games and sacrifices.

Sassanid (or Sassanian) empire the state in Persia, established by the Sassanid dynasty, which succeeded

the **Parthian** empire and ruled from AD 225 until Arab Muslims conquered the region in *c.* AD 636.

senate the governing body of the Roman republic. Members of the senate had to possess significant property and, ordinarily, to have held the office of quaestor of tribune of the plebs.

Tetrarchy (lit. 'rule of four') the system, named by later historians, instituted by Diocletian to rule the empire. The responsibilities of government were shared by two senior emperors and two juniors.

tribune the main representative of the Roman **plebeian** class. Ten tribunes were elected annually by the 'council of the plebs', a body set up in fifth-century BC Rome. The tribune's powers, an important part of state authority in Rome, were known as the tribunicia potestas.

triumvirate in common usage, any group of three magistrates. The term was applied to the informal political alliance between Pompey, Crassus and Caesar in the fifties BC and, later, to the official board of three established in 43 BC "to set the state in order" that included Mark Antony, Octavian and Lepidus.

Vestal Virgin servant of Vesta, the patron goddess of the Roman hearth and home. The Vestals were charged with keeping alight the eternal flame, symbolizing the enduring strength of the state, at the Temple of Vesta in the forum.

vicarius (lit. 'substitute, stand-in') term used in the early Roman empire to denote a deputy to a provincial governor. Following Diocletian's administrative reforms in the third century AD, the term denoted an office-holder who was responsible for the day-to-day administration of one of the three **dioceses** under the jurisdiction of each of the empire's four praetorian prefects.

villa the buildings of a Roman country estate, traditionally comprising living quarters, storehouses, stables, workshops, farm buildings, and so on. Lavish villas became the preferred residence of many Roman emperors, who ran the business of empire from there, when not in the capital or on campaign.

virtus the manly quality of service to the state, much prized as a quintessential Roman characteristic that helped create social cohesion from the early days of the republic onward.

Index

Further reading

Section I

Fergus Millar's *The Crowd in Rome in the Late Republic* (Ann Arbor, 1998) and the narrative chapters in the second edition of the *Cambridge Ancient History*, volume 9 (especially those by T.P. Wiseman) offer a splendid introduction to the history of the Late Republic. The best biography of Caesar remains M. Gelzer, *Caesar: Politician and Statesman* (Cambridge, MA, 1969), which, though dated, displays a masterful command of the sources. For the issue of how Romans of the post-Augustan age thought about the Republic see the fascinating discussion in A.M. Gowing, *Empire and Memory* (Cambridge, 2005). The fundamental study of the rise of Augustus and, indeed, of the imperial system as a whole remains R. Syme, *The Roman Revolution* (Oxford, 1939), though it must now be supplemented with J. Osgood's *Caesar's Legacy* (Cambridge 2005), G. Rowe, *Princes and Political Culture* (Ann Arbor, 2002) and P. Zanker, *The Power of Images in the Age of Augustus* (Ann Arbor, 1988). The best starting points for the later Julio-Claudians are A.R. Barrett, *Caligula* (London, 1989), B.M. Levick, *Claudius* (London, 1990), and M.T. Griffin, *Nero* (London, 1984).

Section II

For Flavians and Trajan see B.M. Levick, *Vespasian* (London, 1999), and the excellent chapters in the second edition of the *Cambridge Ancient History,* volume 11. For the later years see A.R. Birley's *Hadrian. The Restless Emperor* (London, 1997) and *Marcus Aurelius. A Biography*, 2ND ED. (London, 1987). For the social and administrative history of the empire see P. Brunt, *Roman Imperial Themes* (Oxford, 1990) and chapters in the second edition of the *Cambridge Ancient History* volume 11 by W. Eck and B. Shaw, as well as the essays collected in D.S. Potter and D.J. Mattingly, *Life, Death and Entertainment in the Roman Empire* (Ann Arbor, 1999) and D.S. Potter, *A Companion to the Roman Empire* (Oxford, 2006). For the position of the emperor, F. Millar, *The Emperor in the Roman World*, 2ND ED. (London, 1992) remains central. For the history of religion the starting point remains R.J. Lane-Fox, *Pagans and Christians* (London, 1989).

Section III

For the early Severans see A.R. Birley, *The African Emperor. Septimius Severus*, 2ND ED. (London, 1988). For a narrative of the history of the third century and age of Constantine see D.S. Potter, *The Roman Empire at Bay* (London, 2004). T.D. Barnes, *Constantine and Eusebius* (Cambridge, MA, 1981) is the starting point for contemporary study of Constantine, while H. Drake, *Constantine and the Bishops* (Baltimore, 2000) provides a significant alternative view. S. Mitchell, *A History of the Later Roman Empire AD 284–641* (Oxford, 2006) offers an up-to-date and vigorous discussion of the period, giving equal weight to the histories of the eastern and western Roman empires.

Section IV

For a narrative of the period down to Theodosius see Potter, *The Roman Empire at Bay*, and Mitchell, *A History of the Later Roman Empire*. For the period after Constantine the fundamental works remain J.F. Matthews, *Western Aristocracies and the Imperial Court AD 364–425* (Oxford, 1975) and *The Roman Empire of Ammianus* (London, 1989). For administration in general see C. Kelly, *Ruling the Later Roman Empire* (Cambridge, 2004). For the time of Valens and Theodosius I see N. Lenski, *The Failure of Empire* (Berkeley, 2002) and N.B. McLynn, *Ambrose of Milan: Church and Court in a Christian Capital* (Berkeley, 1994). For the fifth century see P. Heather, *The Fall of the Roman Empire* (Oxford, 2006), and, for an account of scholarly difference between those who generally see the period in a positive light, a viewpoint best represented in the essays collected in G.W. Bowersock, P. Brown and O. Grabar, *Late Antiquity: a guide to the post-classical world* (Cambridge, MA, 1999), see B. Ward-Perkins, *The Fall of Rome* (Oxford, 2006). For the period of Theodosius II, K. Holum, *Theodosian Empresses* (Berkeley, 1982) is splendid, as is F. Millar, *A Greek Roman Empire: power and belief under Theodosius II 408–450* (Berkeley, 2006). In terms of sheer style and brilliance of exposition, E. Gibbon, *The Decline and Fall of the Roman Empire* has no peer.

Picture credits

Designed and edited by BCS Publishing Limited, Oxford.

Metro Books
122 Fifth Avenue
New York, NY 10011

ISBN: 978-4351-2962-7

Printed and bound in China

1   3   5   7   9   10   8   6   4   2